THE DANCE
OF
THE MILLIONS

Latin America and the Debt Crisis

by Jackie Roddick

First published 1988
© Latin America Bureau (Research and Action) Ltd
1 Amwell Street, London EC1R 1UL

Written by Jackie Roddick
Additional material and editing by Philip O'Brien and James Painter

Case studies: Brazil by Sue Branford, Peru by John Crabtree and
Costa Rica by Trevor Petch.

The Contributors

Sue Branford is a journalist at Christian Aid specialising in Latin
America.
John Crabtree is a writer on Latin American affairs, formerly *The
Guardian* correspondent in Peru.
Philip O'Brien is a lecturer at the Institute of Latin American Studies,
Glasgow University.
James Painter is a researcher/writer at the Latin America Bureau.
Trevor Petch is a freelance journalist specialising in the Caribbean and
Central America.
Jackie Roddick is a research fellow of the Institute of Latin American
Studies, Glasgow University.

Thanks are due to the Economic and Social Research Council (ESRC)
for financing the research project of Philip O'Brien and Jackie
Roddick, 'The Politics of Debt Renegotiation in Brazil, Argentina and
Peru'.

Thanks also to Oscar Ugarteche, Roberto López and David Stansfield

ISBN 0 906256 30 0 pb
ISBN 0 906156 37 8 hb

Cover by Sergio Navarro
Printed in England by the Russell Press Ltd, Bertrand Russell House,
Gamble Street, Nottingham NG1 4ET

Trade distribution by Third World Publications, 151 Stratford Road,
Birmingham B11 1RD
Distribution in the USA by Monthly Review Foundation

Contents

List of Figures

List of Tables

A Note on Vocabulary

Discussion of the debt crisis is hampered by a mass of technical jargon, largely incomprehensible to the general reader. We have therefore included a glossary of the terms most frequently used in the book. Other terms or phrases which occur only once or twice in the text are explained the first time they are used.

A number of phrases like 'the Third World', 'less developed countries'(LDCs), 'the West', and 'the OECD countries' are used loosely as a form of verbal shorthand despite the diversity in the size, economies and geographical positions of the countries involved.

The term 'band-aid solution' first mentioned in chapter one and discussed more fully in chapter three refers to the hurried patch-up measures applied by Western governments, banks and the IMF to Latin America, and has no connection with the money raised by the Band Aid organisation for sub-Saharan and other African countries.

Some minor discrepancies in the figures used in the text may arise as a result of the different sources used by the different authors.

One billion is one thousand million (1,000,000,000); a trillion is one thousand billion (1,000,000,000,000).

Glossary

Accumulated Principal Increase on the capital sum on which interest is paid.

Aggregate Demand The total effective demand or expenditure of all purchasers of consumer and capital goods within a given market or economic system.

Amortisation Repayment of the principal of a loan spread out over a period of years.

BIS Bank for International Settlements, representing OECD central banks.

Bond A piece of paper given in exchange for a borrowed sum of money, and a written promise to repay the sum on a certain future date. Governments, local and national, sell bonds when they want to raise money.

Buying Forward A promise to buy securities or commodities on a future date at fixed prices.

Central Bank Central government authority charged with managing a nation's currency, protecting its value and regulating the growth of the money supply. In Britain it is the Bank of England, in the US, the Federal Reserve Board.

Commercial Bank A privately owned bank (owned by shareholders) which operate current accounts, receive deposits and make loans (including to Third World countries) with the explicit purpose of maximising profits. They are to be distinguished from Central Banks.

Debt-Equity Swaps A commercial bank holding a country's debt may be willing to sell it at a discount of maybe 30 to 50 per cent.

A potential investor can purchase the discounted debt in foreign currency, and sell it at full value or sometimes less, depending on local regulations, to the Central Bank of the country, in local currency. The investor can then buy shares or whole local enterprises. (see box p.122)

Debt Service Ratio The ratio of debt repayments to a country's export of goods and services or Gross National Product (GNP).

ECLAC Economic Commission for Latin America and the Caribbean.

Equity Capital The value of the stockholder's investment.

External Public Debt That proportion of the national debt, debts of local government authorities and the debts of public corporations, owed by one country to foreign banks, IFIs and governments.

Federal Reserve Board The Central Bank of the US. (see Central Bank)

Floating Bonds When returns on bonds are in keeping with fluctuating market conditions.

Grace Period The number of years before capital repayments (amortisation) can begin.

Group of Seven The group of seven most industrialised countries — US, France, UK, West Germany, Japan, Italy and Canada.

IFIs International Financial Institutions such as the IMF or the World Bank.

ILO International Labour Office.

Libor London Interbank Offered Rate, the rate of interest at which money is traded between private banks in the international money market.

Money Centre Banks While not a technical term, an expression generally referring to the 10 largest US banks with the most extensive international financial operations — Bank of America, Citicorp, Chase Manhattan, Security Pacific, Bankers Trust, Morgan Guaranty, Irving Trust, Chemical Bank, Continental Illinois and First Chicago.

Money Supply Total value of bank deposits of commercial banks plus total amount of cash in banknotes and coins; to be controlled in monetarist economic theory to constrain or stimulate the economy.

Multiyear Rescheduling see **Rescheduling**.

NICs Newly Industrialised Countries (e.g. Brazil and Mexico in Latin America).

NOPECs Developing countries which are not major oil producers or exporters.

OECD Organisation for Economic Cooperation and Development, consisting of 24 of the world's richer nations, mostly of Western Europe, but also including the US, Canada, Japan and Australia.

Offshore Banking Centres Banks, mainly in the Caribbean, attractive to foreign bankers due to a less restrictive system of taxation.

Paris Club An informal gathering of creditor nations who meet to discuss rescheduling requests from debtor nations of the loans outstanding to official agencies and governments. The governments involved in the Paris Club are the Group of Seven countries, plus Austria, Belgium, the Netherlands, Norway, Spain, Sweden and Switzerland.

Prime Rate The lowest interest rate a bank is prepared to offer, even to its best customer.

Provisions Reserve money set aside by banks in case their loans are not fully repaid. They are not write-offs involving the cancellation of debt owed by debtor countries.

Rate of Return Pre-tax profits expressed as a proportion of assets.

Reflation Macroeconomic policy designed to expand aggregate demand in order to restore full employment levels of national income. A typical reflationary measure includes the expansion of the money supply with consequent reductions in interest rates, increases in government expenditure and reductions in taxation.

Reschedule To revise or postpone dates on which capital repayments are supposed to be made. **Multiyear Rescheduling** is a rescheduling of interest and amortisation payments due over several years rather than the one in course.

Roll over Used loosely to refer to the replacement of a maturing short-term loan with a new loan. More tightly defined, it refers to an agreement between borrower and lender to have the option to repay or extend a loan, at specified intervals, under the terms of the original loan agreement.

SDRs Special Drawing Rights were created in July 1969 as a form of international reserve asset to replace the dollar as the IMF's official unit of account. They are allocated to members as a supplement to other reserves and they function as credits in the member countries' accounts with the IMF, which can be used to buy hard currencies from the IMF in times of debt or balance of payments problems.

Secondary Market Market for the purchase or resale of loans to developing countries.

Spread The difference between Libor and the actual interest rate on a loan paid by the borrower.

Stagflation A combination of economic stagnation and inflation.

Suppliers' Credits The same as trade credit. Credit extended by suppliers (e.g. of materials) to others (e.g. manufacturers).

Supply Side The forces considered by some economists to determine output; the availability or supply of capital and labour, and the state of technology.

Syndicated Loans A consortium of banks offering a loan package, with each institution chipping in a portion of the loan.

Terms of Trade The ratio of the index of export prices to the index of import prices. An improvement in the terms of trade follows if export prices rise more quickly than import prices (or fall more slowly than import prices).

Trade Credits Short-term loans granted either by banks, industrial corporations or government agencies to finance the purchase of specific goods.

Value-Added The value added to a commodity at each stage of its manufacture.

Prologue

A Saga of Greed

On 7 July 1987, the Latin American debt crisis came home to the UK. Scotland woke up to find that one of its major banks, the Clydesdale, had become Australian. The owner, the London-based Midland Bank, had been forced to sell by the ripple effects of a decision taken in far-off Brazil. In February 1987, the Brazilian government had decided to suspend any further interest payments on the country's foreign debt, then standing at US$110 billion. The move was bound to affect the Midland, as Brazil was the bank's largest Latin American debtor, owing £1.4 billion.

Midland's response was to sell off the Clydesdale and two other subsidiaries to help cover the cost of setting aside £916 million (US$1.5 billion) in bad debt provision: an insurance against the possibility that a debtor like Brazil might not repay all the money it had borrowed. This was one of a wave of similar, slighty panicky, decisions taken by leading British banks in the wake of the May 1987 announcement by Latin America's largest private creditor, the United States bank Citicorp, that it was setting aside US$3 billion in reserves to safeguard itself against the risks of bad Latin American debts.

The new debt provision meant that informally, banks recognised that the global total of Latin American debts on their books would never be repaid. Formally, they made no such concession. Throughout 1987, British and US banks continued to insist that the whole sum owed to them by Latin American countries formed part of their 'assets', and continued to charge the debtors interest rates in accordance with market rates.

The Australianisation of part of Britain's banking system is thus a tiny element in the 1970s' equivalent of the Great South Sea Bubble. In this extraordinary saga, millions of dollars were transferred at the

1

drop of a hat by supposedly staid, conservative bankers, to a series of Third World governments, some of them democracies, more of them military dictatorships, and most of them in Latin America. Bankers paid little heed to their customers' creditworthiness (or to their record on human rights), and even less to how the money might be used.

In this headlong 'dance of the millions', bankers had the support of Western governments. It was the era of the oil price rises, and the West was frightened that without a deliberate policy of recycling oil producers' new earnings, a major world recession would ensue. Recycling the surpluses to Latin America helped to maintain the demand for Western-produced goods, and keep Western factories in production.

Meanwhile the bankers credited the interest charges from Latin America into their accounts, yielding welcome profits. When Latin American countries could not pay, the banks loaned them more money to keep the interest payments sweet in their accounts — still more money, making a still bigger debt, and earning still more interest. Time passed, and interest rates rose steeply.

The difference between the South Sea Bubble and this twentieth century scandal is that eighteenth century capitalists knew for a fact that magic would never make their millions return. Modern bankers and Western governments have refused to admit that any of the speculative gold of the 1970s, or its accumulated real and fictitious earnings, has actually been lost.

The twentieth century bubble burst in August 1982, when Mexico declared that it could no longer keep up its interest payments. Fearing the collapse of their banks, Western governments moved in to take charge. Political and economic pressure ensured the continued extraction of interest, not only on the money the bankers originally lent out, but also on the new money. For the past five years, the debt has thus officially continued to be a growing asset. Bankers have credited the rising interest charges to their publicly declared profits. While living standards plummeted in the Third World, the big four British banks increased their dividends, and their share prices rose. In 1986 they showed record profits of £3.2 billion.

The dance thus whirled on throughout 1987, in spite of Brazil's February moratorium, which sent shivers through the banking world. The Brazilian episode ended in compromise. In November 1987 Brazil agreed to make a token payment of US$1.5 billion on its interest arrears of US$4.5 billion accumulated since February. The bankers themselves contributed the remaining two-thirds of the year's lost interest in new loans, adding yet more to Brazil's paper mountain of unpayable debt.

2

Between 1980 and 1986 the Third World as a whole transferred to the developed countries about US$321 billion in repayments of principal and US$325 billion in payments in interest, equivalent to about 5 per cent of their annual GNP since 1982. These payments presented enormous difficulties for the countries concerned, and the poor suffered particularly. Yet despite the sacrifice of living standards, and the amount of money sent abroad, the overall debt burden has actually increased. By the end of 1987, the Third World's external debt topped the staggering figure of US$1,000 billion.

Some economists argue that the notorious looting of India by the British East India Company in the eighteenth century pales in comparison with the current outflows. Latin America alone transferred US$121 billion between 1982 and 1986, an average of US$24 billion a year.

Africa and Latin America are the major victims of this scandal. They have suffered a depression worse than the 1930s in terms of its duration, and more significantly, in terms of the damage done to long-term development prospects. As always, the people who suffer most are the poorest and most vulnerable. The 1987 UNICEF study, *Adjustment with a Human Face*, suggests that in these two continents living standards have dropped 10-15 per cent since 1983, describing the situation as 'unprecedented'. Child malnutrition has worsened, fewer children are continuing past the first and second year of primary school, and adults and children have both become more vulnerable to disease. The debt crisis has undermined the human capital on which all development is finally based. Other kinds of capital, like roads, factories and hospitals are disintegrating as a result of the drastic contraction in investment imposed by governments forced to cut spending by International Monetary Fund (IMF) adjustment programmes. Children are growing up in a worse condition to face the future, and the future has become a worse prospect for them to face.

Meanwhile, Western governments who deliberately encouraged the dance of the millions when it began and lauded the social responsibility of their own banks for managing it, now refuse to accept responsibility for the collapse of the future of Latin America, stone-walling each and every proposal by the region's governments to reduce the weight of the debt burden. With Western banks surviving, why should they care?

1. The Dance of the Millions

In December 1986, Bolivia's tin miners began a long march on their capital city, La Paz, in a vain attempt to stave off a government threat to close their mines. The marchers had already survived four long years of economic disaster, in which wages were paid only after long delays and workers on the mine face could not get replacements for broken tools. They had successfully endured spiralling inflation which reached a peak of 8,170 per cent in 1985. Their families were subsisting on bread because they could not afford other foods — there were periods when even bread was scarce. The miners were clinging to a fast-disappearing vision of themselves as people who might be poor, but who had nonetheless a certain degree of power over events — a vision fired by memories of years spent battling military dictatorships, culminating in 1982 with the withdrawal of the military from government and the return to civilian rule under President Siles Zuazo.

The march was a hopeless cause before it began. The miners could rid themselves of the Bolivian military, but not Bolivia's debt. Bolivian trade unionists campaigned for the repudiation of the debt from the moment the military withdrew, and provided political support to the decision by Siles Zuazo in March 1984 to suspend interest payments. Neither the miners nor Bolivia's creditors regarded Siles Zuazo's moratorium as particularly radical — Bolivia was suffering from a failed harvest, and simply could not pay, as its creditors publicly recognised. The moratorium did not even imply a refusal to accept the legitimacy of debt contracted by an illegal military dictatorship. Until the time of the announcement of the moratorium the Siles Zuazo government had already paid its creditors US$1.1 billion — US$677 million in interest and US$441 million in repayments on principal, money which the mines, and the miners, could well have used.

Yet in spite of the country's inability to pay, in spite of its previous transfer of desperately needed funds abroad, in spite of the failed harvest of 1983 and the threat of widespread hunger in the *altiplano* (highland region), Bolivia's creditors did not cede an inch in response to the moratorium. Governments and bankers held firm to the view that the debtors must pay, or suffer the consequences. Suppliers' credits began to dry up, and the state mining company's accounts in the National Bank of Washington were frozen as collateral against the unpaid bills of other state agencies. Bolivia's ability to import parts and equipment from the industrialised world began to disappear.

In 1985, with popular discontent boiling over, Siles Zuazo resigned. His successor, President Paz Estenssoro, gave up any effort to reconcile social objectives with the demands of Bolivia's creditors. In August he committed himself to a new and drastic economic plan, modelled on the classic pattern of IMF programmes of 'adjustment'. The aim was to achieve IMF approval, thus paving the way for bankers and Western governments to reschedule debt repayments, postponing a burden of debt service costs which threatened to eat up half of Bolivia's export earnings on interest payments alone.

In line with traditional IMF policies, government subsidies to consumers were cut back drastically. Freed from such subsidies, the price of bread rose four-fold. As the state gas and oil companies began to charge 'economic prices' to consumers, the price of a bottle of domestic gas went up twenty times, a litre of petrol seven times. At the same time, wages were frozen below the rate of inflation, and employers were freed from all existing legal controls on their right to dismiss staff at will, or any obligation to pay compensation. But the IMF plan had other, long-term changes in view. The key to its success was to be the removal of the state from its traditional role at the centre of economic activity: an important point of principle for the IMF, its Western political masters, and the banks. The state mining company was to be broken up into smaller regional companies, prior to privatisation, as was the state oil company.

Miners were not the only group to suffer from the new economic strategy. It had savage consequences for the 80 per cent of Bolivians whom the International Labour Office (ILO) estimates to be living in absolute poverty, as it triggered a drastic rise in their living costs. But miners were one of the principal targets of the new regime. The price of tin, long Bolivia's main export, was declining on world markets, and by 1986 had fallen by a half over the previous year, wiping out the mines' commercial viability. Tin miners were no longer useful contributors to the process of debt repayments. Within a year of taking office in 1985, President Paz Estenssoro dismissed 20,000 of the 27,000 workers employed by the state mining corporation, COMIBOL.

5

Paz Estenssoro may well have felt he had no alternative. The Bolivian economy was not strong enough to face down a Western blockade. His good behaviour secured formal approval from the IMF in February 1986 and a rescheduling of the country's debt burden on very favourable terms — which were never conceded when Bolivia faced the spectre of famine. Even Western governments gave aid in a programme to rebuy its debt on the secondary market (see chapter six) at rates which recognised that Bolivia could not realistically be expected ever to pay back its debt.

But the miners also had few alternatives. They could migrate to the cities, where open unemployment was already running at 20 per cent and local industry was in a state of virtual collapse (due to past and present IMF policies). They could stay at home and attempt to turn the arid mountains into subsistence and market gardens. Or they could take their luck with migration to the more prosperous north-eastern areas producing coca for the cocaine trade, where they would run the risk of confrontation with the drug mafia or with US soldiers brought in by a compliant Bolivian government to suppress cocaine production at its roots.

In a decade notable for the self-righteousness of Latin America's Western creditors, the plight of the Bolivian tin miners mirrors the fate of the majority of Latin America's poor.

The Scissors Crisis

Bolivia has suffered more than most Latin American countries from the debt crisis, not so much because of the spectacular collapse of tin prices (Bolivia has other exports) as because it is the poorest country in South America and consequently has fewer resources to cope with an emergency. In some respects the Bolivian debt is not representative of all Latin American debts — at US$4.5 billion it is small compared to most other South American countries (see table 1.1). Furthermore, the money is owed more to Western governments, who in theory, and in recent practice, are more flexible creditors than private banks.

Nonetheless, the elements which combined to create a crisis in Bolivia from 1981 to 1986 are typical. During this period, Latin America has been squeezed between burgeoning debt payments and shrinking export revenues, in a classic scissors crisis. The region has been earning less and less for its exports, not just in terms of their prices on world markets, but also in terms of what the revenue from them can purchase in Western manufactured goods — what economists call their 'terms of trade'.(see figure 1.1) At the beginning

6

Table 1.1
Latin America and the Caribbean, Debt by Country, 1987
(US$ billion)

Argentina	54.5
Bolivia	4.5
Brazil	116.9
Chile	20.5
Colombia	15.7
Costa Rica	3.8
Dominican Republic	3.7
Ecuador	9.6
El Salvador	2.3
Guatemala	2.7
Haiti	0.7
Honduras	3.1
Mexico	105.6
Nicaragua	6.2
Panama	4.9
Paraguay	2.0
Peru	15.3
Uruguay	5.6
Venezuela	32.2
Total	**409.8**

Source: ECLAC, *Balance Preliminar de la Economía Latinoamericana*, Santiago, December 1987, Table 16.

of 1987 commodity prices were lower compared to the price of manufactured goods than at any time since the Second World War.

Western firms and consumers benefit from cheaper commodities — cheaper copper, tin, soya, orange juice, coffee and ultimately, oil and gas as well. Western banks have lost nothing through the fall in commodity prices, because they have been successful in insisting that regardless of the fate of their exports, Latin American countries must continue to pay their debts by exporting more. Multilateral agencies such as the IMF and the World Bank have cooperated with this scenario, helping to police a further shift of Latin America's productive resources away from production for use to production for exports, thus ensuring a vicious circle of further competition and lower prices in the world markets for the exports the region needs to sell to pay off its debt.

Meanwhile the debt burden has risen to unprecedented levels. In 1987, Latin America and the Caribbean together owed a total of US$410 billion, and paid US$30.1 billion in annual interest charges —

Figures rounded up to nearest US$ billion.

nearly four times as much as they owed in 1977, and nearly four times as much in interest payments.(see figure 1.2)

Caught in this scissors crisis, Latin American governments have found the effort to pay back Western banks and governments an enormous strain, depriving them of their traditional mechanisms for

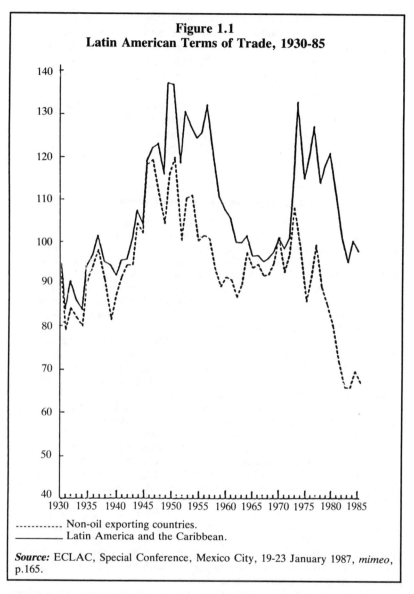

Figure 1.1
Latin American Terms of Trade, 1930-85

------------ Non-oil exporting countries.
―――――― Latin America and the Caribbean.

Source: ECLAC, Special Conference, Mexico City, 19-23 January 1987, *mimeo*, p.165.

containing urban poverty, such as subsidies on food, transport and energy, which the IMF insists on removing as part of its strategy to manage the debt crisis on the West's behalf. Expenditures on health, education and housing have also been slashed. This in turn has aggravated social tensions, which in Bolivia's case were directly responsible for the resignation of President Siles Zuazo before the end of his term of office. Elsewhere Presidents have survived, but year after year, one Finance Minister after another has fallen victim to the impossible pressures of the debt crisis.

Meanwhile the illegal and criminal economy has been growing, sometimes compromising whole economies. Peru, Colombia and Bolivia have all become more and more dependent on selling the one commodity for which there is still a booming export demand — cocaine. (see box below)

The 'Scissors Crisis' and Cocaine

As Latin America faces the double threat of reduced export earnings and ballooning debt charges, a large chunk of the continent has become increasingly dependent on the export of cocaine. The illicit drug industry, according to a US Presidential Commission, is worth an estimated US$110 billion in the US alone. World-wide, the turnover of the industry is supposed to be equivalent to that of the Organisation of Petroleum Exporting Countries (OPEC). Cocaine earns Colombia more than its main legitimate export, coffee. It earns Peru and Bolivia more than the value of all their official exports put together.

Growing coca may have provided an alternative source of income to hundreds of Bolivian peasants and sacked tin miners, but according to official figures, it has clearly failed to pull the majority of Bolivians out of the poverty trap. Per capita income had fallen by 1985 to US$840, US$150 lower than it was in 1970. Arguably, it has contributed more to Colombia, which both produces and trades in the drug — Colombians control about 75 per cent of the supply of the drug to the US. Of all the Latin American countries, Colombia has had the greatest success in insulating itself from the 'debt crisis'. Some experts argue that cocaine production has also helped to alleviate the crisis in Peru, underpinning President García's refusal to pay more than 10 per cent of Peru's export revenue on the debt by providing an inflow of cheap dollars to keep the country's black market under control.

The cost, to Colombia and Bolivia at least, has been a further deterioration in overall political stability and the threat of arbitrary violence. Colombia has murder gangs run by cocaine bosses, who have assassinated judges attempting to bring the trade's practitioners to book. Bolivia's armed forces have developed ties with the trade, inspiring the 'cocaine coup' of General García Meza in 1980.

In both countries, it has been suggested that cocaine ought to provide the solution to the 'debt crisis'. Rumours periodically reinvent the scenario in which a well-known cocaine baron offers President Reagan the ▶

► settlement of Bolivia or Colombia's entire national debt, in exchange for the release of a son or close colleague who has been arrested in the US. Similar stories are reported in the popular press.

Wishful thinking is not just a Latin American phenomenon. In the middle of 1987, European creditor governments offered to fund — anonymously — a Bolivian government effort to buy back its debt from banks at the much discounted rate at which Bolivian debt trades on the secondary market, on condition that in return Bolivia should reduce the flow of cocaine. It was not made clear how Bolivia was supposed to guarantee a reduction in the flow of cocaine without a sustained programme of new investment to provide substitutes for both cocaine and tin, and a massive expansion of state employment to police the vast hinterland in which coca was grown. But the banks were undoubtedly pleased with any opportunity to extricate themselves from the Bolivian quagmire.

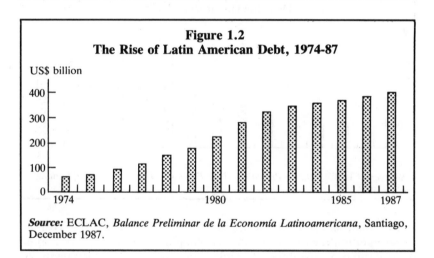

Figure 1.2
The Rise of Latin American Debt, 1974-87

US$ billion

Source: ECLAC, *Balance Preliminar de la Economía Latinoamericana*, Santiago, December 1987.

Who Pays?

Poverty did not arrive in Latin America because of the debt crisis: what the debt crisis has done is to exacerbate the misery which was already there. Nor is there anything new in the existence of governments closer to the values and philosophy of international bankers than to the pressing needs of their own citizens. Over the past two decades, Latin America's elites have fought consistently to preserve their own Westernised patterns of consumption and their access to international accounts, at the expense of alternative development strategies focused

11

on basic needs. As we show in chapter four, in the 1970s this set of preferences met with considerable favour in international banking circles and helps to explain both why Latin American debtors were regarded as creditworthy and the colossal waste of resources during the dance of the millions.

Nonetheless, when it comes to the nefarious alliance between local elites and Western economic interests — old history in Latin American terms — the debt crisis is a special case. As we show in chapter two, the original recycling of the petrodollars and the extrordinary growth of interest rates are developments which have their roots in problems tangential to Latin America, but central to the preoccupations and rivalries of Western governments.

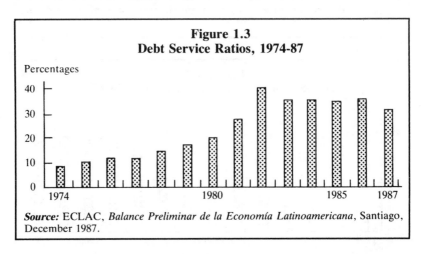

Figure 1.3
Debt Service Ratios, 1974-87

Percentages

Source: ECLAC, *Balance Preliminar de la Economía Latinoamericana*, Santiago, December 1987.

The 'band-aid solution' to the debt crisis put in place by Western governments after 1982 is reviewed in chapters three and five. Chapter three outlines its essential principles, and chapter five documents its impact on Latin American economies and the Latin American poor. For the West it was a 'minimum cost' effort: no sacrifice for the banks, and no additional aid from Western governments to buy out the banks' staggering mountain of unpayable debt. Least cost for the West has meant much heavier costs for Latin America: a tax annually creaming off around 35 per cent of the value of the region's exports (see figure 1.3) and forcing it to transfer between 4 and 7 per cent of individual countries' GNP to Western banks and governments. The burden on Latin America is more than double the level of post-First World War reparations imposed on Germany at the Treaty of Versailles and

12

widely held to be a major factor in the tensions contributing to the rise of Hitler.

The rationale for this high cost solution (low cost for the rich, high cost for the poor) has been the need to protect Western banks from bankruptcy, as we show in chapter six. No considerations of development or social justice have been allowed to interfere. Nor has there been any attempt to square payment of the debt with the market principles in which Western governments profess to believe, leaving the banks themselves to absorb the cost of bad judgements made during the 1970s. On the contrary, when Latin American governments have been forced to declare private companies bankrupt, Western pressure has ensured that they accept the responsibility for the firms' foreign debts, thus increasing the costs of repayment for the poor.

It is therefore a double irony that Western governments, agencies and banks see the present debt crisis as an unparallelled opportunity to introduce the kind of market-oriented reforms that they have long favoured, as we outline in chapter three: a reduction in protection for local industries against Western competition, a reduction in the state's role in development, and a reduction in the overall costs of state programmes which are of direct benefit to the urban poor. These reforms will undoubtedly benefit Western business interests who have always complained about the restrictions on their access to local markets in Latin America, even while the Western powers, faced with their own internal economic crises, are themselves increasingly turning to new forms of protectionism, as we show in chapter ten.

As the debt crisis has evolved, the headlines in the Western press have focused on a fast-changing kaleidoscope of trouble spots. In 1982, the spotlight fell on Mexico, the pioneering partner in all Western 'solutions' to the debt crisis from then to the present day. Argentina looked dangerously close to default in 1984, when a combination of falling grain prices and the end of an unpopular military regime produced a civilian government, which looked initially as though it might take a stand on the illegitimacy of debts contracted under the previous, extremely brutal military regime.

Brazil, the biggest debtor in Latin America, was once self-defined alongside Mexico as among the most 'responsible', i.e. conciliatory, debtors. But in 1985 the government decided to attempt to grow their way out of the debt problem and go it alone without the IMF. Then throughout 1987, Brazil was the focus of tension-laden negotiations with bankers, following its declaration of a unilateral moratorium on interest payments, and an abortive attempt to force Western governments to face the nature of the debt crisis as a political crisis. Chapter seven analyses the origins of the Brazilian debt, the social cost of servicing the debt, and the failure of the Sarney government to push through a viable solution.

Peru was the first problem debtor in Latin America in 1985, as the newly elected government of Alan García took a unilateral decision to limit debt service repayments to private banks, setting a ceiling on such transfers to 10 per cent of Peru's annual export earnings, and triggering a campaign by the Western powers to prevent the example from spreading. The fate of Alan García's mild effort at defiance is examined in chapter eight.

The fruitless attempts of these Latin American powers to unite and force a redefinition of the nature of the debt crisis and the West's handling of it, are documented in chapters three and ten. But not all Latin American countries are important political actors in negotiations, as they do not by themselves threaten the world's banking system. Most are relatively small, and their bargaining power, like Bolivia's, essentially very weak. In chapter nine, we look at one such country, Costa Rica, a small debtor (in absolute, but not in per capita terms) caught in the trammels of US policy not only towards the debt crisis, but also towards Central America.

Debt Peonage

Collectively, by 1987 the countries of the region had easily repaid all the millions they were loaned during the 1970s. Between 1974 and 1981 Latin America received a real transfer of US$100.7 billion from abroad (including direct investment by foreign companies), once profits and interest payments remitted back have been discounted. From 1982 to 1986 the countries of the region have been exporting capital to the developed world to the tune of US$121.1 billion.(see figure 1.4 and table 1.2) The industrialised world is thus already US$20.4 billion richer for its original loans. Even discounting profit remittances by multinationals, the West has made a profit on recycling the oil funds of the 1970s, roughly equivalent to the entire GDP of a Colombia or a Venezuela in 1985.

Today's debt crisis resembles the old system of debt peonage in which a reluctant local labour force is tied to the land at minimum rates of pay. The landowner advances goods to his low-paid agricultural workers on the security of their future wages. Then, by charging high rates of interest, he ensures that the peon remains eternally in his debt and cannot afford to move elsewhere in search of a better-paid job.

Like the landowner, Western countries have not only become adept at securing payment of unprecedented rates of interest, they have also done very well out of the low cost of Latin America's exports to the

14

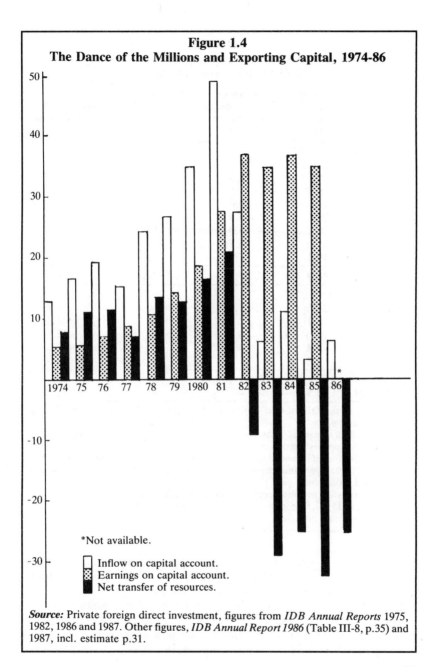

Figure 1.4
The Dance of the Millions and Exporting Capital, 1974-86

*Not available.

☐ Inflow on capital account.
▦ Earnings on capital account.
■ Net transfer of resources.

Source: Private foreign direct investment, figures from *IDB Annual Reports* 1975, 1982, 1986 and 1987. Other figures, *IDB Annual Report 1986* (Table III-8, p.35) and 1987, incl. estimate p.31.

Table 1.2
The Dance of the Millions and Exporting Capital, 1974-86
(US$ billion in current values)

	Inflow on Capital Account (1)	Of which Direct Foreign Investment (1a)	Earnings on Capital Account (2)	Net Transfer of Resources (3) = (2)−(1)
The Dance of the Millions:				
1974	13.1	1.9	−5.4	7.7
1975	16.5	3.3	−5.8	10.6
1976	18.7	1.5	−7.1	11.6
1977	15.6	3.0	−8.6	7.0
1978	24.2	3.9	−10.6	13.7
1979	26.7	5.0	−14.2	12.4
1980	35.0	5.7	−18.7	16.4
1981	49.1	7.5	−27.8	21.3
Total	**198.9**	**31.8**	**−98.2**	**100.7**
Paying the Piper:				
1982	27.6	5.7	−36.8	−9.2
1983	6.1	3.5	−34.9	−28.8
1984	11.6	3.4	−37.1	−25.5
1985*	3.4	4.0	−35.9	−32.6
1986*	6.2	n.a.	n.a.	−25.0
Total (1982-6)	**54.9**	—	—	**−121.1**

*Estimates from *IDB Annual Report 1987*, Table 49 (Net Balance on Capital Account), and p.3.
(1) Net result of all capital inflows and outflows, including private direct investment, bank loans, suppliers' credits etc.
(2) Sum of inflows of income derived from ownership of foreign financial assets, less outflows. This category includes interest paid on loans and securities, dividends on shares, and profits from enterprises.
Source: Figures for private direct foreign investment from *IDB Annual Reports* 1975, 1982, 1986, and 1987. Other figures from *IDB Annual Report 1986*, Table III-8, p.35, and 1987, estimate on p.3.

West. This is a critical factor in keeping inflation down in the industrialised countries, which is more usually credited to the virtuous behaviour of Western governments themselves.

In the late 1980s, with export prices still low and with a new recession facing the West, the chances of paying off the principal and ending this export of capital are small. Latin America as a whole is still carrying a level of debt four times its export earnings in any one year: in the case of weaker countries such as Bolivia more than seven times. Even on the optimistic assumptions about world trade set out by the IMF, Latin America's debt in 1990 will total US$410 billion, with interest payments due of US$38.5 billion, thus ensuring that the perverse flow of capital from poor to rich will continue into the next decade.

As we conclude in chapter ten, under present conditions, this outflow of funds will go mainly to feed an insatiable market for credit in the world's richest country, the US, where deficit spending has been greatly exacerbated by President Reagan's re-armament programme. Money from Latin America will be used to help US industry cope with West German and Japanese competition, and to preserve the right of the US consumer to more and better houses, cars and videos, in spite of the crisis facing the US economy. The poor of Latin America are being squeezed to fund not only the consumption, but also the power struggles, of the governments of the world's most prosperous societies.

2. The Giants Play Monopoly

'To find respectable arguments for default, we might note that the US itself effectively defaulted on a foreign debt of US$68 billion in 1971, when it reneged on the Bretton Woods Agreements to convert foreign holdings of dollars into gold at US$35 an ounce.'
Claude Cockburn, *The Wall Street Journal*, 7 January 1986.

The leaders of the West have never had any doubt as to the real storyline of the 1982 debt crisis. The victims were the Western banks. The nightmare ending was the collapse of the world's entire financial system as one after another of the West's leading financial institutions went bankrupt. The task facing Western governments was therefore to ensure that the banks received a sufficient supply of money from their Latin American debtors, at least in the form of regular payments of interest, to keep them from having to declare a formal default on loans.

For the poor of Latin America, this vision of priorities is the stuff of purest Western self-delusion. Bankers are well fed — if anything, their salaries have increased during the debt crisis. Their children do not die of malnutrition. The children of Latin America's urban slums and neglected rural areas often do. For Western governments however, dark memories of the stock market crash of the 1930s combined with a sense of guilt. If the banks had overextended themselves in the 1970s on loans to poor credit risks in Latin America, some of the blame attached not just to their head offices, but to the IMF and the Finance Ministries of Western governments, who not only abdicated all responsibility for supervising the banks' international lending, but provided every form of official encouragement to the banks to make the loans.

Ultimately, the real roots of the debt crisis lie in a quiet struggle for economic advantage between the great capitalist powers, as the US

18

attempts to preserve its dominant role in the world economy in the face of growing competition from West Germany and Japan. Latin America's debts were created in the course of one manoeuvre in this struggle, when the great powers could not agree on a programme of economic reflation or an increase in IMF and World Bank funding to counteract the effect of the OPEC price rises of 1974 and 1979 and agreed instead to turn the problem of recycling petrodollars over to the banks. The debts became totally unmanageable in the course of a second manoeuvre, as President Reagan bolstered arms spending in an attempt to assert both US military superiority over the Soviet Union and US technical leadership over other Western economies.

Even the existence of an international banking system operating under conditions of almost total freedom from government surveillance, and able to take such huge risks, is largely due to the game of Monopoly which the Western powers have been playing since the late 1960s, with the international financial system as their board.

Finance, Debt and Default before the Second World War

In the nineteenth century, international trade was financed through the exchange of gold, while the financial institutions which organised world flows of credit were rooted in the British Empire and were based in London. International loans took the form of bonds issued on the London market and bought by large numbers of individuals, thus spreading the impact of default in what was an extremely risky business. This financial system began to collapse during the First World War, which weakened the Western powers' financial position and forced them for the first time to declare that their currencies could no longer be converted into gold. The Great Depression in the 1930s set the final seal on its disappearance, as international trade first of all foundered and then became the focus of political competition between Germany, Britain and the US.

For developing countries, the collapse was to prove incomparably less dangerous than the situation which confronted them in the 1980s. Latin American countries which owed large debts to foreigners before the Great Depression almost all defaulted in the wake of the Great Crash. These defaults sometimes triggered the fall of a government, but they had very little strategic significance for the superpowers in a world strongly marked by their political rivalries. If anything, rivalry protected the defaulters' interests, as none of the great powers was prepared to allow a defaulter to be forced by economic problems into the hands of a potential rival. In any event, Latin America's debts were owed not to the West's leading banks, but to thousands of individuals who had bought them as bonds in the way others had bought stocks and shares, whose values had also plummeted in the Great Crash. As their economies revived, Latin American governments were able to redeem these bonds at a greatly reduced price and relatively easily recover their credit status.[1]

The Bretton Woods Alternative

In 1944 the Allies came together for a conference at Bretton Woods in the US to establish the rudiments of a new international financial system. The agreements they reached there reflected the trauma of the Crash and the desire of all parties to recreate a new framework for international trade. The gold standard was replaced with a system of pegged exchange rates, policed by the newly-created IMF. The reemergence of rival trading blocs, seen as a cause of the Second World War, was to be avoided through a slow negotiated progress towards the elimination of all national customs barriers, an aim later given institutional form in the General Agreement on Trade and Tariffs (GATT). The self-evident need for some mechanism to encourage financial transfers from prosperous North America to nations devastated by the war, led to the creation of the International Bank for Reconstruction and Development, later known as the World Bank.[2]

For all its good intentions, the Bretton Woods Agreement nonetheless reflected the lop-sided economic circumstances behind its creation. While some of today's Less Developed Countries (LDCs) were represented at the conference, most of them were still suffering from colonial rule. The US was clearly the world's dominant economy, being the only power to emerge from the conflict with its productive system intact, the obvious lender of last resort for the new system, and the source of funds for reconstruction. Its representatives were determined that the new monetary system should work to its advantage. The British were prepared to make concessions on the structure of the new world trading system in return for US financial support.

Thus, contrary to the initial proposals put forward by the British economist, John Maynard Keynes, the new international monetary system essentially reflected the interests of the US. The new international currency was no longer gold, nor a neutral international currency such as the 'bancor' which Keynes suggested, but, in the words of the agreement, 'gold and US dollars'. In practice, although the dollar could in theory be freely exchanged for a fixed quantity of gold, the US currency became the indispensable medium for post-war trade and investment. Other national currencies were pegged at a fixed exchange rate to the dollar, and governments were responsible for preserving that value against speculators.

In effect, the US gained the right to coin and spend the world's international currency. This was an enormous advantage to the US in its drive to extend investment abroad and to cover the costs of an expanding worldwide military presence. Furthermore, the less restricted trading system encouraged by GATT, and an unrestricted right for foreign firms to invest in national markets, allowed the quick diffusion of US multinationals and US economic supremacy across the globe.

The Rise of Eurodollar Markets

Privately-owned international banks hardly existed within this framework. The central banks of Europe, Japan and Latin America held the US dollars used to fund the initial activities of US multinationals or to pay the living costs of US servicemen abroad. The rise of international financial markets was made possible by the decay of the Bretton Woods system from the late 1960s onwards, due to the disappearance of US economic pre-eminence, a gradual erosion of its relative industrial strength, and the increasingly desperate attempts of US governments to use a framework intended to underpin world trade to strengthen the individual performance of the US economy to its rivals' cost.

The first seeds of the Eurodollar market were planted in the 1950s, when for political reasons first China and then the Soviet Union decided that they preferred to hold the dollars they earned from international trade in European banks rather than within the US. Real growth began during the Johnson administration (1963-69), when the President was worried that US firms were investing abroad rather than at home, and so tried to restrict the right of US citizens to move capital overseas. His intention was to bolster investment in the US and thus rejuvenate an economy already beginning to suffer from West German and Japanese competition. But US banks and multinationals promptly discovered the convenience of off-shore banking centres, which could hold US dollars free from US government restrictions and thereby service the capital needs of the existing network of multinationals.[3]

Private European banks holding US dollars boomed through the

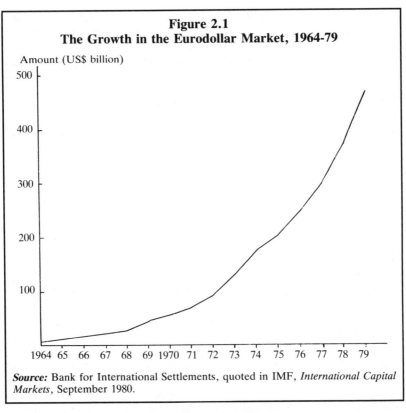

Figure 2.1
The Growth in the Eurodollar Market, 1964-79

Amount (US$ billion)

Source: Bank for International Settlements, quoted in IMF, *International Capital Markets*, September 1980.

late 1960s and early 1970s, as European central banks became increasingly reluctant to hold an ever-growing mountain of US dollars which they no longer had a hope of exchanging for gold at the official rate. 'The watershed,'according to the *Barclays Bank Review*, 'was the intensity of the Vietnam War and the large US budget deficits to which it gave rise, setting in motion an excess supply of dollars and a persistent inflationary process.'[4] Instead of taxing its own citizens to pay for the war effort, which would have been politically unpopular, the US relied on the willingness of the international economy to take an unlimited supply of dollars. But as European central banks became more and more unwilling to hold their own national reserves in dollars, so the role of private, largely European banks, taking dollar deposits and loaning them out again, correspondingly grew.(see figure 2.1)

In the early 1970s, this swelling international banking network came into its own as a result of the next change of rules in the giants' game. In

1971, for the first time since the beginning of the century, the US slid into a trade deficit. The crisis in the competitiveness of the US economy was temporarily resolved in 1971, when President Nixon first formally suspended the right of dollar holders to exchange dollars for gold and then, without consulting the IMF, declared a devaluation of the dollar in order to cheapen US exports — a tactic he repeated in 1973. Nixon's policies staved off the immediate crisis in the US, but the cost was the simultaneous destruction of the world's system of pegged exchange rates. But for European countries already involved in the Eurodollar market — principally, though not entirely, centred in the City of London — there were benefits as well as losses.

From 1973 onwards, the world moved to a system of floating exchange rates, determined by market forces, which many economists at the time favoured for being more efficient. Speculators moved back into the international financial market, where fortunes could be made by correctly guessing the next change in the major exchange rates of the world. Exporters and importers faced increasing uncertainty, with the difference between huge profit and large loss being determined not by the costs of production, but by changes in the rate in which pounds sterling were transformed into US dollars or vice versa. They too began to hedge their bets by buying forward on the international currency markets known as the futures market, and thereby acquiring the right to collect pounds or dollars at a specified price at a certain time in the future.

The managers of multinationals' financial departments discarded the careful tailoring of a conservative banker for the snazzy sportswear of adventurous dealers in international money markets, making vast new profits for the company by playing the exchange markets with the firm's working capital. The era of Casino Capitalism had arrived.[5] The Eurocurrency markets thrived. They were no longer confined to dollars, since they dealt in loans (and speculation) in all the major currencies of the world, nor yet confined to Europe, as the international financial system spread its wings into New York, Chicago, Singapore and Bahrain. By the mid-1980s, the Eurodollar market had become a trillion-dollar business. As *Fortune* reported in February 1985,

'The pool of international capital is enormous. Morgan Guaranty Trust estimates that the Eurodollar market amounts to nearly US$2 trillion nowadays, 20 times the US current account deficit. Daily volume on the New York foreign exchange markets runs to about US$25 billion, according to surveys by the Federal Reserve Board. Barely a tenth of that is connected to export and import business.'

23

The OPEC Oil Price Rises

Economic historians usually blame the oil price rises of 1974 and 1979 for the problems facing Western industrial countries in the 1970s and 1980s. This is partly a myth, though a convenient one for politicians in the West. There were many reasons for the end of the long post-war boom, not least the breakdown in 1971 of the stable world trading system which had prevailed since Bretton Woods, due to the growing competition between the US and other capitalist powers. Rising inflation and declining levels of profit were caused not just by the OPEC price rises, but by the diversion of resources into international finance to cope with increasing levels of uncertainty in the international trading system. Petrodollars alone do not explain the rapid growth in the activity of international financial markets, and arguably not all the money recycled to the Third World was actually accounted for by OPEC deposits.(see figure 2.2)

Nonetheless, there was a real 'oil shock'. The IMF calculates that due to the oil price rises, in 1974 alone oil-producing countries in effect withdrew US$68 billion from the world economy more than they could spend on imports.[6] From the point of view of Western governments, this money had to be used to pay for tangible goods and services. Otherwise its withdrawal would cause a sharp contraction in demand on a world scale, triggering a rise in global unemployment and making

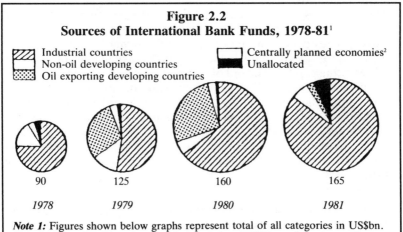

Figure 2.2
Sources of International Bank Funds, 1978-81[1]

Industrial countries
Non-oil developing countries
Oil exporting developing countries
Centrally planned economies[2]
Unallocated

| 90 | 125 | 160 | 165 |
| 1978 | 1979 | 1980 | 1981 |

Note 1: Figures shown below graphs represent total of all categories in US$bn.
Note 2: 'Centrally-planned economies' excludes all IMF members except Hungary, which joined in mid-1982.
Source: IMF, *International Capital Markets, Development and Prospects*, 1982.

The IMF and the Oil Crises

In theory, under the Bretton Woods system, it is the job of the IMF to rescue the international trading system from short-term imbalances among trading partners. Yet the real financial weight of the IMF has declined steadily since the Second World War. In 1945 the funds members pay into the IMF — known as 'quotas' — represented around 16 per cent of all world trade, less than Keynes wanted, but still a considerable sum. By 1971, as quotas fell further behind the expansion of the world economy, the comparable figure was around 8 per cent. Quotas were doubled in 1978-79, but were still too small to halt the overall decline. By 1981, in the wake of the second oil crisis, they represented a mere 3.8 per cent of world trade. The IMF also had to face explicit hostility from the Reagan administration to any kind of increase in members' quotas.

The IMF's professional staff did make an attempt to meet the first oil crisis head-on by relaxing conditions on loans available to members through the *Compensatory Fund Facility* (which is supposed to help countries facing balance of payments crises through a temporary shortfall in export revenues). New loan facilities were also created including an *Extended Facility*, to provide support for members facing long-term structural problems with their balance of payments, a *Trust Fund* for long-term loans at highly concessionary rates, and a *Special Oil Facility*, funded by loans to the IMF from Arab OPEC members which ran for two years.

Member countries gave verbal approval to this loan programme, but they refused to back it with financial resources on anything like the scale needed. Between 1972 and 1984, funds loaned out under all four of the above categories amounted to Special Drawing Right (SDR) 21 billion (US\$25 billion) out of a total IMF loan programme of SDR54.4 billion (US\$66 billion). Over the same period, the current account deficits of NOPECs ballooned to US\$362.5 billion. From 1974 to 1981, with the explicit public support of the IMF's managing director, commercial banks consistently provided NOPECs with between 65 and 75 per cent of the finance for their current account deficits.

it increasingly difficult for Western producers to pay their own increased fuel costs at a time when they were also deprived of sales. Finding customers for the OPEC-swollen balances of international banks thus suited the major Western powers. The commercial banks would recycle the petrodollars to selected Third World countries, whose ability to spend them would head off the possibility of a serious recession in OECD countries. As the world's central bankers put it, 'The functioning of the world economy and the international financial system has since 1974, depended on the role of intermediary played by international banks.'[7]

There was an alternative. The weaker capitalist powers, Britain and France, pushed for a coordinated strategy of reflation by Western governments. They argued that the funding of the IMF and the World Bank should be expanded to cope with the new wave of expected current account deficits, on softer terms than had been general in the post-war world. At the same time, to avoid a world recession, the world's industrial powers should take steps to avoid a competitive deflation of their own economies and the collapse of markets for the developing world. If it had been adopted, this approach would have eased European problems with the transition to the new level of oil prices, which were particularly acute for Europe as, unlike the US, it was not yet a major oil producer. It would have allowed Britain to maintain existing levels of expenditure in anticipation of future income from North Sea oil. And it would have lessened the catastrophic impact of the rise in fuel costs for non-oil developing countries (NOPECs), which caused so much havoc in the development strategies of the poorest countries in the Third World.

In the face of the first oil crisis, and with the Carter Administration in office, some attempts were made to use the Bretton Woods institutions (and particularly the IMF) to cope with the global imbalances. (see box p.25) But member countries continued to provide the IMF with minimal resources, only covering a fraction of the balance of payments deficits involved. Although they did come to a formal agreement to avoid a competitive race for adjustment on the part of individual Western industrial countries, they promptly reneged on their promises as the US, West Germany and Japan scrambled to secure their own conpetitive position in the new, post-OPEC world economy at the cost of the rest of the world.[8]

Meanwhile, in this atmosphere of confrontation, the international banks found their traditional role as a haven for footloose capital strengthened. The US was overtly vindictive towards Arab countries after the price rises. Fearing a possible US government move to confiscate their assets in US banks, Arab countries preferred to hold their dollars in Europe's Eurodollar markets. With oil-producing countries holding 60 per cent of all funds on deposit in international capital markets in 1974, it was thus the commercial banks who ensured that OPEC surpluses should be spent somewhere. The sums involved tended to decline sharply over time, but they remained significant — an average of US$35 billion from 1975-77. The original growth in bank loans to the Third World started in the late 1960s, led by US banks. Citicorp was the first to perceive overseas loans as a golden road to increased earnings. In the wake of the oil price rises, bank loans to NOPECs (including Eastern Europe) nearly doubled between 1974 and 1976 and again between then and 1979 — a total of about US$137 billion over the period.

Table 2.1
The Rising Share of Bank Loans in Net Inflows of Capital to Latin America, 1961-78

1961-65	Total: US$1.6 billion	
	Public money	60.2%
	Government aid	40.7%
	Multilateral agencies*	19.5%
	Private money	39.8%
	Suppliers' credits**	7.7%
	Direct investment†	25.2%
	Bonds	5.0%
	Banks	2.1%
1966-70	Total: US$2.6 billion	
	Public money	40.1%
	Government aid	24.4%
	Multilateral agencies*	15.7%
	Private money	59.9%
	Suppliers' credits**	13.8%
	Direct investment†	33.3%
	Bonds	2.5%
	Banks	9.3%
1971-75	Total: US$7.6 billion	
	Public money	25.2%
	Government aid	11.8%
	Multilateral agencies*	13.4%
	Private money	74.8%
	Suppliers' credits**	2.3%
	Direct investment†	26.2%
	Bonds	2.5%
	Banks	43.8%
1976	Total: US$15.3 billion	
	Public money	19.6%
	Government aid	5.2%
	Multilateral agencies*	14.4%
	Private money	80.4%
	Suppliers' credits**	3.7%
	Direct investment†	12.4%
	Bonds	3.3%
	Banks	61.0%
1977	Total: US$15.6 billion	
	Public money	12.0%
	Government aid	4.6%
	Multilateral agencies*	7.4%

▶

►	*Private money*	88.0%
	Suppliers' credits**	5.8%
	Direct investment†	20.1%
	Bonds	14.8%
	Banks	48.3%
1978	Total: US$21.8 billion	
	Public money	7.3%
	Government aid	4.2%
	Multilateral agencies*	7.4%
	Private money	92.7%
	Suppliers' credits**	9.8%
	Direct investment†	16.0%
	Bonds	10.3%
	Banks	56.6%

*IMF, World Bank, Inter-American Development Bank.
**Credits for pre-payment of imports and finance of exports, used in trade.
†Investment by foreign companies in subsidiaries' plant.
Source: S. Griffith-Jones and O. Sunkel, *Debt and Development in Latin America*, Oxford, 1986, Table 5:4.

Over the eight years following the first rise in oil prices, 74 developing countries from giant Brazil to tiny Grenada chalked up individual debts with the banks of more than US$500 million.[9] The lion's share of funds went to those developing countries seen as having good economic prospects, mainly those which were themselves developing a manufacturing base (with the cooperation of Western multinationals) or those which seemed to have a future as oil producers.(see chapter four) Two-thirds of developing country debts to the banks were thus accounted for in 1981 by only five countries — Mexico, Brazil, Venezuela, Argentina, and South Korea.

The majority of Latin American governments were willing borrowers, as most faced higher bills for oil imports and borrowing was cheap in real terms. Prior to 1971, the bulk of Latin America's foreign capital had come from direct foreign investment, with the exception of a brief period from 1961-65 (the Alliance for Progress) when most of the inflowing funds came from US government aid or from multilateral agencies under strong US influence.(see table 2.1) Between 1975 and 1982 however, it was the banks who loaned out a total of about US$60 billion to Latin America. But in the rush to lend, the banks were often prepared to break cardinal rules of banking and to take undue risks in their lending policies. (see box p.29) A major factor behind their apparent lack of caution was the new competitive environment in international banking.

Can the Banks be Blamed?

Officially, UK and US bankers blame OECD governments, the IMF and the BIS for pressurising them to recycle the OPEC surpluses. They say they were urged to make the loans to cover the balance of payment deficits of developing countries who could not immediately manage the new price of oil. Banks were thus forced to break a cardinal rule of banking, under which international loans should never be used for such deficits, which is the job of the IMF to fund.

Unofficially, bankers sometimes tell a different story. In the fierce competition for reliable customers, bankers offered money even to relatively poor countries like Bolivia and Peru, whose past history might have dictated a degree of caution. As one economist from the Economic Commission for Latin America and the Caribbean (ECLAC) has written,

'In 1973-4, Peru's loan syndications were often oversubscribed, meaning that banks offered more money than the government and its lead banks had solicited [...] There were also oversubscriptions to Bolivian syndicates beginning in 1976. Particularly revealing is an incident in which Chase Manhattan was so eager to lend to the country that it broke ranks with the tradition of creditor solidarity and entered a syndicate even though the government was in default on some turn of the century bonds that had been underwritten by Chase. The bank's legal advisors were horrified by the marketing department's lack of discretion. The legal department eventually won, but as Chase withdrew it was replaced by another institution.'

Countries which were a better credit risk were simply overwhelmed with offers. Angel Gurria, head of Mexico's Office of Public Credit, recalls:

'The banks were hot to get in. All the banks in the US and Europe and Japan stepped forward. They showed no foresight. They didn't do any credit analysis. It was wild. In August 1979, for instance, Bank of America planned a loan of US$1 billion. They figured they would put up US$350 million themselves and sell off the rest. As it turned out, they only had to put up US$100 million themselves. They raised US$2.5 billion on the loan in total.'

Old rules of caution were scattered to the winds. One such rule says that no country should be allowed to borrow beyond the point at which 50 per cent of its exports revenues are committed to paying debt service charges. But by 1979, Mexico was already paying 65.6 per cent of its export revenues in debt service charges, yet bankers were queueing up to loan Mexico more funds on the basis of its prospects as an oil-producer. The herd instinct common to financial and other markets took over. Banks which *failed* to develop a portfolio of international loans were labelled 'inefficient'. For ▶

▶ example, when the Bank of Scotland faced a takeover battle in 1979, the financial press cited its lack of international loans as a weakness!

In retrospect, the most remarkable feature of the bank loans was the weakness of the information on which they were willing to lend. In the 1970s and early 1980s, banks had few economists on their staff with expertise in the developing world. Nevertheless, they were undaunted by the general inadequacy of economic data from debtor countries, and did not even begin to attempt a comparison of the political risks involved until the dance of the millions was well under way in the early 1980s. Worst of all, they tolerated the lack of any systematic local monitoring of the scale of private debt until the debt crisis broke in August 1982.

Banks simply did not pay adequate attention to the growing debt burdens, or to the damage done by the interest rate shock of 1979, the subsequent world recession and the declining export prices. Like politicians in the debtor and creditor countries, bankers put their faith in the efficiency of the markets. They saw their own scramble to lend as a confirmation that lending was economicaly viable, just as debtor politicians saw it as confirmation that their national economic policies were sound, and the growing debt burden ultimately manageable. When market conditions turned sour after 1979, bankers were forced into a hole from which there was no obvious escape.

The Banks Play Monopoly too

'I am far from alone in my youth and inexperience. The world of international banking is now full of aggressive, bright, but hopelessly inexperienced lenders in their mid-twenties. They travel the world like itinerant brushmen, filling loan quotas, peddling financial wares, and living high on the hog. Their bosses are often bright but hopelessly inexperienced twenty-nine year old vice presidents with wardrobes from Brooks Brothers, MBAs from Wharton or Stanford, and so little credit training that they would have trouble with a simple retail instalment loan.'
S.C. Gwynne, 'Adventures in the Loan Trade', *Harper's* 267, no. 1600.

The large-scale lending during the 1970s suited the macroeconomic priorities of OECD governments, the IMF and the World Bank, who wanted to limit global recession in the face of the OPEC price rises. It had a second, quite independent, rationale, when looked at from the point of view of the banks.

Between 1977 and 1980, Western banks began to face a similar problem to the one which troubled governments after 1970: the transition from stable financial markets almost completely controlled by the US, to unstable markets in which US institutions faced a strong challenge from the Europeans and Japanese.(see table 2.2)[10] In 1970, six of the world's top ten banks were North American, and between

Table 2.2
Top Ten in World Banking, 1970-85

	1970		1975		1980		1985	
1.	Bank of America	USA	Bank of America	USA	Citicorp	USA	Citicorp	USA
2.	Citicorp	USA	Citicorp	USA	Bank of America	USA	Dai-Ichi Kangyo	Jap
3.	Chase Manhattan	USA	Credit Agricole	Fra	Credit Agricole	Fra	Fuji	Jap
4.	Barclays	UK	Chase Manhattan	USA	Banque Nacionale de Paris	USA	Sumitomo	Jap
5.	Nat. Westminster	UK	Banque Nacionale de Paris	Fra	Credit Lyonnais	Fra	Mitsubishi	Jap
6.	Manufacturers Hanover	USA	Deutsche Bank	Ger	Societé Generale	Fra	Banque Nacionale de Paris	Fra
7.	Banco Nazionale del Lavoro	Ita	Credit Lyonnais	Fra	Barclays	UK	Sanwa	Jap
8.	Morgan Guaranty	USA	Societé Generale	Fra	Deutsche Bank	Ger	Credit Agricole	Fra
9.	Western Bancorp	USA	Barclays	UK	Nat. Westminster	UK	Bank of America	USA
10.	Royal Bank of Canada	Can	Dai-Ichi Kangyo	Jap	Dai-Ichi Kangyo	Jap	Credit Lyonnais	Fra

Note: Not all the banks listed are overseas lenders (Credit Agricole for example is almost purely a national bank). Also, ranking by global assets reflects sharply changing currency valuations. The strong dollar in the early 1980s increased the apparent value of US banks, and the strong yen in the mid-1980s has the same effect on Japanese banks. Nevertheless, the trend of increasing Japanese domination is still valid.

Source: The Banker, 'The Top 500', June 1971, 1976 and 1981; July 1986.

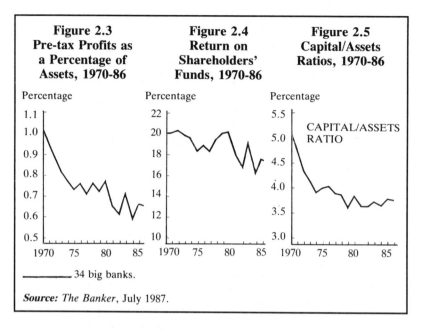

Figure 2.3
Pre-tax Profits as
a Percentage of
Assets, 1970-86

Figure 2.4
Return on
Shareholders'
Funds, 1970-86

Figure 2.5
Capital/Assets
Ratios, 1970-86

——————— 34 big banks.

Source: The Banker, July 1987.

them they controlled 70 per cent of the top ten's total assets. By 1980, only two of the US majors remained in the top ten (Citicorp and Bank of America), compared to seven European and one Japanese. By 1985, the Japanese had increased their presence to five. Despite the continued importance of the London and New York financial markets, the old banking powers in the US and the UK were struggling to maintain their market share in the face of a strong overseas challenge.

One important by-product of this competition was a collapse in the average rate of return on the banks' loans between 1970 and 1982.(see figure 2.3) Spurred on by the need for new sources of profit, bankers abandoned their traditional conservatism, opting instead to become speculators on foreign exchange markets and travelling salesmen for a new range of cheap recycling loans, guaranteed to be good business by the IMF and the world's central banks, speaking through the Bank for International Settlements (BIS). While cheap in historical terms, loans to LDCs still carried a high risk premium and were therefore more profitable than loans to the industrialised world. This money could have been put into loan loss reserves, but instead it was used to sweeten declining pre-tax earnings and preserve the return which the banks offered their shareholders.(see figure 2.4). Over the 1970s, the seven leading US banks experienced a substantial rise in the

Table 2.3
Growth in Foreign Profits of US Banks, 1970-82

	Foreign Profits (US$m)			Foreign Profits as a % of Total Profits		
	1970	1981	1982	1970	1981	1982
Citicorp	58	287	448	40	54	62
Bank of America	25	245	253	15	55	65
Chase Manhattan	31	247	215	22	60	70
Manufacturers Hanover	11	120	147	13	48	50
JP Morgan	26	234	283	25	67	72
Chemical New York	8	74	104	10	34	39
Bankers Trust New York	8	116	113	15	62	51

Source: F.F. Clairemonte and J.H. Cavanagh, 'The Spectre of Third World Debt' in *Raw Materials Report*, Vol.5, No.1, Table 2, p.6. Calculated from data from Salomon Bros. in *The Economist*, 14 January 1978 and *Forbes*, 7 May 1982 and 4 July 1983.

percentage of profits they received from foreign, rather than domestic, loans.(see table 2.3)

The squeeze on profits accompanying this inter-bank rivalry also explains some of the eagerness with which the US banks began to organise syndicated loans. The lead bank in a syndicated loan stood to earn a guaranteed fee representing an average one per cent of the loan's total value and perhaps as much as 20 per cent of the profits.[11] Thus, on a US$200 million loan package, the fee for the lead bank would be US$2 million. Even when the US majors began to doubt the wisdom of increasing their loan portfolios to LDCs (and their share in new lending actually fell from 53 per cent in 1974 to about 33 per cent in the early 1980s[12]), they nonetheless continued to play a vital role in organising syndicated loans for other banks. The determination of European and Japanese banks not to be left out of a profitable market meanwhile prolonged the dance of the millions far beyond the point at which a reasonably alert banker might have seen warning signals. As for the US banks, their acknowledged centrality to the syndication process left them in a key role as the coordinator of the international banking system's response to the debt crisis when it became public in 1982.

Competition also helps to explain the dramatic figures plastered across the world's press in August 1982, which showed US banks as having dubious loans in Latin America's problem debtor countries worth '250 per cent' of their capital. A bank's capital is its safety cushion against bad loans or runs on the bank by depositors. For very good reasons, most governments make the existence of this safety cushion a legal requirement before a bank sets up business. Banks have to have some resources in reserve to offer depositors making sudden large withdrawals, beyond the list of outstanding loans due from their debtors in ten years' time. They also need an implicit hedge against possible bad loans. Currently the US Federal Reserve Board considers an adequate capital:assets ratio (i.e. the percentage of a bank's outstanding loans covered by its own capital) to be six per cent.

During the 1970s the international banking system had allowed its capital:assets ratio to deteriorate substantially.(see figure 2.5) Thus, when the Mexican crisis hit the headlines in 1982, comparisons of the major banks' potential losses from doubtful Latin American loans were astounding, and certainly enough to scare not only the Reagan administration, but also members of the Latin American elite holding their deposits in New York banks. Other measures of the risk to the banks in fact gave a more reassuring picture: in 1982, the US$350 billion owed by all developing countries represented only 20 per cent of the US$1,800 billion worth of assets on the books of the entire Eurocurrency market, or 13.9 per cent of the total US and foreign assets of US banks.[13]

The Impact of Reaganism

Latin America's debt crisis of the 1980s thus has its origins in a convenient 'solution' to the OPEC crisis of the 1970s, a solution whose long-term viability was given too little attention by the Western actors involved. It suited the world's industrial powers because they were saved from an even worse crisis of deflation than that which they actually suffered in 1975-76, as they were provided with new export markets in the developing world. It suited the banks in their new competitive environment as the operation became highly profitable — in 1983, at the height of the debt crisis, 20 per cent of Citicorp's global profits came from profits on loans to Brazil. Initially it suited Latin American countries, in their search for money to meet balance of payments difficulties and development programmes. Local borrowers ignored the additional risks implicit in contracting commercial loans at variable interest rates, which would rise and fall with the general rate of interest on world markets.

In the period when Latin American countries were contracting their debts, rates of interest were at an all-time low. Adjusted for inflation, US real interest rates for dollar loans averaged one per cent between 1970 to 1980. Faced with a determined cutback of economic activity by major Western countries, banks could hardly find sufficient customers

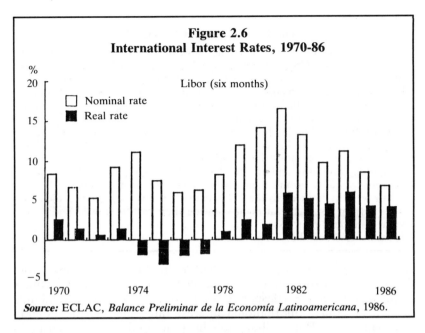

Figure 2.6
International Interest Rates, 1970-86

Libor (six months)

☐ Nominal rate
■ Real rate

Source: ECLAC, *Balance Preliminar de la Economía Latinoamericana*, 1986.

for their loans, a fact which was reflected in basic rates of interest which were below the rate of inflation in the industrialised West.(see figure 2.6)

The economic recovery of major Western powers from 1977 onwards helped change this picture, sucking funds back into OECD countries to pay for newly profitable home-based activities. More important still was the determination of OECD governments to contain inflationary pressures by restricting their money supplies, thus making capital harder to come by in OECD countries, and driving up interest rates as a result. But in 1981 the election of Ronald Reagan as President of the US gave these pressures an enormous boost. Reagan brought to power a generation of 'supply side' economists, who believed that the tendency of the US economy to lag behind German and Japanese competition could be cured by cuts in taxes and the restoration of incentives to those with money to invest. Taxes were duly cut. At the same time, government expenditure boomed, as Reagan dramatically increased the US defence budget in an effort to restore US military superiority over the Soviet Union and its technological pre-eminence over its rivals in the West.

One immediate consequence was that capital within the world economy became enormously expensive. Interest rates in the US rose

35

as the government and other US debtors tried to attract money from the rest of the world. Interest rates elsewhere rose in parallel, as other countries engaged in a desperate competition to keep the capital they needed at home. International interest rates such as the London Interbank Offer Rate (Libor), to which the service charges on Latin American debt were fixed, rose in parallel with those in the US. By 1983, the nominal interest rate was over 15 per cent and the real interest rate about 8 per cent — the highest since the Second World War.

The reverse side of the coin was a marked deterioration in the US balance of payments. Prior to 1981 the US was an important source of capital for the rest of the world. By 1983 the Reagan revolution had successfully reversed this position, with the rest of the world providing capital for the US. In just five years between 1981 and 1986 the US went from being the world's largest creditor nation to the world's largest debtor with a total debt approaching US$250 billion. (see box above)

For deeply-indebted countries in the Third World, these developments were nothing short of disastrous. One US economist has estimated that the costs to NOPECs of the initial rise in interest rates was US$20 billion a year between 1980 and 1981. This coincided with a deterioration in the terms of trade which cost them a further US$79 billion, and a fall in the real volume of exports because of the recession in the West. The final figure for the cost to NOPECs over the two years alone was US$141 billion, a staggering economic shock which was entirely externally-produced.[14]

Service charges became an impossible burden. Between 1978 and

1984, Latin America's total interest payments increased by 360 per cent, and the total amounts owed or guaranteed to international financial markets by its governments increased 250 per cent. By 1984, every 1 per cent rise in interest rates was adding US$700 million to the annual service charges of the Brazilian debt alone. The debt crisis had become inevitable.

However, the perverse effects of Reaganism on the Third World were not confined to rising debt charges. The demand for capital in the US acted like a vacuum, sucking up capital from all parts of the world economy. Euromarket capital available for rescheduling debts became much more scarce, as banks could do better business in the US. European and Japanese multinationals were also scrambling to gain a foothold in what was now the world's most secure and prosperous market. Latin America was by now facing obvious economic problems and was much less attractive to additional multinational investment, adding a famine of foreign capital from this source to the growing famine of capital from the banks. Local sources of savings also tended to migrate northwards, as local elites throughout the developing world began to send their money abroad in ever increasing amounts, encouraged by high rates of interest in the US and on international capital markets. In the case of Latin America, new sums were added to the traditional flight of capital into Florida real estate and US Treasury bonds. (see chapter four, box p.65) The world Bank estimates that Mexico alone lost US$26.5 billion in capital flight between 1979 and 1982.

The Reagan spending spree offered other OECD countries some benefits. Above all, it secured a certain level of growth in the world economy at a time when other capitalist countries were still holding back on consumer spending. Some Latin American debtors, and particularly Brazil, were thus able to find markets for their exports in the US as others closed, though not on a scale sufficient to compensate for the cost of rising interest rates or declining commodity prices.

In the long run, Reaganism has been counter-productive, even from the point of view of the US. Although it may have helped encourage US businessmen to invest by providing them with vigorous markets in defence and other areas, and a new technological drive, it also produced an immediate worsening in the underlying competitive position of the US and increasing tension betwen the US and other capitalist powers. The influx of foreign capital alone was enough to take the international value of the US dollar to new heights, which caused US exporters to be squeezed out of foreign markets. As the US trade deficit with the rest of the world expanded, so pressures within the US for more consistent protection of local markets against foreign competition grew by the day. The final legacy of the Reagan years would be an exacerbation of the world's economic imbalances and political tensions they threatened to unleash.

Over the next five years, the West's chosen solution to the debt crisis would compound world economic instability, as Latin American countries began a vigorous campaign of exports to pay their interest bills, and the US's own traditional trade surplus with Latin America slumped into a trade deficit in Latin America's favour, amounting to US$16 billion a year by 1985.

3. Can't Pay, Will Pay

'There was no Toscanini. There was no Beethoven. It was more like Arnold Schonberg improvising as he composed,' replied Donald Regan, the then US Treasury Secretary, when asked who orchestrated the handling of the Mexican debt crisis of August 1982.[1] This was not quite true. The banks had already learnt from their experience of renegotiating the Polish debt in 1981 the importance of an effective bankers' cartel (see box p.40), and from their attempts to control Peruvian economic policies in 1978 the importance of having the IMF as a watch-dog with real teeth to monitor Third World economies. Yet for Western governments, it *was* the truth. In August 1982 the possibility of Third World debt default was not included in their economic scenarios, and there was no agreed machinery for dealing with the crisis. In the circumstances, the Reagan administration's on-the-spot invention of 'the band-aid solution' pre-empted more careful planning for the resolution of the debt crisis. In practice, it also leaned heavily on the wisdom of the banks.

The Band-Aid Non-Solution

For Reagan and Regan the essence of the 1982 debt crisis was the threat that the failure by a Latin American government to keep up interest repayments might trigger a collapse of confidence in one or more of the major US banks. The threat was acute because the banks' books were already in bad shape (see chapter six), and under US law, loans on which interest had not been paid within 90 days were legally non-performing, so that interest payments from the debtors could not legally be credited to a bank's accounts. After six months of unpaid interest, loans became value-impaired, and banks could no longer credit the full value of the debt as part of their assets.

The band-aid solution was essentially a rescue mission for the banks.

39

The Bankers' Cartel

Since the debt crisis broke, Western newspapers have been full of rumours that Latin America's debtors might form a debtors' cartel, and Western governments have firmly insisted that debt negotiations must be bilateral, between individual debtors and the banks. But ironically, it is the banks who have confronted the debt crisis with a formal cartel. They first formed a cartel in 1975 when Peru's creditors created a negotiating committee chaired by Citicorp in response to Peru's threatened default. Since 1983, their coordination has been strengthened by the creation of the Institute of International Finance in Washington, to keep them better informed about the political attitudes of Western governments and the credit risks of their clients.

There is an advisory committee of bankers for each Latin American debtor, invariably chaired by a leading figure from one of the major US banks. The Mexican Advisory Committee for example, consists of a chairman, William Rhodes of Citicorp, and representatives of twelve other major banks. Rhodes is Citicorp's senior Vice-President for South America and also chairman of the advisory committees for Argentina, Peru, Uruguay and Brazil. He is in close and constant contact with US government officials and those of the IMF on issues involving the debt.

The formal task of each committee is to coordinate information and activities of a large number of smaller creditors (Mexico, for example, has 1,400 individual creditors). Within these committees, individual banks assume specialist responsibilities. In the Mexican case, Lloyds of Britain is responsible for discovering who owes what to whom, while Morgan Guaranty is responsible for monitoring the economy.

Without a parallel debtors' cartel, no Latin American country can count on a similar source of information on the vulnerability of individual banks to default. They have no specialists to tell them the current state of their nationals' deposits in Citicorp and Lloyds. Nor do they have any single agency to monitor the performance of the US government's debt and its impact on the world economy and world interest rates, and use this information in bargaining with the US Federal Reserve Board.

The price the debt crisis has exacted in terms of political instability exacerbates this weakness. When President Paz Estenssoro took over from President Siles Zuazo in Bolivia, all but three of the fifty-strong team till then responsible for negotiating Bolivia's debt were fired. In Brazil, seven Presidents of the Central Bank have represented the country in its discussions with Paul Volker of the US Federal Reserve Board since the debt crisis began.

Before the 90-day deadline expired, the US Government and the Bank for International Settlements provided crucial bridging loans, ensuring that debtors kept up payments until a new commercial agreement on rescheduling could be organised between the debtors, the banks and the IMF. Rescheduling eased the burden on debtors by postponing repayments of the original loan, making it feasible for debtors to pay the interest, with some additional help in the form of new loans ('new money') from the banks. The IMF was brought in to reorganise debtors' economies, in such a fashion as to secure the banks their interest payments in the future: essentially by switching local economic resources from domestic consumption to exports and slashing imports to produce a trade surplus. New loans and the rescheduling of old loans were made dependent on IMF conditionality. (see box p.42)

From the debtors' point of view, rescheduling temporarily eased the present burden a little at the cost of an increase in the absolute size of the debt. In fact, it postponed the problem without offering a solution. In the early years of the debt crisis, it meant postponing the problem only for a single year, until the next rescheduling. Latin American governments ceased long-term planning, and instead struggled to manage the economy for the next ten months, closely supervised by the IMF.

In their critical short-term role of avoiding a debt default, the US Treasury, Federal Reserve Board and the IMF gathered together the key threads to ensure their political control over the crisis. There was no need for government pressure on the major US and British banks, as their own personnel were playing an active part behind the scenes in the management of bilateral negotiating committees. Pressure had, however, to be maintained on the smaller banks, who had taken a stake in syndicated loans in the heyday of lending, and now needed to be forced to keep up small additional loans when their best commercial instincts dictated a rapid withdrawal from the field.

In fact, the real targets for Western government pressure were not mid-Western banks, but possibly recalcitrant Latin American debtors. Here the Polish debt negotiations provided a model. In 1981, faced with the defeat of the independent trade union movement, Solidarity, the US government briefly considered using the negotiations to destabilise the Polish economy. As *The Economist* said at the time, a blockade on crucial trade credits and parts for Western-installed machinery would have given the West real political leverage.[2] In Poland, this shameless economic blackmail was not used as the West German banks were anxious to preserve their ties with Eastern bloc economies. However, it played a crucial part in securing the compliance of Latin America governments, whenever they threatened to challenge the legitimacy of debt payments. Deputy Secretary of the US Treasury McNamar made open reference to it in a speech to the US Chamber of Commerce in 1983, when he outlined the sanctions available against a defaulter:

IMF Conditionality

Conditionality, the right to demand policy changes from governments which ask for loans from IMF funds, is the hallmark of the IMF. Governments come to the IMF as a lender of last resort when their balance of payments deficits reach crisis levels. In a typical stand-by programme, they are offered IMF funds and an IMF seal of approval which virtually guarantees a rescheduling of debts with individual OECD governments through the Paris Club of creditors (on which the IMF has its own representative), and should also guarantee a parallel rescheduling with commercial banks. The IMF's stand-by programme usually lasts a year, and funds are repayable over the next five years.

In return, the IMF demands changes in government economic policy to correct the deficit. These changes are negotiated with an IMF mission of economists, embodied in a formal letter of intent from the government, and enforced by a careful spacing of the stand-by loan into tranches at three month intervals. To secure each successive tranche — and the relief from other creditors that comes with it — a government must show that it has complied with the IMF's policy demands and met the successive economic targets specified in the letter of intent (such as reduced public sector deficits, increased exports, and reduced inflation), and policy targets like devaluation of the currency or the introduction of measures to attract private foreign capital. Failure to meet these agreed targets attracts the risk of loss of the next tranche of the loan and withdrawal of the IMF's seal of approval. In effect, IMF experts sit down with the government's own economic ministers to plan development of the local economy throughout the year covered by a stand-by loan.

Conditionality is the creditors' answer to balance of payments problems, and is designed to reassure OECD governments, OECD exporters, and the international banks. It did not appear in the original Bretton Woods agreement, given Keynes' insistence that surplus countries, like today's Japan and West Germany, were as much responsible for balance of payments problems as those countries which registered a deficit. Latin America was the first visible target, when the US invented the concept and steered it through an Executive Committee meeting in 1952. In 1954, when Peru signed the first ever stand-by agreement, it took very much its present form. By way of contrast, the UK, drawing several tranches of IMF funds in 1956, was exempt from any formal agreement to conditions.

By 1952, conditionality clearly had other goals than a simple correction of balance of payments deficit. Following the Great Depression and the Second World War, Latin American governments built a series of direct government controls over imports, differential exchange rates which used the profits from the export sector and turned them towards investment in local industry, and massive programmes of state investment in the economy. IMF policy prescriptions were part of a US campaign to roll back these so-called siege economies, and open up the continent to foreign trade ▶

and investment, strengthening the position of US and other foreign businessmen in the face of a developmentalist drive by the local state. With the proviso that it should always act so as to further the expansion of international trade built already into its articles of association, the IMF was a useful ally. But other agencies were also dragged into the campaign. The Pentagon was involved in the setting-up of the US-Brazil Mutual Defence Treaty of 1959, which endorsed the principle that the Brazilian state should not set up government monopolies and favour these suppliers over foreign corporations.

'The foreign assets of a country would be attached by creditors throughout the world: its exports would be seized by creditors at each dock where they landed, its national airlines unable to operate and its sources of desperately needed capital goods and spare parts virtually eliminated. In many countries even food imports would be curtailed. Hardly a pleasant scenario.'[3]

How serious this threat was in practice is a difficult question. Given the willingness of the US, Japan and Germany to risk disruption of the entire world economy in the pursuit of their own competitive interests during this period (as shown by the tensions between the US and West Germany over Poland), the threat was probably not particularly serious. In the event of default, the industrial power which failed to abide by this stern programme of sanctions could have expected to make substantial gains from trading with Latin America on its own account. Nonetheless, Latin American governments, economists and businessmen were unprepared to take the risk.

Band-Aid and the IMF

With the support of Western governments, the IMF was now cast in the dual role of crisis manager and policeman. There was a certain irony in this development. In the 1970s, as commercial bank loans took over, the role of the IMF as a major source of loans to developing countries with balance of payments problems declined. At the same time, in response to the emergence of global economic shocks such as the oil crisis, its lending policies softened considerably, and new longer-term facilities were created to help developing countries such as the Extended Fund Facility (allowing countries to prolong their adjustment programmes up to three years). (see box, p.25) But in 1982 neither the banks nor the US government were in any position to impose the cruel restructuring of local economies necessary to ensure continuation of interest payments. As the Vice-President of the Royal

Bank of Canada explained, 'there certainly is a need for [the IMF] to be in there, as a lender and as a disciplinarian and that's the thing all of us like about the IMF. They, perhaps like no one else, can make conditions on loans, which ensures some tightening of the belt.'[4]

The advent of the Reagan administration in late 1980 paved the way for a tougher IMF attitude towards developing countries with balance of payments problems. In late 1981 the US implemented a conditionality freeze, restricting the IMF use of low conditionality funds and longer-term agreements by the single expedient of voting against any loan agreements which did not conform to the traditional pattern of the year-long stand-by loan. Even the softer loan facilities which were already in operation were subject to high conditionality. The Reagan administration's attitude received explicit support from the commercial banks, who told the IMF openly that softer stand-by agreements were jeopardising its role as a seal of approval for further commercial lending.[5]

The debt crisis of 1982 gave the IMF some new money and unprecedented powers. In 1983 the member governments of the IMF increased their subscriptions by almost 50 per cent, and reached an agreement allowing the IMF to borrow still more funds from OECD governments' central banks at need, thus almost doubling the total resources the IMF had available to US$100 billion. The new funds were explicitly for high conditionality loans only; the resources available for softer loans facilities remained frozen at the previous level.

The IMF had given vigorous support to the recycling of the OPEC surpluses. Now it changed its tune. International financial flows to the developing world in the 1970s had made possible 'weak domestic policies and delays in adjustment measures [...] Demand-management policies had been lax'.[6] Debtor countries were held to have contributed to the crisis through supply side weaknesses, due to price distortions in their local markets and a reluctance to devalue. The debt crisis with all its ramifications was thus assimilated into the IMF's traditional policy prescriptions for countries with balance of payments difficulties. If the Fund had any doubts about the value of prescribing increased exports simultaneously to large numbers of primary exporters, in the face of already-depressed markets, these were not publicly expressed.

The IMF's new role also implied a certain gentlemanly coercion of the banks themselves, with the IMF 'insisting' (before the debt crisis, it would have 'hoped') that they should agree to new loans before the IMF credits were transferred. These new loans were known as involuntary lending, though the terms for the new loans and the costs of rescheduling were left up to the banks to negotiate with the debtors. Greater support for the IMF had to be forced on the banks as an essential part of the band-aid solution, because the experience of the 1976-81 period showed that commercial banks were ever less willing to support the IMF's seal of approval with new commercial loans.[7]

With the IMF as a prop, OECD governments thus secured a definition of the nature of the debt crisis which has dogged Latin America ever since, the so-called 'case by case' or 'bilateral' approach. The debt crisis became the sum of a series of individual problems between country negotiators and their creditors with the IMF acting as arbiter. The only appropriate solution was effective adjustment on the part of the individual debtors, without any concessions to the weight of external trade conditions and long-term structural problems during the 1970s. The OECD countries, whose economic mismanagement created the debt crisis, were saved the embarrassment of having to fund a large-scale government bail-out of the debtors.

Squeezing a Continent

Between the end of 1982 and the end of 1983, the IMF band-aid was applied to no less than fourteen Latin American countries. From the IMF's point of view, it was clearly a success. Before the onset of the crisis in the late 1970s and early 1980s, Latin America's exports just failed to cover the cost of its imports by US$2-3 billion a year. By 1983, in spite of stagnating exports, the region had built up a US$30 billion trade surplus, which was not eroded until 1986.(see table 3.1) This surplus, mainly caused by a drastic cut in imports, was the by-product of the IMF's successful strategy of demand-management, i.e. a deliberately-induced and savage compression of local public and consumer spending. Its benefits were passed directly to Western bankers. Latin America's net transfer of capital from 1982-86 reached a staggering US$121 bilion (see chapter one, table 1.2), US$20 billion

Table 3.1 Latin America's Trade Balance, 1980-86 (US$ billion)							
	1980	1981	1982	1983	1984	1985	1986
Exports (FOB)	93.9	100.7	86.3	91.5	100.9	95.3	80.1
Imports (FOB)	95.5	102.9	78.9	61.4	63.1	62.9	62.0
Trade Balance	−1.5	−2.1	+7.3	+30.1	+37.8	+32.4	+18.0
Source: IDB Annual Report 1987, Table II-4, p.10.							

The IMF Traditional Recipe

- **Demand-Management**, i.e. a cut in the spending power of local consumers. Too much local spending power is assumed to be the reason behind every balance of payments deficit. Cuts are usually achieved by a government-imposed controls on real wages — the one government control which the IMF favours. Deflation and increased unemployment usually follow in demand-management's train.

- **Devaluation of Currency**, which makes a country's exports cheaper, and arguably more attractive to foreign buyers. But devaluation also makes its imports more expensive for local consumers, which may lead to a cut in import bills (because consumers can no longer afford to buy), or higher inflation (because workers push for higher wages).

- **Liberalisation of Foreign Trade**, the elimination of government-imposed import controls, whether these operate directly or indirectly (such as through the government fixing different exchange rates for different categories of goods). Broadly, this means that imported goods go to those who can best afford them, and governments cannot attempt to save foreign exchange by banning imported luxuries and allowing only investment goods or food.

- **Liberalisation of Prices**, usually involving the elimination of price controls, which in the short run also generates inflation.

- **Reduction in Budget Deficits** especially by removing state subsidies to food, fuel and transport, and reducing social expenditure.

- **A Restructuring of Relative Prices** i.e. large price increases to benefit particularly important sectors such as energy, agriculture and exports, at the cost of consumers, generating further inflation.

- **Raising Interest Rates to their Natural Market Levels** to discourage capital flight. This also discourages local private investment (generating deflation), giving multinationals a marked advantage in the battle for investment resources over local firms without foreign financial connections, and making government borrowing on local financial markets much more expensive (generating higher public deficits and more inflation).

- **Elimination of Artificial Government Subsidies on Investment** which again gives an advantage to multinationals over local firms.

- **Reduction of State Investment in the Economy**, on the theory that state activity crowds out the efforts of private sector firms to obtain credit and forces up their costs by raising taxes.

The IMF is against inflation and in favour of reducing public sector deficits. Fund policies tend, however, to produce a surge in inflation — thus justifying even more drastic controls on wages to reduce inflationary pressures. Policies which raise government costs, like those which force up local interest rates to provide local investors with a risk premium over what they would get in the US, likewise force debtor governments to take even sharper measures to reduce public sector investment, public sector services, and the wages of government employees.

more than the total net transfer of resources Latin America received during the entire dance of the millions after 1974. Even so, the debt kept growing, albeit at a slower rate. Without new money from their commercial creditors, Latin American countries could still not afford to pay all the interest due on their old debts.

This squeezing of Latin America was achieved principally through the adoption of traditional IMF policy prescription. (see box p.46) There was, however, some bending of the rules to serve the greater needs of the banks. For example, exchange controls and import tariffs are generally not liked by the IMF. But a cut in imports on the scale achieved would have been impossible if the IMF had not accepted the right of governments such as Mexico and Brazil to introduce statutory import controls to meet the emergency. Likewise, band-aid letters of intent concentrated on devaluation as the best technique for currency management, but the IMF also accepted direct government controls over foreign exchange (as in Brazil and Mexico), and even dual exchange rates in some cases, merely demanding that governments provide the foreign exchange to cover private sector debt.[8]

Drastic cuts in public sector expenditure were a crucial policy prescription, with the IMF demanding that Mexico should halve its public sector deficit within a year, and Brazil eliminate it entirely. The IMF also put open pressure on governments to reduce public spending on investment and cut government subsidies to local consumers and producers. None of this prevented the IMF from offering tacit support to Western banks in their campaign to have the local private sector's debts nationalised, thus greatly increasing the real burden of foreign debt on public sector finances.(see chapter six)

Other customary prescriptions were followed rigorously. Governments were pressurised to free prices in general and raise local interest rates to levels capable of keeping capital within the country, regardless of the impact of local capital costs on local private sector investment. Such measures brought about a severe deflation of economic activity, thus compounding the direct cuts in local consumption brought on by government wage controls. Falling demand from workers in the private sector and falling demand generated by the government combined to confront local industrialists with a dramatic contraction in their markets. The theory was that having no alternative, they would turn to exports. Few among Latin America's small businesses were in any position to take this step. The immediate consequence of IMF programmes everywhere was thus a dramatic fall in economic output. The effect on the continent's poor was catastrophic and jeopardised any prospect of development until the 1990s.(see below, chapter five)

The Cartagena Non-Solution

If no Toscanini was available to conduct the response of Western governments, and if Western banks had to make do with the musical abilities of Citicorp's William Rhodes, then Latin America lacked not so much a good conductor as the entire orchestra. For the next five years, Latin American countries were to be bedevilled by their own inability to forge a united front against the West's band-aid solution to the crisis. In the face of such weakness, the West was able to maintain the principle that debt negotiations should always take place between a single debtor and all its commercial creditors combined. Periodic declarations of support for this ironically-labelled principle of 'bilateralism' were extracted from the debtors, and those willing to negotiate on the West's terms were intermittently used against more recalcitrant governments.

In the early days of the debt crisis, there was no cooperation at all among Latin American governments. Stories even circulated of two of the major debtors negotiating on the same day in the same bank — but on different floors — with each being totally unaware of the other's existence. When collective action came, it was typically cautious: whereas Western politicians had taken immediate action to resolve the crisis in their favour, Latin Americans' first response was to look to the regional international agencies to produce a documented analysis. In February 1983, the then President of Ecuador, Osvaldo Hurtado wrote to the Economic Commission for Latin America (ECLAC) and to the Latin American Economic System (SELA), a coordinated listening post for Latin American governments in Washington, asking them to undertake a social and political analysis of the implications of the crisis.

In raising the question, Hurtado was voicing the real concerns of the new wave of civilian politicians gradually replacing military dictatorships, that the debt crisis could threaten the fragile stability of the new democratic governments. Ecuador had been one of the first countries to return to civilian rule in 1979. As Hurtado himself put it, 'what is at stake is the social and political peace of the nations and the stability of the democratic system', and darkly warned about the 'possibility of a total disaster'.

By May 1983 ECLAC and SELA had written a document which was first discussed in Quito, then in Santo Domingo and then at the Organisation of American States (OAS) meeting in Caracas in September, where the US contemptuously brushed aside attempts to raise the issue, arguing that it was only a temporary problem. The Latin Americans learnt their lesson and deliberately did not invite a

US representative to the meeting in Quito in January of 1984, which adopted the so-called Quito Declaration.

This declaration, signed by all the Foreign Ministers, was the first and most radical in a long series. It called for a continuing flow of information and coordination among the Latin American debtors, and outlined a set of demands which the debtors agreed to put to their creditors in negotiation: no increase in the costs of debt through re-negotiation; longer grace and amortisation periods on rescheduled debt; increased resources for the IMF, including new SDRs for indebted countries; and debt repayments to be linked to export earnings. As a result of the Quito meeting, the first approach was made to the OECD countries asking for a discussion of the debt problem between governments. Once again, the response was cursory: the OECD governments refused the request, arguing that the debt was a private issue between debtors and the banks.

In early 1984 the Alfonsín government in Argentina — itself a newly elected civilian regime, desperate to maintain popular standards of living — declared a six-month moratorium on interest payments in the hope of negotiating a better deal. It could have been a moment to inspire some hard collective bargaining on behalf of all Third World debtors. The New York Federal Reserve Board was coincidentally hosting a conference on the debt to consider the possibility of more global solutions. Instead, Mexico, Colombia, Brazil and Venezuela cooperated with the US government to preserve the fictional economic buoyancy of the US major banks, offering Argentina a loan to cover its interest payments before the termination of the 90 day limit.(see box p.50). The message was clear: Argentina would be totally isolated in any attempt to call the banks' or the US government's bluff. Shortly after, Alfonsín capitulated, changed his Minister of Finance and began negotiations with the IMF.

However, collaboration did continue at the level of public statements denouncing the developed world's lack of interest in the debt. The continuing rise in interest rates throughout 1984 stung the previously cautious Presidents of Brazil, Colombia and Mexico, together now with Argentina, to issue a public letter in May, calling for international action and summoning other Latin American countries to participate in a meeting 'to define initiatives and more adequate forms of action'. Headlines appeared in the Western press suggesting that the banks were threatened with the appearance of a debtors' cartel. But Latin American governments' intentions were still basically conciliatory. In June, the Presidents of these four countries, together with those of Ecuador, Peru and Venezuela, wrote a very polite letter to the Group of Seven meeting in London, calling for a

---

Political Pressure on Argentina

Few developments have done more to dispel bankers' anxieties about Third World debt than those that brought Argentina to swallow the IMF's medicine last year [1984]. They showed how much pressure can be brought to keep a country from becoming an outcast of the international financial community. Of all the major debtors caught up in the crisis, Argentina was the most likely to default. It is self-sufficient in food and energy and, as the Falkland Islands war proved, unpredictable. But when Argentina took a tough stance with its banks early in 1984 and refused to pay interest, it found itself virtually isolated.

Four Latin American countries came to Argentina's aid with portions of a stop-gap loan — not because they sympathised but because they wanted to keep Argentina involved in the debt-restructuring process. Latin American finance ministers, economists from the IMF and commercial banks and officials from major industrialised countries dropped by to remind the government of the consequences of defying the lenders.

The US Treasury came up with another bit of persuasion: a list of items that would become scarce in various major debtor countries if they defaulted and imports came to a virtual standstill. R.T. Macnamar, Deputy Treasury Secretary, emphasises that the list did not single out Argentina. But he says it raised such interesting questions as: 'Have you ever contemplated what would happen to the president of a country if the government couldn't get insulin for its diabetics?'*

* *At the time the US company solely responsible for the manufacture of insulin was threatening to close down its operations in Argentina.*

Fortune, February 1985.

---

constructive dialogue between debtor and creditor countries over the debt. The Group of Seven made no concessions.

Two weeks after the failure of this initiative, all of the above, together with Bolivia, Chile, Uruguay and the Dominican Republic, met at Cartagena to adopt the Cartagena Consensus. Even at this point, Argentina's call for a debtors' cartel was undermined by Brazil and Mexico. The Consensus set out a list of international bodies to which the Latin American governments could address further appeals for dialogue. If anything, the tone was less aggressive than it had been in Quito and the propositions for a common platform in debt negotiations less clear.

Subsequent meetings of the Cartegena group added little to this programme. Undoubtedly, the very existence of the group helped to reduce the monopoly rents being charged by the banks on rescheduling.(see chapter six) Exchanges of information ensured that any gains made by one country in the course of negotiations would immediately figure as demands in the negotiation strategy of other

Castro on Cartagena

'The Latin American countries piously meet to implore that they be taken into account, saying they are starving, and they write letters. In this situation, they set up a small group, the so-called Cartagena Group, and started writing moderate, careful, elegant, polite letters:

"Look, sir, please we need to have political dialogue to settle these problems, to discuss the question of debt. Look, sir, give us a break: increase the basic funds of the IMF and the Special Drawing Rights; and make provisions for a special fund earmarked to cover excess interest. Help us."

And so the spring meeting of the IMF was held in April in Washington. Well, the Cartagena group wrote its letter, made its proposals, pleaded, implored, and was left waiting. The matter was settled in 15 minutes. They were told "No". and that was that.

"That's ridiculous; forget about it; work hard; export; be austere; economise so you can pay the debt; and moreover, develop." '

Fidel Castro, Meeting on the Status of Latin American and Caribbean Women, 7 June 1985.

debtors (although they did not guarantee that countries would receive the same treatment). Nevertheless, at the end of the day, there was no political dialogue, and no substantial concessions on debt relief. Declining oil prices and persistent difficulties in rescheduling agreements caused by the reluctance of regional banks to commit new resources continued to dog the band-aid negotiations throughout 1984 and 1985.[9]

Three events in the second half of the 1985 helped persuade the US government that the band-aid solution was not working. First, in July Alan García took the unilateral decision to limit debt repayments to 10 per cent of the value of Peru's exports, and called for collective action by all Latin American debtors to impose the same kind of restrictions, convening a timely meeting of the Cartagena group in Lima to add weight to the threat. Bankers meeting in their own Group of Fourteen forum in Paris began to worry that Peru's action might just trigger a domino effect.[10] Coincidentally, Fidel Castro also chose July to host a series of conferences on the debt issue with representatives of Latin American churches, businessmen, military officers, trade unions and women's groups, exhorting all of them to consider the prospects of relief through a general repudiation of the debt burden, and pointing out the limitations of the Cartegena group. (see box above)

Finally, Mexico, which in the first eighteen months of the crisis had been the IMF's much touted success story, was also running into problems as a decline in oil prices on world markets made nonsense of

Table 3.2
Official Loans from OECD Sources Replace Commercial Financial Flows, 1981-85
(US$ billion)

| | Net Flows of External Finance to Latin America* | | | | | |
| | Official** | | Commercial | | Overall Total | |
	Total	%	Total	%	Total	%
1981	4.5	8.6	47.2	91.4	51.6	100
1982	6.3	17.1	30.3	82.9	36.5	100
1983	13.5	40.3	19.9	59.7	33.4	100
1984	8.4	120.5	−1.4	−20.5	7.0	100
1985	11.1	104.8	−0.5	−4.8	10.5	100

*Financing in the form of growth of the external debt. Figures exclude the Bahamas, Panama and Surinam.
**Financing by the IMF, other multilateral agencies and foreign governments.
Source: IDB Annual Report 1987, Table III-6, p.32.

a second and softer rescheduling agreement finally signed in March. In August, the Mexican Finance Minister went on record with a warning that debtor countries could be expected to withhold interest payments if they had insufficient access to new funds.

In September Mexico fell foul of IMF performance targets and was threatened with the loss of a tranche of its current loan. Hard on the news of the IMF's displeasure came the shattering earthquake in September. With little sense of timing or tact, bankers rushed into print and onto newscreens, demanding that the catastrophe should not be allowed to delay Mexico's repayment schedule or justify any loosening of the economy to allow for the cost of the physical rebuilding of Mexico City.

In October 1985, the US government suddenly reversed its existing policy of public indifference to the debt negotiations, and dropped its hostility to increased funding of debtor countries through World Bank loans. A dramatically new approach to the crisis was unveiled by the US Treasury Secretary James Baker at the annual IMF meeting in Seoul, South Korea in October 1985, and was promptly christened the Baker Plan. The US now tacitly recognised the existence of a fundamental flaw in the band-aid solution: in practice, controls over lending by private banks had not prevented them from quietly withdrawing funds from Latin America to invest in more profitable and safer projects in the US and Europe, leaving the IMF and other International Financial Institutions (IFIs) to cover their interest bill. (see table 3.2) Central to the Baker Plan was the conviction that commercial banks would have to be cajoled and bribed into renewing the flow of private loans.

At Seoul, the Reagan administration reluctantly accepted the principle against which it had fought within the IMF in 1981: multilateral agencies had to provide some compensatory flow of funds to debtor countries, and allow some time for the reorganisation of the local economy to cope with changes in international markets. Baker saw a revamped World Bank, traditionally chaired by a US citizen, as the appropriate channel for these compensatory flows of finance. World Bank sectoral and structural adjustment loans would allow investment in debtors' export sectors while simultaneously resolving all those unsolved problems with Third World development strategies such as too large a state sector, too high local tariffs, and too many inefficient nationally-controlled industries, all of which had irritated the US for so long.

The Baker Sham

'Despite the setback in developing country debt problems over the past year, the principles of the US-sponsored Baker Plan remain valid .... The deterioration in the balance of payments of the heavily indebted countries covered by the Baker Plan was due to a combination of weak raw material prices and economic mismanagement.'
Financial Times. 16 June 1987, quoting BIS Report.

The Baker Plan was a political success, staving off any threat of collective action by Third World debtors into the far future, and postponing the spread of unilateral action to major debtors by eighteen months. Some care went into the deliberate isolation of Peru. (see chapter eight) Technically included in the original fifteen, Peru was only able to benefit from the Plan if García announced a radical change in his debt repayment policy. Other Latin American debtors were induced to downplay any feelings of solidarity they might have had, in the hope of receiving World Bank funds. They cooperated by letting it be known at the Seoul IMF meeting that they considered the Peruvian action to be rash. The meeting of the Cartagena group which followed the Seoul meeting formally rejected any possibility of regional moves along Peruvian lines and gave the Baker Plan public support, as a political step in the right direction, though one which did not go far enough.

Yet, however much the Baker Plan represented a breach in the determination of Western governments to leave the debt crisis to private negotiations between the banks and Third World

Table 3.3
The Fifteen Major Debtors, 1985

Country	Foreign Debt in 1985 (US$ bn)	Interest Owed in 1985 (US$ bn)	Interest as % of 1985 GNP	Debt Owed to US banks (US$ bn)
Brazil	103.5	11.8	5.8	23.8
Mexico	97.9	10.0	6.3	25.8
Argentina	50.8	5.1	7.9	8.1
Venezuela	32.6	4.1	8.1	10.6
Philippines	27.4	2.1	6.2	5.5
Chile	21.9	2.1	12.9	6.6
Yugoslavia	20.0	1.7	3.6	2.4
Nigeria	18.0	1.8	1.9	1.5
Morocco	14.4	1.0	8.2	0.9
Peru	13.9	1.3	10.8	2.1
Colombia	13.9	1.3	3.3	2.6
Ecuador	7.9	0.7	6.0	2.2
Ivory Coast	6.3	0.6	8.7	0.5
Uruguay	4.9	0.5	9.8	1.0
Bolivia	4.2	0.4	10.0	0.2
Total	**437.6**	**43.5**		**93.8**

Source: Fortune, December 1986.

governments, in economic terms it was a disappointment. In theory, the Plan offered the fifteen biggest debtors a total of US$32 billion in new loans over three years. Of this, US$20 billion was to come from commercial banks, as their voluntary contribution to resolving the crisis. The remaining US$11.7 billion was to consist of loans for economic restructuring channelled through multilateral agencies, principally the World Bank, with the funds coming from the flotation of World Bank bonds on the world's financial markets.

Over the same period, US$2.7 billion was to be made available to the IMF to allow a roll-over of the outstanding debts owed to it by the poorest developing countries. This sum was just about enough to cover the repayments due to the IMF from sub-Saharan Africa, while reinforcing the IMF's power to keep local economies in a strait-jacket. Even for Africa, the Baker Plan did nothing to relieve the crippling impact of interest charges — amounting to US$12 billion for 1985 alone — or to resolve the underlying crisis. The remaining US$29 billion was to be directed to the fifteen major debtors listed in table 3.3, whose total debt amounted to US$438 billion (of which US$93.8 billion was owed to US banks alone). The annual interest charge on

The World Bank and Restructuring

The World Bank has traditionally funded big development projects like irrigation systems, highways and agricultural and reforestation programmes. Though supposedly governed by long term considerations of social welfare, these loans are charged at commercial rates of interest, reflecting the fact that the bank itself gets most of its funds by floating long-term bonds on international money markets. The Bank has a subsidiary, the International Development Association (IDA) which does provide loans to poor countries at less than the commercial rate, but the IDA has always been starved of adequate funds.

Since the early 1970s the Bank has been the target of criticism from Left and Right. In spite of its market interest rates, and the fact that its President is traditionally a US government appointee, US businessmen distrust the Bank, arguing that it has financed and approved the massive expansion of state power throughout the Third World. Non-governmental development agencies and environmentalists dislike the Bank for other reasons. Dams and irrigation systems are criticised because they dispossess large numbers of poor peasants and destroy existing agricultural or forest land, in return for an increase in the productivity of land controlled by the rich — usually to increase export production, sometimes only for a relatively short time, and rarely in a fashion which will spread employment and income through the ranks of the dispossessed.

As President of the Bank in the early 1970s, Robert MacNamara made grand promises about using its resources to secure 'Growth with Redistribution'. But the Bank's loan programme continued to be governed by the need to earn short-term returns on capital borrowed from the international markets, and the promises disappeared in a flurry of projects promoting the Green Revolution in agriculture, and further dispossession of the Third World's rural poor. For all the publicity surrounding the Bank's new 'environmentally sensitive' policies, the era of Reagan and James Baker has intensified the integration of Bank policies with the needs of Western exporters.

In 1980, the World Bank introduced its first Structural Adjustment Loans (SALS). Many Third World countries were facing serious balance of payments problems and now needed foreign currency loans to cover the cost of servicing their existing imported technology — not just new development projects. In theory, SALS were loans paid to Third World governments for taking action to increase or save foreign exchange. Loans were offered for a year, with the possibility of a new SAL being negotiated as the old one came to an end, allowing a five to nine year programme amounting to supervised, long-term adjustment in place of the short, sharp shock characteristic of the IMF.

With very few exceptions, these loans were offered to countries already in the throes of IMF adjustment programmes. Under the SALS, World Bank conditionality was intended to reinforce and prolong the ▶

▶ conditionality already imposed by the IMF. In 1983, this programme was strengthened with the introduction of Sectoral Adjustment Loans (SEALS), aimed specifically to strengthen export production.

Where SEALS boost exports, SALS have been targetted on encouraging very specific global reforms:

- reduction in government expenditure and the size of the government sector
- an end to the creation of new public enterprises
- rationalisation, and sometimes privatisation, of those already in existence
- higher prices for public-sector produced goods
- higher interest rates to discourage capital flight
- tax reform
- steps to make trade policy more outward-looking, such as the
- removal of trade and exchange controls, and the reduction of effective protection against imports.
- higher prices for agricultural producers, especially exporters.

SAL improvements to the recipient's economic policies were thus of a very special kind. Like the IMF, the World Bank defines improvement as that which strengthens the international economy at the expense of local political initiatives, which, it argues, only represent special interests threatening the rationality of market forces — ignoring the special interests represented on its own Board of Directors, all representing countries for which the strengthening of international trade and exports is a special concern.

this debt came to US$44.5 billion, more than the entire value of the Baker Plan.

The Baker Plan carefully preserved the myth that the debt crisis could be solved by the banks and their clients with just a little help from governments. It did more. New money coming to Latin American debtors through the World Bank now carried with it all the baggage usually associated with the IMF conditionality. (see box, p.55) The money from the World Bank was increasingly policy-based, designed to restructure Latin American economies, removing their existing barriers to foreign trade and investment, reducing the economic power of the state, privatising state enterprises, and strengthening export sectors which would be needed in the future to pay for an expanded schedule of imports from the developed world. The burden of long-term planning was thus shifted from debtor country governments onto the back of the World Bank — with the chosen growth model being similar to the IMF's and one which most suited the interests of the US.

The sums involved were pitifully insufficent — about half as much again as the World Bank and the regional development banks were already spending in the fifteen countries concerned. The new multilateral loans amounted to a mere seven per cent of the fifteen debtors' three-year bill for interest charges, or two per cent of their accumulated debt. Since the loans had to be paid back with interest, and the World Bank had to repay its private sector creditors out of the proceeds, the concessions were minimal.

OECD governments were happy with the Plan, since they continued to be spared any contribution to the piper, yet they continued to dictate the tune. The banks too gave the Plan their public support as it safeguarded two basic points of principle in the band-aid scheme: the principle of bilateral negotiations — all the banks confronting each individual debtor, and no debtors' cartel — and the principle of conditionality as new money was made provisional, as a minimum, on the adoption of economic programmes which would raise national export surpluses at the expense of satisfying the demands of local consumers. The liberalisation of trade and financial barriers foreseen in the World Bank's restructuring programme could not be expected to contribute much to the immediate ability of the debtor countries to keep up their payments, but in the long run, it would further the interests of the world's banks by securing them free access to local financial sectors, from which government legislation often kept them barred.

Bankers Refuse the Dough

Two years after the introduction of the Baker Plan, the BIS and other international organisations were still willing to go on record in its public defence. Yet in economic terms, it might best be described as a non-starter. Far from producing an increase in financial flows to developing countries, over and above what they were paying out in repayments on old loans, the first year of the Baker Plan witnessed a *decline* in the flow of funds from banks and multilateral agencies alike.

Funds flowing into developing countries from all sources during 1986 fell by a further US$10 billion, to roughly two-thirds of the levels prevailing in 1982.(see table 3.4) Private sector loans fell by a further US$11 billion in the course of the year. By the end of 1986, private sector contributions of new money stood at just about half their level during the panic-stricken months of 1982. These are World Bank figures, and relatively optimistic. BIS estimates of total commercial lending, covering both long- and short-term loans, suggest a much

Table 3.4
The Failure of the Baker Plan
Flows of Long-Term Finance to the Third World, 1982-86
(US$ billion)

	1982	1983	1984	1985	1986
*Total Debt**					
109 developing countries	551.2	630.2	673.4	730.9	775.0
17 major debtors**	276.5	329.2	354.0	367.6	382.0
Total Debt Service Payments					
109 developing countries	97.4	90.8	99.0	108.0	101.0
17 major debtors	56.6	48.2	51.6	50.1	47.0
Disbursements of New Finance from Private Sources					
109 developing countries	83.9	63.9	56.1	52.1	41.0
17 major debtors	50.9	29.7	22.5	13.6	12.0
Total Disbursements of New Finance from All Sources					
109 developing countries	115.8	96.5	88.3	81.7	72.0
17 major debtors	60.1	39.7	32.3	22.4	21.0
Net Transfer of Resources					
109 developing countries	+18.4	+5.7	−10.7	−26.3	−29.0
17 major debtors	+3.5	−8.5	−19.4	−27.7	−26.0

*Disbursed and outstanding.
**The Baker 15 plus Jamaica and Costa Rica.
Source: World Bank data quoted in the *Financial Times*, 6 March 1987.

grimmer picture, a total outflow from the Third World to the banks of US$1.8 billion in 1986.[11]

The highly indebted countries who were the Baker Plan's principal target may have fared a little better. On World Bank figures, overall lending in their direction tended to stabilise at just less than the level existing in 1985. From 1985 to 1986, overall capital flows fell by a total of US$1 billion, while flows of private capital fell from US$13.6 billion to US$12.0 billion.(see table 3.4) However, when these sums are measured against the levels of funding available when the debt crisis began, the extent of the squeeze on local resources is very clear. Private finance was providing just a quarter of the level of capital in 1986 that it provided during the first year of the debt crisis, and overall capital flows had declined to a third of what they were then — and these are generous estimates. The countries on whose behalf Baker was supposedly mobilising urgent assistance, still accounted for the bulk of the net transfer of capital flowing out of the Third World and into the developed countries of the West — US$26 billion out of a total of US$29 billion.

As for the increased role for multilateral institutions promised by the Plan, the IMF celebrated the first Baker year by taking back US$4.7 billion in debt repayments from developing countries [12], and found itself facing a sharp rise in the number of its own debtors who were now in arrears. Bankers broke new ground in June 1987, with the suggestion that, lender of last resort or not, the IMF must be prepared to roll over existing loans — waxing indignant at the thought of the Fund 'withdrawing money from the international financial system at a time when the commercial banks are being pressured to increase their exposure to highly indebted middle-income countries'. [13]

Funding increases for the World Bank were delayed by quarrels between the White House and Congress, while the Bank agonised through its own process of restructuring, as a new Reagan appointee struggled to transform it into an adequate instrument for imposing market-oriented reforms. Thus it, too, failed to provide a conduit for new resources. The scale of new World Bank loans on offer for such policies as sectoral adjustment rose, but the scale of old loans falling due for repayment was also rising. The real funds which the World Bank transferred to borrowers fell from US$2.8 billion in 1985, to US$2.4 billion in 1986. [14]

By 1987, the failure of the Baker Plan was an accomplished fact. At best, it slowed down temporarily the rush by commercial bankers to withdraw funds from Latin American debtors, persuading them instead to withdraw funds from elsewhere in the developing world. At worst, because the counterpart of Latin America's trade surplus, out of which the banks were paid their interest charges, was a US trade deficit with Latin America growing by leaps and bounds, it contributed to the underlying instabilities of the world economy which were to resound throughout the world on Black Monday: 12 October 1987, the day the world's stock markets crashed.(see chapter ten)

But even had it succeeded, the Baker Plan could never have provided a real solution to the debt crisis, because like the band-aid solution, it offered debtor countries no relief on their accumulated burden of past interest charges, nor any lowering of current interest rates below commercial levels, but only a little additional finance at commercial rates with which to keep current interest payments going. With this kind of remedy, the total burden of debt on the debtors was bound to keep growing, as indeed it did: in the case of Latin America, from US$377 billion in 1985 to US$388 billion in 1986, in the case of the 'Baker's dozen plus two' from US$417 billion in 1985, to US$437 billion in 1986 and US$477 billion in 1987. [15] Only the failure of the Baker Plan to mobilise more adequate capital flows from the commercial banks prevented it from growing even more.

4. Debt and Development I: Lending in the 1970s

In principle, development experts have always argued that the natural answer to the shortage of capital in developing countries must be foreign investment and borrowing. The rich countries of the world ought to provide a transfusion of capital for the development of those who are poor. The dance of the millions was just such a transfusion — perhaps not as much as the US$380 billion that Latin America owed by 1987, but a substantial amount — equivalent to a net inflow of US$100 billion between 1974 and 1982, according to IDB calculations. What happened to all this money? Did the dance of the millions make a real contribution to development? Did Latin Americans squander it, thus contributing to the debt problem? And why did all that money have so little impact on the living standards of the poor?

Answers to these questions are often buried under thick layers of special pleading. Bankers and US Treasury Secretaries have a vested interest in believing that Latin American countries were guilty of economic mismanagement in the 1970s. (see box p.61) If this is the case, the West can be more justified in placing the blame for the debt crisis of the 1980s at their doors, and forcing them to carry on footing the interest rate bill. This explains why US Treasury Secretary James Baker publicly complains about capital flight from Mexico, even though the US Treasury is simultaneously trying every possible trick to attract foreign funds into the US to finance the US government deficit. The allocation of blame is also an important benchmark in the struggle over what kind of economic policies will be adopted by Latin American countries in the future, as detailed in chapter three.

Carlos Díaz-Alejandro pioneered an attack on the West's most cherished myths about Latin American responsibilities for the debt crisis, with the comment, 'Blaming the victims is an appealing evasion of responsibility, especially when these are far from virtuous.'[1] There were plenty of guilty parties in Latin America during the 1970s: hard-

Did Latin American Governments Overvalue their Exchange Rates?

One of the common charges against Latin American governments is that during the 1970s they allowed their exchange rates to become overvalued, so that US dollars and other hard currencies were worth less than they should have been in *pesos* and *cruzeiros*, making imports cheaper and exports dearer and therefore more difficult to sell. The argument is that this policy error significantly increased the debt, by encouraging imports unnecessarily and pricing exports at a level unattractive on world markets. However, the notion that their mismanagement of exchange rates was somehow responsible for the debt crisis is absurd.

In the 1970s, Latin American governments faced a similar economic problem to Mrs Thatcher's struggles with the British 'petrocurrency' in the early 1980s. Like earnings from oil, a massive influx of foreign capital could be expected to push up exchange rates. It would also be inherently inflationary, because more locally-produced resources would have to be found for which there was no import equivalent, as increased economic activity meant more workers to feed, more contractors to pay, and more wood and concrete to be found.

Mrs Thatcher's answer was to let the exchange rate of the pound rise, or become overvalued. British exports to the rest of the world suffered because they became much dearer, but imports became much cheaper, holding the rate of inflation down. (The overvalued pound was the death-knell for British industry, which could no longer compete with its international rivals, and did not regain its old levels of production until 1987.) Latin American governments faced a similar choice during the dance of the millions. They might be forgiven in retrospect for making the same choice as Mrs Thatcher, and even for the costs of this decision in increased capital flight, as local businessmen found it cheaper to buy dollars and invest in the US. After all, Mrs Thatcher would have approved of the argument which said that when funds cannot be invested productively at home, it is wise to invest them abroad.

In fact, taken as a regional average, exchange rates in Latin America during the dance of the millions were not noticeably overvalued compared to earlier years.(see figure) In real terms (i.e. corrected for inflation in both the region and its trading partners), local currencies consistently bought more in the way of foreign exchange than they had done in 1970. There were only two exceptions, in 1974 and 1980, the two years following the two rounds of oil price rises. This kind of performance must indicate substantial government pressure to keep exchange rates down rather than up — a better performance in terms of securing the interests of local exporters than was characteristic of Mrs Thatcher's Britain.

In practice, the regional average hides country variations. Throughout the 1970s, Brazil and Colombia practised a policy of mini-devaluations, keeping their currencies low to help boost manufactured exports. The weight of the Brazilian economy in regional figures explains a good part of ▶

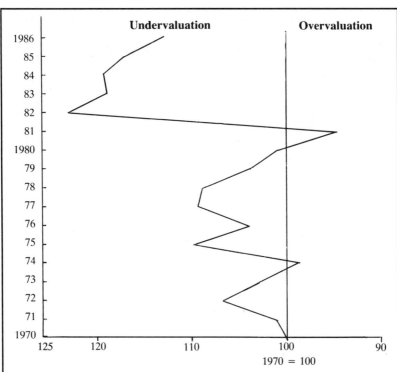

The real effective exchange rate for Latin America and the Caribbean, 1970-86 (*pesos* or *cruzeiros* per unit of foreign currency).
Source: *IDB Annual Report 1987*, Table II-5, p.14.

the region's resistance to overvaluation, although Brazil paid the price in high rates of inflation — and any bonus in increased exports was wholly insufficient to resolve its debt problems after 1982. Argentina, Mexico and Chile deliberately took the opposite path, using the influx of capital to keep their currencies overvalued and so reduce inflation, Argentina from 1976, Mexico from 1977 and Chile from June 1979.

During 1980-81, overvaluation did rise sharply as governments found it the only way to save private debtors from bankruptcy. As interest payments on past debts ballooned, dollars had to be kept cheap if local banks and companies were to be able to pay their bills. This emergency juggling with the exchange rate lasted a brief two years until the 1982 Mexican crisis. It was followed by a wild swing towards undervaluation, as countries attempted to increase their exports by making them cheaper, in the hope of paying off their debts. Overvaluation was thus just as much a consequence of the dance of the millions as an independent cause.

hearted military governments more interested in parading with up-to-date military equipment than in the poor; profligate civilian politicians; an urban upper class more than willing to spend the easy-gotten gains of the dance of the millions on tourism in the US and Europe and *pieds-à-terre* in Miami; and businessmen who calculated that investments in the US would produce a higher and safer return than those made at home. But bankers are afflicted with highly selective memories. Throughout the decade of the 1970s, these people were their local allies, who made the dance of the millions possible by finding uses for surplus funds, and like fools or villains, committed their countries to foot the bill when the dance was done.

The reasons why Latin America achieved so little development for its money, and the poor even less, lie in the convenience of this political alliance for all the parties, and the ideas about development which were its common currency.

To Recycle or Cut?

'Ever since the first oil shock of 1973, a cloud of "managed money" has been drifting around the world, first showering riches and then unleashing economic squalls wherever it happened to descend.

The cloud first wafted from the Middle East to the international banks in New York and London and from there to Latin America. These days, the cloud forms above the industrial centres of Japan and carries money across the Pacific to the US Treasury in Washington, casting its shadow over most of US industry as it passes.'
Anatole Kaletsky, in the *Financial Times*, 22 July 1985.

In all the arguments of the 1980s over whether the debt should be repaid, the original logic behind the official encouragement to commercial bank loans to Latin America is easily lost. Recycling was introduced not just to compensate NOPECs for oil-generated balance of payments deficits, but also to protect their ability to buy goods from developed countries, in the hope of limiting recession in the industrialised world. Faced with the pressures of oil price increases and the bonus of freely available capital to compensate for them, Latin American governments were easily persuaded to facilitate recycling. Though not suffering on the scale of sub-Saharan Africa, many countries were in real difficulty. In 1974 only Bolivia, Ecuador, Venezuela, and Trinidad were net oil exporters, and of these only Venezuela and Trinidad were sufficiently flush with money to generate a current account surplus in the wake of the 1974 and 1979 price rises. The rest of the continent saw its trade deficit rise from US$0.3 billion in 1973 to US$7.9 billion in 1974.[2] In Brazil for example, the cost of oil imports doubled between 1973 and 1974, and the impact of the second oil price rise was so serious that by 1980-81 half the value of Brazil's imports was accounted for by fuel.[3]

Nor was this the whole story. Traditionally, Latin America always runs a deficit on services, even when its exports are prospering and able to foot all or more of the import bill. Throughout the 1970s, some US$4 billion was being sent abroad every year to cover profit remittances by multinationals.[4] Even from 1972-74, interest payments on existing foreign public debt were taking between US$1-2 billion a year.[5] After the 1974 oil price rise, with exports no longer covering the import bill, the cost of meeting this deficit on services was increasingly paid by commercial loans. Altogether, Latin American countries ran a current account deficit of nearly 4 per cent of the region's GDP in 1974-75.

By borrowing petrodollars, Latin America locked itself into a dependence on commercial finance which was self-perpetuating. The weight of interest payments in the region's current account deficits continued to rise — by 820 per cent between 1969 and 1980 — compounding the impact of the second round of oil price rises, and pushing the region's total current account deficit above 5 per cent in 1980[6], even before the Reagan hike in world interest rates. Without further loans, the balance of payments could not be made to balance.

Thus, recycling was a success. The banks did well. (see chapter six) So did exporters in the West, who supplied two-thirds of the region's imports. Latin American growth rates were half as much or more than those of the OECD countries, well above the historical norm.[7] Imports were growing even more than the Latin American economy as a whole, and the share of Latin America in world imports was slowly rising, thanks to the plentiful supply of foreign exchange made available by the banks. Recycling postponed the outbreak of a severe recession in the region until the second oil price rise of 1979, holding down open rates of unemployment — an indirect benefit for which Latin American governments would pay after 1982 by assuming responsibility for the entire cost.

Investment

'In 1980, an investment project to be financed with external debt, without resort to subsequent refinancings, would have to generate an income stream that would permit the debt to be paid in the first three and half years. Very few projects in the countries of the region could be launched under those conditions.'
IDB Annual Report 1982, p.68.

Capital Flight

In 1987, suitcases of money arrived in France and Hawaii, in the luggage of Baby Doc Duvalier, ex-dictator of Haiti, and Ferdinand Marcos, ex-dictator of the Philippines. The coincidence of two such visually convincing instances of capital flight, has helped highlight the fact that the elites of the Third World have billions of dollars in bank deposits, real estate, jewellery, and valuable paintings held in the developed countries of the West.

However, the real news on capital flight in the 1980s is to be found elsewhere — in the accounts of an international banking system which has made it easier to ship capital out, and in the introduction of electronic technology which has made it even easier. Behind a veil of secrecy one account in Buenos Aires can be quietly debited while quietly adding to another in New York. These developments in the world's banking system combined with the increased financial flows from private banks to swell the absolute size of the sums involved. The banks encouraged these practices, often with the tacit collaboration of capital-hungry Western governments.

Accurate figures are difficult to find. Academic estimates usually assume that the errors and omissions category in balance of payments accounts more or less represents capital flight. At the world level, the balance of payments does not balance at all, with US$80 billion a year missing. Official US sources suggest that by the end of 1983 non-government assets owned by Latin American and Caribbean investors in the US alone amounted to US$168 billion, although some of this money came from international banking centres set up on Caribbean islands and thus perhaps originally from Europe or the Middle East. Taking into account these problems and the existence of other destinations for deposits, Professor Felix of Washington University has estimated that the figure for the total assets held abroad by Latin Americans in 1985 was US$180 billion.

Anecdotal evidence confirms the picture. In 1985, a Mexico City newspaper published the names of 537 Mexicans each with over a million dollars on deposit with foreign banks. Citibank, with the biggest portfolio of loans to Latin America, is alleged to have as much as US$13 billion in Latin American deposits among its liabilities and may thus actually owe more money to Latin Americans than it is owed.

There is agreement on the fate of funds associated with the debt. 'Much of the money being borrowed from abroad was funnelled straight out again,' wrote the World Bank, which it described as 'a recipe for disaster'. The Bank was citing information provided by the world's central bankers which suggested that between 1979 and 1982, US$19.2 billion left Argentina, US$26.5 billion left Mexico and US$22 billion left Venezuela: 64 per cent, 48 per cent and a staggering 137 per cent respectively of the gross capital inflows to those countries.

Latin American governments can only compete with the high US ►

> interest rates at the cost of high bankruptcy rates among the local firms that foot the bill for the high local interest rates. Nor can they compete with the security of real estate in Miami or Hawaii, or US banks. Without international support it is doubtful whether Latin American governments can do much to stem capital flight.

Latin American countries have always been careful investors, in spite of the temptation to private investors to send their funds abroad. This practice dates back at least as far as the Bolivian tin magnate, Patiño, who built his house in Paris, his smelter in Britain, and his company headquarters in Delaware, USA — and before he died, owned tin mines in Malaysia.[8] Traditionally, if private investors fail or move elsewhere, the Latin American state has always taken up the slack.

Investment in the region continued to grow as a percentage of GDP during the 1970s as it had done in the early 1960s, reaching a peak of nearly 25 per cent in 1981.[9] The enormous influx of capital during the dance of the millions conceivably protected this rising trend against the depressing effect of the oil-generated slumps. However, over the decade of the 1970s, there is a lot of evidence to suggest that the dance of the millions was less of an *addition* to locally-available capital resources than a *substitute* for them. This new influx of money freed the local rich from existing claims on their capital resources, and allowed them to swell their consumption of expensive foreign imports or take advantage of the unprecedented availability of dollars to make investments in the developed world. Increased capital flight provides the clearest proof that a high percentage of these millions were wasted. (see box p.65) So too does the ease with which governments built up official reserves of foreign exchange, which increased by US$10 billion over the decade, or 10 per cent of the total net capital inflow, much of it held in the very international banks making the new loans.[10]

The region's major debtors, Mexico and Brazil, did attempt to use the influx of capital resources being pressed upon them to finance investment and create new export incentives. These efforts, though laudable, were not always efficient. Successive Brazilian Presidents marked their period in office with massive works of infrastructure — highways, dams, nuclear power stations — which humbler Brazilians have aptly labelled 'pharaonic', and which, given their incursions into the Amazonian rain forest, have been widely viewed as a criminal attack on the ecological balance of the globe. This kind of *folie de grandeur* may help to explain the declining efficiency of investment throughout the region as a stimulus to new economic growth, which the IDB detects during the period 1974-80.[11]

66

It would have been much more efficient to distribute this influx of resources among smaller firms and independent producers, raising their capital and productive efficiency, and spreading the benefits much more widely. One of the strengths of the Japanese economy at the turn of the century and of the contemporary East Asian economies is supposed to be the local sympathy and support for smaller firms. But international bankers do not commonly have contacts with small entrepreneurs. The huge projects organised by the state and the megalomanic acquisition policies of local private sector conglomerates better suited the bankers' need for a quick distribution of their surplus money.

In Mexico, investment was focused on oil, as the government attempted to transform the country from an oil importer into a major oil exporter in the shortest conceivable time. Oil installations require large-scale imports of plant and machinery, yet between 1979 and 1982, Mexico managed to re-export capital to the US, covering 48 per cent of the gross capital inflow, proof enough that the country was being offered more capital that it could reasonably use.[12]

Besides offering the private sector financial bribes to export, the Geisel dictatorship in Brazil (1974-79) used the 1970s' bonanza to press forward with the building of local factories producing steel, chemicals, petrochemicals, pulp and paper, fertilisers, and fuel from sugar cane alcohol — all in an effort to save on future import bills. There was a deliberate strategy behind this investment drive: if oil prices continued to rise in the future, Brazil would be able to pay for them out of the savings on other imports. If sugar cane alcohol worked as a petrol substitute, it might even have the technology and the primary materials to offer the world an alternative to oil-based fuels. Brazil could thus claim to have made the most productive use of the millions flowing into the region, despite its governments' addiction to creating large monuments. Moreover, Brazil managed to avoid capital flight on the Mexican scale. But all this investment, good and bad, was consistent with a massive build-up of internationally-held reserves, which suggests that even here capital inflows on the scale of the dance were not needed.(see chapter seven)

So, even where governments were vigorously pursuing viable investment programmes, they seemingly could not make use of all the resources on the scale provided by the dance of the millions. Still less could they find investments which generated returns on the scale and with the speed required by the build-up of interest charges after 1980. The scope of the money flooding in made it difficult for Latin American governments, or foreign financiers, to direct resources towards poorer producers, who could sensibly use US$5,000 or even

US$50,000 — but could hardly hope to repay US$500 million.

Moreover, neither governments nor bankers showed any public concern over the unequal distribution of resources in Latin America during this period, when Brazil was regarded as the ultimate in a model of efficient economic administration, even though its military regimes regarded their own poor with contemptuous indifference, arguing at their most liberal that development would solve poverty automatically through a trickle-down process, and at their most brazen that the problems of the poorest 60 per cent of the population were none of their concern.

Winds of Change

'The US .. completely rejects the idea that there is such a thing as "development economics"...'
A Reagan appointee to the Asian Development Bank, quoted in the *Financial Times*, 30 May 1985.

The decade of the 1970s saw rapid change within the Third World, and an even more abrupt reversal of economists' views about what developing countries should do. This was the era of the Newly Industrialised Countries (NICs), when South Korea, Taiwan, Hong Kong and Singapore began to distance themselves from other developing economies, especially those which were 'really poor'. Economists such as Bela Balassa seized upon the successes in East Asia to argue for a sea-change in government economic policies throughout the Third World, bringing them more closely into line with free market theories as to what should be done within OECD economies. They recommended a more generalised openness to the international market place, manifested in lower tariffs against OECD products, counterbalanced by export drives making it possible to finance the increase in imports which would inevitably result.[13]

Governments who set up protective tariffs, it was now argued, only gave local businessmen an effective monopoly and a means of squeezing economically-unjustifiable profits out of consumers. Development economists in the World Bank disowned the old modes of government planning and investment — of which Latin America and India were typical examples. State companies were even more inefficient, centres of waste and unnecessary expense undisciplined by market controls. Low wages were a positive virtue, allowing a country to keep its exports cheap on international markets. The 'in' words were export-led growth.

Belassa's views have continued to dominate the thinking of

The South Korean Alternative

When Latin Americans complain about the failure of recycled surpluses to deliver development in the 1970s, bankers have a ready answer. If only Latin American economies were run more like the Asian NICs — Hong Kong, Singapore, South Korea and Taiwan — there would never have been a problem. South Korea, after all, is also one of the world's major Third World debtors: US$29.1 billion in 1985. Why can't Latin America be more like South Korea?

For a start, South Korea (like Taiwan) began the post-war era with something which has seldom been achieved in Latin America: a comprehensive land-reform. After the Second World War, the US forces of occupation turned over confiscated Japanese landholdings to poor peasants. The South Korean government itself later extended the process to locally-owned property, in the course of the Korean war.

Land reform may help explain another surprising fact. In spite of its history of military dictatorship, South Korea has a better record on income distribution than Latin America has ever had — in 1986 the poorest 60 per cent of South Korean households controlled 32.3 per cent of the nation's total household income. In Brazil, they make do with 16.4 per cent, and in Peru 18.0 per cent. The gap is still impressive in Mexico where the figure is 21.9 per cent, and in Venezuela 23.2 per cent.

Nor is South Korea precisely the *laissez-faire* ideal. Imports of goods needed by the manufacturing sector rate very low tariffs, but the domestic economy has benefited from substantial tariff protection throughout South Korea's post-war history. On some estimates, the state controls two-thirds of all local investment. Formal and informal government controls of the private sector's behaviour are highly developed. Some development economists call it state capitalism. Others suggest that the real difference between South Korea and Taiwan, and Latin American debtors, is that the former are strong states, whereas Latin American governments are politically weak, and less able to impose the short-term sacrifices necessary for development on their own richer classes.

Perhaps Latin American governments are also weaker when it comes to managing the invasion of multinationals. In South Korea, foreign capital is only allowed to invest in designated areas of economic activity, and the rules governing its operation are at least as strict as in any Latin American nation. More to the point, the South Korean state (like Taiwan and Hong Kong) at an early stage directed its manufacturers away from the production of Western consumer durables, targetted on local elite markets, and towards the production of cheap non-durable consumer goods which were easier for the local poor to buy and also easier to market in the West.

Table 4.1
Who Gained from the Dance of the Millions? 1977-80
(US$ billion in current dollars)

	Net Foreign Loans to Central Government*	Net Foreign Long-term Dividends and Loans* to the Private Sector
Mexico	0.9	9.8
Argentina	−0.7	7.9
Brazil	n.a.	6.4
Chile	−0.9	2.6
Venezuela	2.2	2.4
Bolivia	0.3	0.4

*Figures on loans to state firms are not included: they would show heavy lending to this sector in Brazil and Mexico.
Source: IDB Annual Report 1982, Tables 23 and 50.

development agencies throughout the 1980s, in spite of growing doubts about the applicability of his theories to the East Asian success stories. (see box p.69) Today, the same arguments justify the IMF's practical drive to increase exports at the expense of production for the local economy, and the World Bank's emphasis on lower tariffs, liberalisation of trade, and the reduction of state controls in its restructuring programmes, (see chapter three, box p.55)

In this context, the myth of state intervention as the Achilles heel of Latin America's development problems has been very convenient for bankers, economists and politicians, who would like the proposed remedies of the 1980s to be as different as possible from the experience of the 1970s. They are thus convinced beyond any need to analyse the evidence that 'whereas in Korea much of the debt was held directly by the private sector, it was held by the public sector in Latin America, as a result of high budget deficits in the years preceding the debt crisis'[14], because they already know that public sector deficits are the real explanation for Latin America's economic inefficiency, and that everything would be different if the private sector were in charge.

As it happens, this view of cause and effect in the debt crisis is wrong. Outside Venezuela, Latin American governments in the main debtor countries made no significant attempt to use the dance of the millions to finance government deficits, which continued to be funded by local capital markets.(see table 4.1) Smaller Caribbean and Central American countries were guilty of this practice, but before the debt crisis of 1982 expanded governments' debt obligations and pushed up domestic interest rates, the larger countries were not involved.[15] In

Table 4.2
Unguaranteed Private Sector Debt as a Percentage of Total Debt, 1980

Venezuela	59.6
Argentina	57.3
Chile	51.3
Ecuador	43.6
Colombia	41.3
Mexico	33.3
Brazil	33.0
Peru	25.9
Jamaica	19.2
Bolivia	15.6
Haiti	14.4
Costa Rica	9.8
Nicaragua	0.0

Source: IDB Annual Report 1982, Table 4 and 29.

fact, there is good evidence to suggest that the bulk of the bank loans went to private companies. Two-thirds of US bank loans, for example, were made to the private sector.[16]

Figures on the state's relative importance as a debtor in the 1970s are obscured because some of these loans were made to state-owned firms (particularly in Brazil, Mexico and Venezuela), and because most global calculations of the burden of debt add together debt contracted by the government itself with those private sector debts which governments agree to guarantee, whether contracted by state companies or by private firms. But during the dance of the millions, banks made many loans to private companies without a government guarantee, some of which did not even figure in official statistics until the debt crisis broke in 1982.(see table 4.2) By 1980, private sector debt without a government guarantee amounted to 40 per cent of the total[17], and it is safe to assume that outside Venezuela (where state firms contracted debt without the government's knowledge or support) most of this total was loaned to *bona fide* private sector firms.

But what about the bankers? Broadly speaking, Belassa's views had their support in the late 1970s. The dance of the millions gave them an unprecedented opportunity to back their economic judgement with positive finance, as well as the prestige which then and now allowed them to give individual countries the seal of viability. Did they use it?

In retrospect, one puzzling feature of recycling is that the funds it provided went first and foremost to Latin America, not East Asia.

Table 4.3
External Debt Characteristics of LDC Regions, 1984 .

Region	Total Debt (US$ bn)	Percentages of		
		Debt: Exports	Debt: GDP	Interest: Exports
Latin America	351.1	280	46.0	28.9
Africa	126.8	162	39.8	11.3
Asia	210.9	86	23.7	6.0

Source: R. Dornbusch, 'Policy and Performance Links between LDC Debtors and Industrial Nations', *Brookings Papers on Economic Activity*, 2:1985.

Table 4.4
Debts of Major Latin American Debtors Owed to Commercial Banks, June 1983 (US$ bn)

	All Commercial Banks	US Banks
Mexico	65.5	32.3
Brazil	62.8	23.3
Venezuela	26.8	10.8
Argentina	25.5	11.2
Chile	10.9	5.2

Source: R. Dornbusch, 1984, citing BIS and Federal Reserve Board data.

Either bankers did not regard the East Asian economies as a good, practical bet for recycling, or East Asian governments were too wise to accept the poisoned gift. From 1977 to 1980, Latin America took US$80 billion in net commercial bank loans, while all the Asian countries put together took a mere US$36 billion.[18] The outcome of this very skewed distribution of resources was that by 1984, Latin American countries were carrying twice the level of debt in comparison to GDP and three times the level of debt compared to exports, as their Asian counterparts.(see table 4.3)

Within Latin America, resources were also distributed in a very skewed fashion. 90 per cent of US bank loans went to just five countries: Mexico, Brazil, Venezuela, Argentina and Chile.(see table 4.4) 60 per cent went to just two of these, Mexico and Brazil. Mexico was clearly the most important target as a non-OPEC country on the border of the US, with large potential oil reserves of crucial strategic significance.

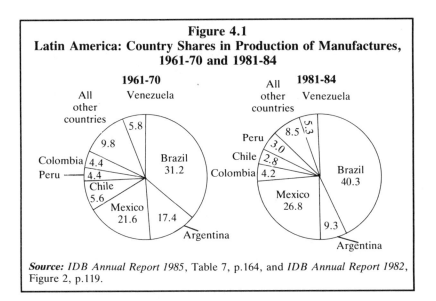

Figure 4.1
Latin America: Country Shares in Production of Manufactures, 1961-70 and 1981-84

1961-70

All other countries

Venezuela 5.8

9.8

Colombia 4.4

Peru 4.4

Chile 5.6

Brazil 31.2

Mexico 21.6

17.4

Argentina

All **1981-84**

other countries

Venezuela

8.5 5.3

Peru 3.0

Chile 2.8

Colombia 4.2

Brazil 40.3

Mexico 26.8

9.3

Argentina

Source: IDB Annual Report 1985, Table 7, p.164, and *IDB Annual Report 1982*, Figure 2, p.119.

If the banks lent to Mexico because it was an oil producer, Brazil was seen as a potential competitor of the East Asian NICs. The apparently unquestioned power of its military regime offered (in bankers' eyes) a sure guarantee of stability, as did the sheer size of the country: more than 100 million souls, 20 million of them consumers, providing a profitable local market for multinationals who could then expect to make further profits (with the state's generous financial assistance) by expanding into foreign markets. The flow of international funds in turn sweetened the so-called Brazilian miracle of the late 1960s and 1970s, further inflating a middle class consumer boom at the cost of a deliberate squeeze on workers' wages.

Together, between 1961 and 1970, these two countries accounted for half the region's total production in manufacturing, though only a quarter of its manufacturing exports, about the same as Argentina and Chile.(see figures 4.1 and 4.2) A decade of lavish funding from the banks increased the comparative size of their economies and industrial sectors, largely at the expense of comparable growth in Latin America's less lavishly funded medium sized industrial producers. Mexico kept pace with Brazil in its industrial growth largely thanks to its own state-directed and state-financed industrialisation programme, which bankers presumably financed as yet another set of Brazil-style pharaonic projects which could usefully absorb resources. Paradoxically, Mexico's relative share in the region's manufactured

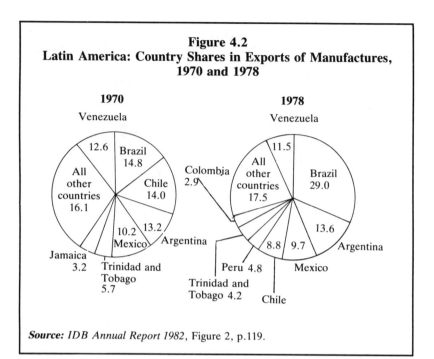

Figure 4.2
**Latin America: Country Shares in Exports of Manufactures,
1970 and 1978**

Source: *IDB Annual Report 1982*, Figure 2, p.119.

exports actually fell. By 1978, Brazil alone accounted for 29 per cent of the region's exports of manufactured goods.

Having thus given a sharp push to the forces within the region making for increased specialisation and greater inter-regional imbalance, the banks refrained from any intervention in the Mexican and Brazilian governments' chosen style of development. They were equally complaisant in the case of Venezuela, the third most important target for their loans. Venezuela was an established oil producer and member of OPEC. Commercial bank loans here financed central administration to an exceptional degree, as well as investment in both the private sector and state companies. Venezuelan irresponsibility with this loan bonanza was to become a byword among creditors in the wake of the debt crisis. The government itself had no notion as to how much state-owned companies had borrowed. The private sector used the ready availability of dollars to make capital exports amounting to a third more than the country's entire foreign debt — a figure without precedent in any other Latin American country.[19] But Venezuela managed to preserve its share in regional manufacturing, against the trend towards concentration in the region's economic giants, and also

Rockefeller and Argentina

David Rockefeller's visit to Argentina last week was the first in what could be a series of calls paid by foreign dignatories seeking to bolster the image of the economy minister José Martínez de Hoz. The head of the economic team seems determined to use them to end his five-year term in office in a blaze of glory.

Officially, Rockefeller visited Argentina to take part in Chase Manhattan's annual convention in Iguazú. Two plane-loads of Chase executives were flown in for the convention, and Rockefeller also hired the Teatro Colón in Buenos Aires to give a special reception for Chase officials and their friends. But the main objective of the exercise was to convince the military authorities that current economic policies must be continued when the new government comes in next March.

No opportunity to extol the virtues of Martínez de Hoz's economic programme was missed. Rockefeller described his meeting with the economy minister as 'historic'. He also made it clear that if present policies were continued, he would personally do his best to ensure greater international investment in Argentina.

But the praise was not well received by the press; the signs are that the military, too, are more concerned with the current state of the economy. This is hardly the moment, they believe, for exaggerated claims about the success of the economic programme. [..] Earlier successes in moderating inflation may turn out to be temporary. The annual rate is now running at 89.4 per cent.

More serious, however, is the extremely shaky state of the financial system and many of the large industrial companies. Estimates of the banks' and finance houses' bad debts range from US$6 billion to US$8 billion. Debt clubs and repeated roll-overs are staving off the crash, but it is generally felt that the government will have to prop the system up.

The press has taken a particularly jaundiced view of Rockefeller's role. It has been pointed out that Chase Manhattan has done particularly well out of the collapse of local banks such as BIR earlier this year.

Much has also been made of Martínez de Hoz's long personal friendship with Rockefeller, and the fact that he has worked for Chase Manhattan and the Trilateral Commission. The *desarrollista* newspaper *Clarón* has emphasised these connections, while the weekly *El Economista* has described the visit as 'an elegant way of interfering in a neighbour's affairs.'

Latin America Weekly Report, London, 21 November 1980

kept its status as a major exporter of manufactured goods.

Elsewhere it was a different story. Argentina and Chile rank fourth and fifth in the banks' table of Latin American debtors. Both were controlled by military dictatorships willing to experiment with the new, liberal form of economics — lower wages, reduced government deficits, higher interest rates, reduced import tariffs and the privatisation of state-owned firms. In spite of its relative economic stagnation during the 1960s, bank lending to Argentina made some sense: it has the third largest economy in the continent, with a substantial oil supply of its own. Even so, international bankers clearly took an interest in giving the experiment explicit political support. (see box p.75)

In Chile, there was no need to give the liberal revolution an overt political boost, since the Chilean 'Chicago Boys' (graduates of Milton Friedman's Department of Economics at the University of Chicago) were firmly in control. But Chile clearly did receive an economic boost from the banks: more commercial finance than the size or status of its manufacturing sector would have warranted. In terms of its 1970 GDP, it was already smaller than Peru and Columbia, though its manufacturing sector was a little stronger (something the Chicago Boys quickly corrected), and it was very much more important as a contributor to regional exports of manufactured goods (a role they also cut down to size). Unlike both Peru and Columbia, it was not an oil producer. Why would bank funds flow into Chile, rather than Peru?

In practice, the banks provided the Argentine and Chilean business sectors — not their governments — with copious funding to cover the costs of a pioneer effort at restructuring. Restructuring here meant selective deindustrialisation — the closing of inefficient manufacturers oriented towards the domestic market — and the encouragement of new non-traditional industries much more closely tied to the agricultural and mineral products which bankers felt were a natural focus for specialisation: cheap tinned fruit for the US market, copper tubing, whisky and wine. The restructuring process did not require large-scale investment, except in the sense that local businessmen may have felt the need to compensate for the investments now being made in Miami and New York. In Chile, total investment in the economy was actually less in 1978 and 1979, measured in constant dollars, than it was in 1970 — in spite of a net influx of bank loans and dividends to the local private sector amounting to US$1.75 billion.[20] Overall, industrial production in both countries grew very slowly. While value-added in manufacturing was doubling in Mexico and nearly trebling in Brazil over the decade of the 1970s, in Argentina it grew by a mere 14 per cent and in Chile by 12 per cent.[21]

Meanwhile, much of the money provided by international bankers was consumed in speculation and capital flight. Speculation became a business in itself, as the monetarist policies of local governments drove up the interest rate far above international levels, and huge profits were to be made from borrowing money from the international financial markets and reloaning it locally. In Chile, firms with access to international credit are estimated to have made a profit of US$800 million (about 5 per cent of GDP) on their role as intermediaries in 1976-79.[22]

The Argentine business classes became experts in the round trip: money loaned to firms within the country by some US banks was quickly redeposited under the names of private citizens in the banks' New York branches, only to be turned out again to fund the next Argentine loan. Overall, capital flight took two thirds of the value of inflowing capital funds back out of the country between 1979 and 1982.[23] Like Patiño in Bolivia earlier in this century, Argentine capitalists decided that their country was a fragile reed when it came to the prospects of survival, and the best business strategy was to diversify into investments abroad.

In practice, they survived better than their Chilean colleagues, who took the liberal advice more literally. The inflow of funds helped consolidate the power of a small number of bank-based conglomerates, swollen by the acquisition of firms privatised during General Pinochet's determined demolition of the pre-coup socialist state. They now diversified into areas such as food processing and forestry in obedience to the banks' perceptions of their comparative advantage — as well as into investment abroad. In the end, these conglomerates were top-heavy and unable to generate the level of profits required to pay back their international loans. They duly collapsed in the recession of 1981.

The moral of this story is rather strange, as the next chapter will show. Profligate states and self-denying ones emerged with about equal grace, or lack of it, as the dance of the millions slowed into the debt crisis, with Venezuela and Argentina alike suffering an absolute decline in GDP for five years. The social crisis took its worst toll in Brazil and Chile, the former with a high-spending state (but never on behalf of the Brazilian poor), and the other devotedly following the liberal recipe, only to turn up the worst rates of open unemployment in Latin America.

Whether the long-term lessons of the dance of the millions era will match this picture is another story. On the whole, the region's profligate states did rather better at preserving a broad base for their local economies, in terms of manufacturing capacity and the ability to generate manufactured exports during the 1970s and in the future, than those countries which followed the liberal model. As the prices of primary commodities continued to decline on world markets, their refusal to engage in a premature search for specialisation at the international level, and their care to preserve the domestic market, may yet pay some dividends.

The Banks' Loans and the Poor

'In La Paz today there are many large skyscrapers where once there was only one. They are the fruit of the foreign-funded economic explosion of the 1970s, [when] the foreign debt grew from US$500 million in 1970 to nearly five times that (US$2,400 million) in 1980. The skyscrapers provide flats and offices for bankers.

The ruling elite, however defined, has had a wonderful two decades, laughing all the way to the banks in Miami. In a population of six million, there are perhaps 250,000 people whose lot has improved. For them the jet planes of the national airline, and the expensive new airports all over the country. For them the motorways that link airport and city when, in the rest of the country, virtually no new roads have been built at all — except in zones of minimum population. For them the luxury suburbs of La Paz, the exotic boom areas of Santa Cruz. One Bolivia for a tiny minority, another for the great bulk of the population.'

Richard Gott in *The Guardian*, London, 9 October 1987.

Such is the record of the banks as promoters of development over the decade. The most spectacular characteristic of this period in Latin American economic history, in retrospect, is its colossal waste of resources. 'From dams to arms factories', as one recent study puts it, 'tangible projects account for less than half the debt total in some countries'.[24] Three out of five of the countries (Mexico, Venezuela and Argentina) targeted as most worthy of investment sent half or more of these new resources back to the banks or the US in the form of capital flight. In four countries (Nicaragua, Trinidad, Chile and Jamaica), real levels of investment in industry, agriculture, tourism, and even highways, actually contracted.[25] Nicaragua was suffering the impact of civil war, Jamaica the effects of IMF deflationary policies and the collapse of its bauxite revenues, but Chile was a favoured client of the banks.

The decade of the dance of the millions was essentially a boom era for Latin America's middle and upper classes. From the point of view of the poor, bankers were very bad agents of development. At best, their enthusiasm for international specialisation made them accomplices in the combination of rapid industrial growth in Brazil, with one of the worst records for income concentration in Latin America, and industrial contraction in the Southern Cone countries, where income distribution was better, rates of pay higher, and working conditions, union rights and social security systems incomparably

78

better developed. At worst, they spread the disease of contracting real wages and rising number of unemployed well beyond the Southern Cone, as the region's governments were persuaded by their advice and that of economists like Balassa to study the advantages of a low wage economy.

Under the influence of the new liberal thinking, wages certainly contracted. The 1976 military coup in Argentina slashed wage costs in manufacturing to 55 per cent of their 1974 level. The 1973 coup in Chile brought them down to 40 per cent of their level when Allende came to power. In Peru, following the banks' own attempt to manage an early version of the post-1982 debt crisis, urban wage costs were reduced in 1979 to two-thirds of what they had been a decade earlier, and wages in manufacturing were down by almost 40 per cent.[26] For most Latin American countries, figures show real wage levels in the 1970s as stagnant or declining.(see chapter five, table 5.2)

The decade also saw a gradual worsening of employment opportunities for the poor in the urban areas. In the Southern Cone and much of the Caribbean, rates of open unemployment drifted upwards, and the poor were increasingly forced to invent work for themselves in the urban informal sector — selling goods or offering desirable and not-so-desirable services on the fringes. The trend was particularly noticeable in Chile and Argentina, major recipients of bank loans for restructuring, as industry was less and less capable of providing jobs. Even in Brazil, manufacturing was not a sufficient answer to the population's growing demand for jobs, and the comparative size of urban informal sector only declined slowly.(see chapter five, table 5.3)

The poor everywhere paid a massive price for this decade of financial bonanzas with shrinking expectations of what development might bring. Earlier generations of Latin American politicians and army officers saw development and industrialisation as being linked to the internal market, and therefore put a double value on the possibility of raising the standard of living of the poor: worthwhile both as a means of avoiding social revolution, and because the poor could then provide a better market for local firms. Security of employment for local workers and the development of unions were seen as desirable goals, even by military officers who were vicious opponents of the Left.

By the 1970s, unions, social security systems, high wages and job security were all beginning to be universally characterised as obstacles to economic growth. The very good welfare provision of Argentina and Chile was being run down, in the former case because it was tied to union organisation, and in the latter as part of an explicit government attack on the power of state. The relatively poor provision on offer in Brazil was more acceptable, as it involved lower taxes and social security transfers for businessmen.

The real significance for the poor of this kind of development model would emerge very clearly when the debt crisis exploded in the 1980s, and Brazil — the most advanced industrial producer on the continent — saw its rates of infant mortality rise in a fashion unrepeated in much poorer and more backward countries which had benefited from the earlier, discredited view of what development was all about.

5. Debt and Development II: the Social Time Bomb

The Second Great Depression in Latin America

The scissors crisis of the 1980s — unmanageable debts and falling prices for exports in declining world markets — has produced the second Great Depression in Latin America this century. In broad terms, it has brought to an abrupt end a fairly consistent pattern of growth since the Second World War (see figure 5.1), and because the crisis is far from over — debts have not fallen, interest rates are still highly variable, and foreign markets may be reduced in a new world depression — the damage the crisis has already done may as yet be nothing compared to the damage to come.

The depression in the 1980s has had an unequal impact on different countries. Ironically, Mexico and Brazil — the world's two largest LDC debtors and the two countries taking lead roles in debt negotiations — have been comparatively cushioned from the worst effects of the crisis. Mexico is among the least affected countries (see table 5.1), although its rapidly increasing population makes this advantage something of an illusion.(see figure 5.2) Despite Mexico's reputation among bankers as the IMF 'model economy', the poor have suffered the most from five years of adjustment. (see box p.85)

Until its second economic crisis in 1987, Brazil was also doing relatively well. Weaker economies, carrying less weight in global debt negotiations, have been much less protected against the typhoon. For some, the scissors crisis has brought the spectre of absolute economic decline. Jamaica, for example, suffered from a collapse in the world market for aluminium and an IMF stabilisation programme which has become the *cause célèbre* of anti-IMF campaigns.[1] Throughout the 1980s, the total output of the Jamaican economy remained below 1970 levels. Guyana, another sugar-based economy with a Caribbean-style society, has similarly been transformed from a weak star into a black hole.

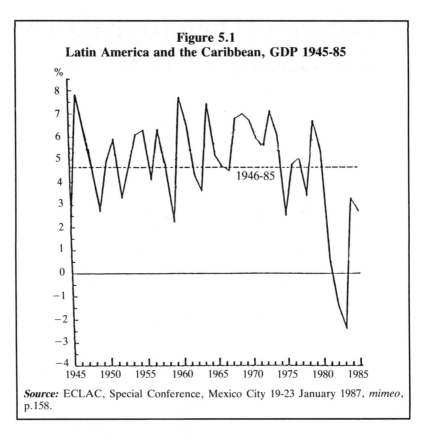

Figure 5.1
Latin America and the Caribbean, GDP 1945-85

1946-85

Source: ECLAC, Special Conference, Mexico City 19-23 January 1987, *mimeo*, p.158.

These are exceptionally tragic cases. Nonetheless, in the five years since the debt crisis broke, most Latin American economies at some point fell back to the level of production they had reached in 1980, and several have failed to struggle back to it. The list of those with smaller economies than they had in 1980 includes many of the countries which figured in the original Baker Plan: among them not only chronically poor Bolivia, but more sophisticated economies like Venezuela (a founder member of OPEC), and the smaller industrial countries of the Southern Cone like Argentina and Uruguay (Chile has been spared a similar fate only by the timely and exceptional recovery in copper prices). Central American countries also found it difficult to escape the combined impact of the scissors crisis and civil war. Guatemala and El Salvador both saw their economies decline in real terms over the post-1980 period.

Table 5.1

Annual Levels of GDP, 1982-86 (compared with 1980 = 100)

	1970	1980	1982	1983	1984	1985	1986†
Four or five years of GDP below 1970 levels:							
Jamaica	108.4	100.0	103.9	105.8	105.5	100.5	102.6
Guyana	84.5	100.0	88.5	82.2	82.5	83.2	77.3
Five years of GDP below 1980 levels:							
El Salvador	72.7	100.0	86.5	87.2*	89.4	91.1	91.9
Guatemala	57.7	100.0	97.0	94.5	95.1	94.2	94.2
Haiti	62.9	100.0	93.4	94.2*	94.8	95.9	95.9
Barbados	84.8	100.0	92.5	92.9	95.0	95.2	99.7
Bolivia	64.6	100.0	90.7	86.3*	90.3*	88.7	86.9
Uruguay	74.2	100.0	91.9	87.7	85.7*	85.6	91.0
Venezuela	66.7	100.0	100.4	94.7	93.5	93.7	96.6
Argentina	77.6	100.0	89.0	91.7	93.8	89.6	94.7
Delayed Shocks:							
Trinidad	59.8	100.0	107.2	103.6	88.3*	83.2	77.9
Nicaragua	96.5	100.0	104.3	109.0	107.3	103.2	102.8
Surinam	n.a.	100.0	104.0	98.1*	98.3	93.3	92.5
Shock and Recovery:							
Costa Rica	57.8	100.0	90.7	93.2*	100.4	101.7	104.6
Honduras	64.8	100.0	99.3	99.0	103.1	105.6	109.0
Chile	77.9	100.0	90.6	90.0	95.7	97.7	106.0
Peru	71.2	100.0	103.9	91.6	95.8	97.7	106.0
Brazil	43.4	100.0	99.4	96.2	100.5	108.8	117.7
Continuing Growth:							
Mexico	52.7	100.0	107.4	101.7	105.4	108.4	104.2
Dominican Rep.	51.1	100.0	109.9	110.0	110.4	107.8	109.2
Bahamas	n.a.	100.0	102.0	103.5	106.7	110.1	112.4
Panama	58.4	100.0	109.8	110.3	109.9	114.3	117.6
Paraguay	43.1	100.0	107.5	104.4	107.7	111.9	111.9
Ecuador	42.6	100.0	105.9	102.1	106.2	110.2	112.2
Colombia	58.4	100.0	103.2	104.2	108.0	111.0	116.7

†Estimated.
*Differences of more than one percentile point between indexed GDP estimates in different reporting years. In each case, the latter estimate has been used.
Source: Author's calculations on the basis of *IDB Annual Reports*, 1985, 1986, 1987.

In other countries — Brazil, Chile, Costa Rica and Peru — the cost of the IMF-dictated programmes of economic stabilisation resulted in fearful losses of economic production lasting two or three years. Nonetheless these economies recovered, sometimes with the help of a deliberate break with the IMF and the adoption of unorthodox

Figure 5.2
Declining Economic Resources of Latin America and the Caribbean, GDP per capita 1980-86

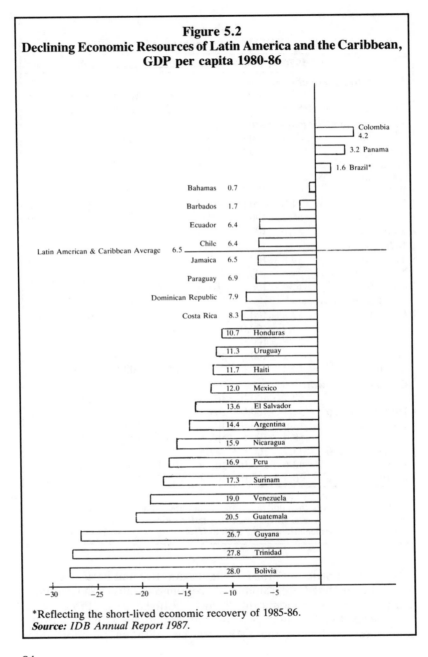

*Reflecting the short-lived economic recovery of 1985-86.
Source: IDB Annual Report 1987.

The Mexican 'Success Story': The Rich Get Richer, the Poor Get Poorer

Since the debt crisis began, Mexico has been the darling of the international financial community and the IMF's local success story. Strategically, it has moved from a position of almost total dependence on oil to one in which it rivals Taiwan and South Korea as an exporter of manufactured goods to the US. In five years, the share of manufactures in Mexican exports has jumped from 16 to 45 per cent. The key has been cheap labour: average wages were slashed 40 per cent between 1982 and 1984, rising again briefly in 1985 only to decline in 1986 and 1987.

A main aim of all the IMF agreements since 1982 has been to cut the public sector deficit. Thanks to greatly-increased prices of locally-produced oil and electricity, and a five per cent increase in VAT, it was slashed from 18 per cent of GDP in 1982 to 7 per cent in 1984. But, as a result of these and other policies, inflation has risen from 18 per cent in 1979 to 28 per cent in 1981, to 102 per cent in 1983 and 86 per cent in 1986.

Price controls and producer subsidies on bread, tortillas, beans, eggs and cooking oils, slashed by the government's cuts in state expenditure, have been replaced by targetted subsidies to poor consumers which are only available at the public sector's food distribution chain, CONASUPO, though not all the poor are able to reach CONASUPO stores. Even here, subsidies declined by almost 43 per cent between 1983 and 1984.

The Impact on the Poor

According to government figures, Mexico has survived the debt crisis better than most. But the Mexican poor would hardly believe it. Trade unions estimated open unemployment at nearly 15 per cent in 1986, when the official government figure was 3.5 per cent. Since 1982, the Mexican labour force has grown by more than four million people, but from 1981-84, 'not a single new job was created', according to the 1986 World Bank Report, *Poverty in Latin America*. Large numbers of public officials were sacked: 30,000 workers from the central administration in 1982, and 750,000 from public sector firms in 1985.

Manufacturing industry completely failed to find places either for the unemployed or for those looking for their first job. For all the growth in US-owned border industries (now employing almost 300,000, most of them women), manufacturing employment in large firms actually shrank between 1981 and 1986, with one worker in ten put out into the streets. Cuts in the government budget in 1985-86 are claimed to have cost 250,000 private sector jobs.

Even before the debt crisis, almost half the working population was earning less than the minimum wage, according to official figures. IMF programmes sent this figure spiralling upwards. In 1982, 13 per cent of workers registered with the Mexican Institute of Social Security were on wages lower than the minimum. By 1985, the proportion was 38 per cent. ▶

Throughout the same period, the purchasing power of the minimum wage was also falling sharply. By 1982, its value was already only two-thirds of the 1976 level. Adjustment shaved off a further 30 per cent between 1982-85, as governments set the legal value in line with expected rates of inflation, some 50 per cent below the actual rate. Leaving aside the cost of rent, cooking fuel and clothes, the cost of providing a minimum diet to a family of four rose from 34 per cent of the minimum wage in 1982 to 52 per cent in 1986.

And the rich?

The outcome of this success story has been a world in which the rich get richer, and the poor get poorer. In December 1985, *Fortune* reported that Mexican figures on exports to the US totalled US$14 billion, while US figures put the total at US$18 billion. The Mexican rich were pocketing the difference — US$4 billion in a single year — for investment in US banks and firms. In September 1987, bankers congratulated Mexico on having 'the world's top performing stock market', with a seven-fold rise in share prices in *pesos* during the year, matching a 6,973 per cent increase in reported profits. Even measured in dollars, investors made a gain of 135 per cent over the year. Despite the collapse in the Mexican stock market which followed Black Monday, the government felt compelled to raise interest rates to 160 per cent *every 28 days* in early January 1988, from a 'mere' 127 per cent, in the hope of forcing large local firms and locally-based US subsidiaries to draw on brimming corporate treasuries for working capital, which would otherwise flow back across the border again in increased capital flight.

economic policies stressing growth, as in Brazil and Peru. (see chapters seven and eight) Even here, the recoveries experienced in 1985 and 1986 have been fragile.

Declines in absolute production on this scale would be a severe setback even for countries with relatively stable populations. Latin America's young and growing population gives the crisis the seal of desperation. Since the debt crisis began, the population of the region has increased by 15 per cent: more young people for whom governments had to try to find jobs, more babies being born whose state of nutrition now will affect the intelligence and drive of the labour force in the next generation. The crisis has shrunk the resources which governments have available to provide for them, if one compares the total size of the economy (GDP) with the number of citizens clamouring for a share.(see figure 5.2) Most countries show a decline in GDP per capita way below the regional average of six per cent, because the short-lived expansion of Brazil pulled the figure up sharply. It is hard to find a single case where IMF programmes of

Why IMF Policies Don't Work

● *The IMF tends to assume that excess consumption is the universal villain behind all developing countries' balance of payments problems.* This is not the case. A better explanation for developing countries' difficulties lie in their problems with supply. Local agriculture fails to produce sufficient food for local consumers, which has to be imported. Local industries are geared to producing small numbers of very varied goods for an elite market, and cope poorly with mass demand for basic goods. The investment capital available to increase capacity is extremely expensive, and so is the world market cost of imported technology for countries tied to exports in highly competitive markets, on which they can earn only restricted foreign exchange.

● *Increasing local interest rates is not always a magic answer to capital flight.* It benefits the very rich, who may be persuaded to bring back funds from New York, to earn extortionate rates of interest at home. But many of the small and medium-sized firms whose base is the local economy have to pay these rates of interest on investment or working capital which often results in higher rates of bankruptcy. The local state is also among the losers, facing ever higher budget deficits as the proportion of government expenditure going to pay interest on old debt rises — in spite of its frantic IMF induced efforts to effect spending cuts. Paradoxically, governments may be forced back into the hands of foreign financiers because however high international interest rates have become, they are still less costly than those imposed by IMF policies at home. The numbers of Latin American governments drawing on foreign sources to finance budget deficits has increased since 1982.

● *Increasing exports is not always the best recipe for increasing export revenue. First, it makes foreign markets for the goods in which countries specialise increasingly competitive, forcing down world prices.* In Latin America's case, export volume (the number of goods exported) increased by roughly 7 per cent a year between 1980-84, but export revenue on each unit exported fell by 6.5 per cent. Latin America spent these four years running faster just to maintain its existing revenue from export goods.

● *Secondly, export production is dominated by large firms.* Redistributing resources to encourage it means, in practice, redistributing resources from the poor to the rich, and sometimes directly to firms which are already foreign-owned. In agriculture, it means pushing poor peasants off the land and into the cities, replacing them with farms controlled by the big landowners, and worked by better machinery, producing more perfect food products to be consumed in California, not at home. In manufacturing, it means increasing support for foreign-owned multinationals, who have the local connections and the abilities to ▶

penetrate Western markets, and who already control over 40 per cent of Mexico's manufactured exports and over 50 per cent of Brazil's. In Argentina, Brazil and Peru, a quarter of all national exports are made by multinational firms. In Mexico and Chile, the figure is 20 per cent.

● *Thirdly, the small factories who dominate Latin America's urban centres, are simply not able to switch from production for local markets, to production for foreign consumers.* They do not have the expertise or the knowledge of foreign markets to export to the West, even if they could afford travel bills and hotel expenses. They need a prosperous local market to survive.

● *The local state is not always an economic villain, taking national resources which the private sector would invest more wisely elsewhere.* Government expenditure on investment substitutes for the reluctance of private capital to keep funds in the country. In many Latin American countries, government expenditure on consumption and employment also keeps the local market alive, for the benefit of small and medium-sized firms, and the informal sector of small independent operators on which a quarter of Latin America's urban population depends to survive. If government spending is cut, their possibilities of survival are also reduced — thus paradoxically, also cutting government's tax revenues and increasing, not reducing, the government's budget deficit.

In Keynesian terms, all these policies involve, at best, pushing the economy back to equilibrium at a lower level of overall activity — squeezing out those firms who are locally based, and the poor. Hence the association between IMF policies and reduced economic growth. Studies have shown that even according to its own criteria of success, the IMF has a poor record. In an internal study of the 1980 standby programmes, Fund personnel concluded that the IMF 'cannot be complacent about a situation in which almost half of the cases have not shown any progress towards balance of payments viability.' Studies of the longer-term impact of Fund programmes suggest that they generally failed to contain inflation (one of the key goals of orthodox economic policy) and that in 40 per cent of the cases, the result was reduced economic growth.

adjustment have halted the decline. (see box p.87) In Bolivia, which suffered sixteen adjustment programmes in the four years after 1979 — thirteen of them faithfully following the IMF model — per capita GDP fell every year, giving a cumulative fall of 22.6 per cent.[2]

The Impact on the Poor

'In five years, [in Bolivia] the family sector lost about a fifth of its income, measured in real terms. Taking into account the growth in population over this period, the real income loss for each family amounted to 28.5 per cent overall, a yearly decline in resources of 6.5 per cent.

In the face of this situation, the crisis and the economic adjustment policies introduced to make it possible to pay service charges on the debt, triggered large-scale demonstrations of popular protest. However, politicians who were ignorant in practice of the real impact of economic change, chose to regard these exhibitions of social discontent as manoeuvres by a labour leadership determined to "destabilise democracy".'

Rolando Morales, 'Por qué no se hizo ni se hace lo obvio', La Paz, mimeo, 1987.

Wages and Employment

For the poor, this overall decline in economic resources has been especially traumatic, because they were already in difficulties before it began. Of the few countries who were able to register an authentic increase in wage levels in 1979 above their 1970 levels, Brazil was belatedly compensating for cuts imposed during the early years of military dictatorship from 1964-76, Colombia was engaged in the profitable export of cocaine, and Ecuador was enjoying a boom from the new discoveries in oil. Governments also let the real value of legally-established minimum wages decline in every country except Brazil, Colombia, Costa Rica and Ecuador, and were notoriously lax about enforcing the legislation in Colombia and Brazil.(see table 5.2)

The debt crisis meant that wages were forced down again in line with IMF prescriptions for depressing local demand. ILO figures for the whole of the region suggest a further fall in real average minimum wages of 16 per cent between 1980 and 1985, on top of the damage done in the 1970s. Wages in industry fell by 12 per cent, in construction by 18 per cent and in the public sector by 17 per cent.[3] The contraction in local demand had an immediate impact on the viability of firms producing goods and services for the local market, and thus on the rates of open unemployment, driving them up from an average 6.4 per cent of the urban labour force in 1980 to 8.8 per cent in 1983 — an increase of more than a third over three years.[4] Unemployment doubled in Chile during the crisis, and tripled in Bolivia. Recovery in 1986 (principally in Brazil) reduced the figures a little, but not to 1980 levels.

Figures for open unemployment are never altogether reliable in Third World countries, since the general absence of social security systems[5] encourages the development of hidden unemployment, as those who cannot find wage work set themselves up as odd-job men,

89

Table 5.2
Deterioration in Wages, 1970-85 (1970 = 100)

	1979	1980	1981	1982	1983	Cumulative change, 1983-5 (%)
Minimum Wages:						
1. Well below 1970 levels in 1980						
Argentina	46.8	55.0	53.6	56.8	84.1	27.2/−32.4†
Chile	75.8	76.0	75.3	73.9	59.5	−10.0
Guatemala	53.2	85.1	91.5	91.5	87.2	n.a.
Peru	67.3	83.2	70.8	65.2	62.9	−17.2
Uruguay	84.6	80.7	82.7	83.4	72.1	n.a.
2. Stagnant* in 1980						
Brazil	99.4	101.7	100.6	101.1	89.3	−2.3
Mexico	117.7	110.0	110.7	99.9	80.4	−4.5
Venezuela	64.9	106.9	92.0	84.0	79.0	n.a.
3. Above 1970 levels in 1980						
Colombia	96.0	127.3	124.7	130.7	139.1	n.a.
Costa Rica	151.5	153.5	138.9	131.9	152.7	+9.2
Ecuador	115.5	203.7	175.0	154.2	129.2	n.a.
Industrial Wages:						
1. Well below 1970 levels in 1980						
Guatemala	69.1	68.6	76.4	78.8	81.8	n.a.
Uruguay	50.3	47.8	51.4	50.8	39.3	n.a.
2. Stagnant* in 1980						
Argentina	83.1	93.1	83.1	74.4	96.2	24.9/−16.5†
Colombia	97.4	97.6	98.0	101.8	107.4	n.a.
Chile	92.5	103.6	115.9	112.5	99.9	−3.1
Mexico	121.0	115.4	119.0	117.3	88.0	−1.6
Peru	73.8	87.8	86.1	86.9	68.5	−17.6
3. Above 1970 levels in 1980						
Brazil	147.5	155.5	165.6	177.9	160.0	+3.6
Costa Rica	131.6	131.8	119.0	98.2	112.7	+2.1
Ecuador	140.2	167.9	160.9	157.2	n.a.	n.a.
Venezuela	123.1	122.0	118.4	122.0	118.2	n.a.
Construction Wages						
1. Well below 1970 levels in 1980						
Argentina	56.4	66.5	58.7	52.8	80.2	33.5/−30.7†
Uruguay	68.6	65.3	65.0	56.1	46.2	n.a.
2. Stagnant* in 1980						
Brazil	113.1	113.7	115.4	120.0	101.1	−2.6
Chile	101.0	102.3	108.1	105.0	78.5	−14.6
Guatemala	106.0	111.6	136.4	135.9	126.5	n.a.
Peru	78.0	87.4	86.4	93.6	78.6	−23.0

▶

3. Above 1970 levels in 1980						
Colombia	109.3	117.2	110.6	n.a.	n.a.	n.a.
Costa Rica	133.3	133.7	117.8	93.5	96.6	+10.9**
Ecuador	97.7	123.0	128.9	130.5	n.a.	n.a.
Mexico	114.2	118.5	111.1	102.2	n.a.	+4.5
Venezuela	122.5	119.0	110.1	n.a.	n.a.	n.a.

*i.e. within 15 per cent of 1970 levels.
**1982-5.
†1983-4 and 1985 given separately.
Source: ILO-PREALC, *Mas Alla de la Crisis*, Santiago, 1985. Additional figures for 1983-5, ILO-PREALC, *Adjustment and Social Debt*, Santiago, 1987, p.17.

sellers of matches on street corners and minders of cars for middle-class car-owners — a swollen contingent of workers which social scientists call the informal sector. The best measure of the debt crisis' overall impact on the availability of jobs is thus the combined growth of open unemployment and the urban informal sector.(see table 5.3) In the first five years of the 1980s' Great Depression, Latin America's urban informal sector expanded by a staggering 39 per cent, while the proportion of the urban labour force living off wages shrank from an average of 70 per cent in 1980 to 64 per cent in 1985.[6]

Even these figures fail to capture the real size of the informal sector, because they assume that self-employment and wage work are mutually exclusive. In fact, throughout the crisis years, low wages have forced many *bona fide* wage-earners to supplement incomes which could no longer feed their families, by working after-hours as taxi-drivers, street vendors or even as black market traders. Adding these people to those formally unemployed, those working on contract for firms who failed to register their employment with the government, and those employed in the cocaine trade, Peruvian economists reached the alarming conclusion in 1986 that 70 per cent of Lima's working population was involved in the black economy.[7]

What was it like for a poor family trying to live through the crisis? Forty years earlier, when Latin America was predominantly rural, they could have opted out of the money economy and grown their own food, however miserable their condition. By the 1980s, Latin America was largely urban, and though occasionally churchmen toyed with the idea of teaching urban squatters to grow their own food, very little space for a bean patch was available in the average shanty town. The poor were stuck with an urban labour market for which the debt crisis spelt stagnation or absolute contraction. Even in Brazil the recovery in 1985-86 only brought São Paulo manufacturing activity back to its level of five years before. The crisis was a devastating blow not only to their

Table 5.3
Open and Hidden Unemployment in the Urban Economy, 1970-85

	1970 UIS/OU		1980 UIS/OU		Combined Change* 1980/1970
Latin America†	29.1%	6.8%	26.1%	6.9%	[− 2.9%]
Chile	22.9%	4.1%	36.1%	11.7%	[+20.8%]
Costa Rica	22.5%	3.5%	28.6%	6.0%	[+ 8.6%]
Argentina	19.0%	4.9%	26.3%	2.6%	[+ 5.0%]
Peru	39.8%	8.3%	34.2%	10.9%	[+ 3.0%]
Colombia	30.9%	10.8%	30.2%	9.7%	[− 1.8%]
Brazil	27.5%	6.5%	24.1%	6.2%	[− 3.7%]
Venezuela	30.7%	7.8%	25.6%	6.6%	[− 6.3%]
Guatemala	43.4%	—	31.5%	2.2%	[−11.9%]
Mexico	34.2%	7.0%	24.2%	4.5%	[−13.0%]

	1983		Combined Change* 1983/1980	1985		Combined Change* 1985/1980
Latin America†	29.0%	10.2%	[+6.2%]	30.7%	11.1%	[+ 8.8%]
Chile	37.2%	19.0%	[+8.4%]	37.2%	17.0%	[− 0.9%]
Costa Rica	29.3%	9.9%	[+4.6%]	28.3%	6.7%	[− 0.4%]
Argentina	27.1%	4.6%	[+2.8%]	28.9%	6.5%	[+ 6.5%]
Peru	32.7%	13.9%	[+2.4%]	34.9%	17.6%	[+ 7.4%]
Colombia	33.6%	11.8%	[+5.5%]	35.4%	14.1%	[+ 9.6%]
Brazil	29.6%	6.7%	[+6.0%]	30.1%	5.3%	[+ 5.1%]
Venezuela	27.3%	10.5%	[+5.6%]	26.2%	14.3%	[+ 8.3%]
Guatemala	32.8%	7.6%	[+6.7%]	33.5%	12.9%	[+12.7%]
Mexico	25.6%	6.7%	[+3.6%]	29.5%	4.8%	[+ 5.6%]

Urban Informal Sector (UIS) and Open Unemployment (OU) as a % Non-Agricultural Labour Force

*Increase in open and hidden unemployment together.
†Arithmetical average.
Sources: ILO-PREALC, *Dinamica del subempleo en América Latina*, Santiago, 1981, Table 1, p.16. *Adjustment and Social Debt*, Santiago, 1987, Table 6, p.10 and Table 3, p.5. 1980 figures taken from the latter.

comparative levels of income, but also to their security.

Large factories and commercial establishments which could provide a place for skilled labour under minimally satisfactory conditions consistently laid off workers over the five years. Such private sector jobs as could be found were increasingly only in small firms, notorious for their unwillingness to abide by existing labour legislation.[8]

Table 5.4

Manufacturing Employment and Wages, 1980-85 (% change)

	Employment	Wages
Peru*	−4.7	−13.4
Argentina	−3.2	+ 0.9
Colombia	−2.9	+ 2.6
Mexico*	−2.7	− 8.5
Brazil	−2.5	+ 2.0
Chile*	−1.7	− 5.1
Venezuela	−0.5	+ 0.9
Costa Rica	+7.2	+ 2.6

*1981-5.
Source: ILO-PREALC, *Adjustment and Social Debt*, Table 9, p.17.

Employers' power over their labour force increased dramatically including the power to pay less than the job was worth. In the manufacturing industry, where the drastic cuts in employment and wages were less dramatic than elsewhere (see table 5.4), workers who kept their jobs paid a price in the form of a declining share in the proceeds of production. The value of output from the region's factories fell only marginally over the years of crisis (about 0.4 per cent from 1980-85), but as productivity increased, the share of wages in output fell by 2.0 per cent over the same period.[9] Growing unemployment outside the firm combined with rising rates of inflation to make union activity very difficult. The rare union which succeeded in organising and winning a strike could see everything it had gained in real earnings wiped out by rising prices within a few weeks of going back to work, particularly in countries bedevilled by inflation of 100 per cent and more, such as Brazil, Argentina and Peru.

Women have become almost as numerous as men in some sectors of Latin American industry, particularly in export platform factories in the electronics and textile industries, although their skills are rarely acknowledged and their pay remains comparatively low. They have always provided local manufacturers with outworkers, who work on assemblage at home on a contract basis or help to sell the product through the flexible street-marketing arrangements of the informal sector. The contraction of employment in manufacturing has thus affected them as much as men. Service jobs, such as domestic work and laundry, are traditionally a backstop to which poor women turn when all else fails, but with middle class incomes also contracting, the earnings available inevitably declined.

For many of the men in Latin America's squatter settlements, the

Table 5.5
State Sector Employment and Wages
Average Annual Growth or Decline, 1980-85

	Employment	Wages	Fall in % Total Central Government Expenditure Spent on Wages 1980/84
Chile	−4.6%	− 3.3%	− 7.2%
Venezuela	+0.9%	− 0.7%	−13.1%
Argentina	+1.0%	− 0.7%	n.a.
Costa Rica	+2.3%	− 3.5%	−10.6%
Peru	+2.4%	−16.5%	− 4.0%
Brazil	+4.9%	n.a.	−13.6%
Mexico	+7.4%	n.a.	n.a.

Source: ILO-PREALC, *Adjustment and Social Debt*, Table 9, p.17, and *La protección social a los desocupados*, Table 27, p.58.

construction sector has always been the employer of last resort. But the adjustments hit this sector hard, and in many countries construction work declined by as much as a quarter in the space of a single year, as governments and private firms cut back on capital investment. The existence of large numbers of unemployed construction workers explains the size of the wage cuts taken by those who could find jobs.

Outside Chile, state sector employment continued to expand, roughly in line with the general growth of the labour force — in spite of the IMF's attempts to enforce cuts, in a fashion it would never have dared recommend to industrialised countries faced with a similar recession. In some countries, such as Brazil and Mexico, the state provided a minimal counterweight to the growing jobs crisis, as politicians created or handed out jobs for their personal clients. Employees already on the payroll paid for this crude form of unemployment relief twice over, in declining real wages over and above what they were already suffering from IMF budget cuts.[10] (see table 5.5)

Throughout the years of the debt crisis, only one government developed a new direct employment programme to take the pressure off open rates of unemployment, and a technique for handling recession whose pedigree goes back to Roosevelt's New Deal. This country was President García's Peru. In three others, existing programmes remained in place and were reorganised to meet the new crisis — one in Brazil, one in Pinochet's Chile, and one, ironically, in Panama, one of the countries least affected by the 1982 crisis. In two of these cases, programmes were officially brought to an end, well before the debt crisis could be said to have run its course: the Panamanian programme was closed down in 1982, and the Brazilian programme for the North-East, which had found jobs for some half a million workers over its lifetime, was shut down in 1983.

The Poor as Consumers

Over the five years of the crisis, disappearing employment opportunities and falling income from self-employment have locked the poor into a struggle for survival. Their household economies have suffered (and women have faced an increasing burden) as open unemployment has grown among males. Rapid inflation triggered by adjustment programmes has made budgeting a nightmare, as prices in countries like Brazil and Argentina rose by as much as 20 per cent a month.

While wages were earning less in real terms, the poor have also been paying more for the basic consumer goods which they need to survive — above all, for fuel and food. The price of these goods has risen much more rapidly than the general price level, as governments kept their promises to the IMF and the World Bank and cut back subsidies on wheat and fuel. In Brazil between 1980 and 1985, government expenditure on food subsidies fell from 5.6 per cent of total government spending to 1.7 per cent. There were also reductions in Mexico and Colombia, although not so severe as in Brazil.[11] The diversion of agricultural resources from production for local markets to production for exports (to help pay off the debt) did not help. In Brazil, UNICEF has shown that government promotion of exports and of sugar-cane alcohol as a fuel substitute (saving import bills) actually led to a sharp decrease in per capita food production in 1981-84, with food prices generally increasing more rapidly than the cost of living index.[12] Thus the poor paid over the odds to produce Latin America's trade surpluses, in terms of dearer food and fuel and less of it, as well as through the contraction of their ability to pay.

In many countries, governments were already organising a direct distribution of food parcels to the families worst hit by poverty: Chile, Brazil, Argentina, Uruguay, Peru, Costa Rica and Venezuela all had such programmes. The evidence suggests that even these were not always immune from cuts. Costa Rica cut the number of children benefiting from its supplementary feeding programmes by 20 per cent during a campaign to reduce state expenditure between 1979 and 1982; in Chile, the distribution of milk and food to pregnant women, nursing mothers and children was cut back in 1983, the worst year of the crisis;

Argentina's Food Plan

'In Argentina the need has arisen for a large-scale National Food Program (PAN), administered by the Ministry of Health and Social Affairs. It consists of the periodic distribution of PAN food packages. The highly visible program currently covers about 5.5 million of the country's 30 million people and involves the daily packaging and distribution of about 1,000 tons of food covering about 30 per cent of the needs of an average family of four. The sheer number of recipients in one of the world's best endowed agricultural countries conveys a dramatic image of the social cost of the 1981-82 crisis.'

World Bank, *Poverty in Latin America*, 1986.

and in Uruguay, a programme of food for schoolchildren met with a similar setback.[13] There were some new programmes, such as in Argentina, the so-called bread basket of Latin America. (see box above) Where they existed, they helped to limit the toll taken by the crisis in terms of increased child malnutrition, although they could not always prevent it, given the pressure to keep government expenditure down. (see box p.97) In Costa Rica — by no means the worst affected by the crisis — the cases of people with severe malnutrition arriving at the country's main rehabilitation centre had doubled in 1982.[14]

Programmes such as these — targetted on a specific group of the very poorest — are explicitly encouraged, in theory, by the World Bank and the IMF. Because they *are* clearly targetted, runs the argument, rather than generally available to all urban consumers, they make the most efficient use of government funds. Looked at in a Latin American perspective, however, these attempts at food distribution carry the same message as the equivalent government programmes of direct unemployment relief. Besides being poorly targetted in terms of the countries suffering the worst effects of the 1980s' depression, on a regional scale the amount on offer was small, and even that was vulnerable to cuts. In Brazil, infant nutrition levels fell so low that an epidemic of measles in 1982 carried off so many babies as to raise the infant mortality rate in São Paulo, Latin America's wealthiest and most heavily industrialised city. Nevertheless, a planned expansion of direct food programmes was cut back due to adjustment.[15] Programmes in Peru were also cut back drastically in the second wave of debt-induced retrenchment which preceded the election of Alan García in 1985.(see chapter eight) At best, if they gave the question any thought at all, IMF experts were encouraging only governments with a substantial welfare system, whose costs could be reduced by targetting, to spend money on direct employment or food distribution programmes.

Adjustment and Malnutrition

In Latin America there are numerous indications of increases in malnutrition in various parts of the region. Low birth weight increased in the *North-East of Brazil* from 10.2 in 1982 to 15.3 per cent in 1984. While the recession and ensuing adjustment were found to be primary causes of the increase in low birth weight prevalence, the impact of the recession might not have affected nutrition so strongly had it not been for a prior drought. A recent World Bank Study on the impact of the depression in Latin America reports a higher prevalence of anaemia among poorer families in 1985 as compared with 1973-74. In *Uruguay* the number of malnourished children admitted to the National Nutritional Programme almost doubled between 1982 and 1984. In *Bolivia* the nutritional status of children admitted to the main hospital of Cochabamba showed a marked deterioration between 1980 and 1983. While in 1980, 45 per cent of these children were affected by some forms of malnutrition, the proportion increased to 56 per cent in 1983. Increases of low birth weight babies have occurred between 1979 and 1982 in *Barbados*, from 10 to 16 per cent, and *Jamaica*, from 10 to 12 per cent. For *Mexico*, in 1984 half of low income households suffered from insufficient caloric and protein intake. The cost of a calorie in relation to the minimum salary increased on average between 1982 and 1986 by 65 per cent, with peaks of 130 per cent in the cost of bread, while there were absolute cuts in the food intake of the poor in Mexico in 1983. In Peru the deterioration was acute. Although available data cover only the southern part of the country, the incidence of first-, second- and third-degree malnutrition rose from 42 to 68 per cent of the child population. Third-degree malnutrition, in particular, increased from 0.8 to 3.0 per cent in only three years.

Source: Adapted from UNICEF, *Adjustment with a Human Face*, Volume 1, Clarendon Press, Oxford, 1987, pp.31-2.

The Impact on Health

Poor families struggling to cope with increased stress and smaller budgets for food and heating have been finding government health services less and less adequate to cope with the worsening health problems which are the predictable outcome. The long-term costs implicit in this double deterioration have been ably summarised by the IDB:

'[They] affect the population acutely because of [...] the impact of health on other areas of human behaviour such as education and work. The worsening of the health situation cannot be reversed in the short term: this means that a deterioration, for instance in infant mortality or in nutrition levels, can only be overcome over a long period. [...] A reduction of

97

Table 5.6
Cuts in Health Spending, 1980-84 (%)*

	Health
Bolivia	−77.7**
Guatemala	−58.3
Dominican Republic	−46.5
Surinam	−44.2†
El Salvador	−32.4
Chile	−23.8
Barbados	−21.3
Jamaica	−18.5
Costa Rica	−16.5
Honduras	−15.2
Argentina	−13.9
Uruguay	−13.4

*Cumulative.
**Until 1982.
†Until 1983.
Source: UNICEF, *Adjustment with a Human Face*, Volume 1, Clarendon Press, Oxford, 1987, p.76.

expenditure obliges low-income families to use their own funds for medical care, reducing still further the meager resources they have to provide other basic necessities.'[16]

Figures on health are difficult to collect, but those figures which are available show a clear trend towards a slow-down in government expenditure.(see table 5.6) Of the 15 Latin American governments which provided information to the IDB, 12 had cut the share of overall social service spending in their budgets between 1980-84, due to 'the need to reduce public deficits and the difficulty of cutting other expenditures, such as those for administration and defence', and per capita expenditure on health programmes had fallen in 14.[17] In countries emerging from years of military rule, it was much easier to defend public expenditure on arms than on public health.

Once again, the countries with historically better levels of social service provision (especially in the Southern Cone) weathered the cuts more successfully: not so much because governments kept up health expenditure, perhaps, as because a generation of contacts with relatively adequate health services in the urban areas, had left the poor themselves better educated in health matters, better placed to weigh the importance of sanitation and nutrition, and more determined to buy and self-administer antibiotics in emergencies.

A crude measure of relative health is provided by figures on infant mortality, the number of babies in every 1,000 who die during their first year of life. In Brazil, before the debt crisis hit, the figure was 66 per 1,000 (the figure in the UK is about 10 per 1,000), and declining rapidly: the economic strains of adjustment forced it up within two years to 74, apparently because the government cancelled an immunisation programme due to the cuts.[18] On the whole, Latin America's infant mortality rates have not suffered as badly as expected during the crisis years. Deteriorating states of infant nutrition were counterbalanced in some cases by the development of cheap new medical programmes for immunisation and the treatment of gastroenteritis. This was clearly responsible for holding deaths to the existing level in Bolivia, where the populist government of Siles Zuazo negotiated help from international agencies to preserve an immunisation programme in spite of the cuts.[19] But even outside Brazil, the crisis left its mark in passing. Costa Rica suffered a marginal rise between 1981 and 1982, while in Uruguay figures deteriorated from 28.6 deaths per 1,000 in 1982 to 29.0 in 1984 and 32 in 1985. In Venezuela, deaths due to premature birth rose as a result of the increased strain the crisis put upon pregnant women, though overall infant mortality rates registered only a marginal rise.[20]

Sacrificing the Future

All the data available show that the poor have suffered the most as a consequence of debt-induced recession. Among the poor, as UNICEF points out, it is the 'children and pregnant and nursing women [who] are most at risk and have usually suffered disproportionately'.[21] Economic strategies as dictated by the IMF and the banks — in conjunction with local governments — have spread the costs of the debt burden very unequally, so that those who gained least from the dance of the millions between 1974 and 1980 have had to pay most. With few exceptions Latin American governments were forced into short-term expedients for confronting the Great Depression, locked into permanent negotiations over the debt, and seemingly unable to plan beyond the next few months. Most failed to devise policies which would share the burden more equitably, either by distributing its costs internally or by shifting more of the cost back to the West.

However, the most serious consequences for Latin America's poor and their children are yet to come. Investment in real fixed capital (machinery and highways) has declined drastically as a result of the crisis, compromising future levels of production and exports. Investment in human capital has also been declining. The next

99

generation of Latin Americans will not only be less physically fit, but also less well educated, because governments have been forced to reduce their spending on schools. By the year 2000, this deterioration in the building materials for successful economies will, on ECLAC estimates, mean an additional 20 million Latin Americans living in absolute poverty, who would have enjoyed a relatively decent standard of living if the crisis had not occurred.[22]

Declining Investment

One clear result of the debt crisis has been a decline in the funds available for investment, at a time when capital has been flowing out of Latin America to pay back old debt and keep up grossly inflated interest payments. For Latin America as a whole, the proportion of an already shrunken GDP being put towards investment has further reduced from a regional average of 24 per cent in 1980 to 16 per cent in 1983-86.[23] This represented the end of a twenty-year trend of rising investment, during which time gross investment had increased by an average 7.4 per cent a year, almost without interruption. As the IDB has pointed out, 'for the development of the region, nothing better expresses the present and potential cost of the crisis that began around 1982 and its peculiar adjustment process, than these investment figures.'[24] Between 1980 and 1985, investment fell in economic giants such as Brazil and Mexico by a fifth and a third respectively. Weaker economies did much worse: in Bolivia, the fall was close to 40 per cent in spite of new discoveries of gold and the country's continued importance as a producer of natural gas. Countries such as Argentina, Jamaica, Guyana and Uruguay, facing not only the debt crisis but also a local and international loss of confidence in their future, were actually spending less on investment in 1985 in real terms (i.e. adjusted for inflation) than they had in 1960.[25]

Caught between the Scylla of increasing present misery, and the Charybdis of cutting capital expenditure, governments put the heaviest burdens on Charybdis, as being a less likely source of present complaints. In all seven of Latin America's major economies (Argentina, Brazil, Chile, Colombia, Mexico, Peru and Venezuela), the proportion of GDP going into general government investment and investment by state enterprises, fell in each separate category between 1981 and 1984.[26] General government investment covers highways and hospitals, state firms, investment in industrial equipment and local resources such as oil. The contraction of government investment was thus equally damaging to social capital and the productive sector.

In the theories of restructuring expounded by the IMF and the World Bank, this should have been beneficial, shifting Latin

100

America's pattern of economic activity from excess dependence on the state and towards more active investment by the private sector. Unfortunately for theory, private sector investment was also falling everywhere. Latin American businessmen were looking at the future, and feeling distinctly discouraged. Thus, in spite of the contracting *real* resources which governments were putting into fixed capital, their share of the national investment effort actually *rose* during the 1983-84 period in five out of the seven major economies.[27]

Nor were foreign businessmen any more sanguine about Latin America's prospects. In real terms, the influx of foreign direct investment fell by 30 per cent in Brazil between 1981 and 1984. Elsewhere its collapse was even more drastic. In Argentina, by 1984, funds for foreign direct investment were coming in at a third of the 1981 level. In Chile — where IMF theories were being adopted with maximum enthusiasm — the inflow was a little over a fifth of what it had been just before the beginning of the debt crisis. In Mexico, whose long border with the US makes it an ideal base for export development, the inflow was just 17 per cent of what it had been before 1982.[28]

This investment famine is doubly serious. By failing to expand productive capacity and leaving bottlenecks in production unresolved, it weakens the ability of governments to introduce any future form of economic programme which expands employment and thus popular demand. The factories to provide the consumer goods needed by a growing population are not being put in place. Governments which take the risk, face the prospect of their efforts to reintroduce economic growth running into a log-jam of frustrated consumers and rapidly inflating prices, which could quickly derail any attempt to pull local economies out of the Depression, as it did in Brazil in 1986-87, when the Cruzado Plan collapsed.

Over a longer time span, it also means that Latin America is failing to keep up with the technological revolutions of the present era — failing to realise the dream of its ruling and middle classes, of a modern economy which can offer the same kind of consumer civilisation as Europe or the US. This aspect of the continent's decline is likely to be catastrophic, because it will encourage Latin American ruling classes to send more of their capital abroad to earn money, and establish an alternative home, in more dynamic economies elsewhere.

Education

Government figures on school enrolment suggest that over the past five years, right across Latin America, poor families have made enormous sacrifices to ensure that the present depression should not jeopardise their children's future. The proportion of adolescents continuing in school has risen in every country, in spite of the temptation for parents to withdraw children from school to eke out shrinking budgets by earning a little income of their own.[29] This picture may be a trifle rosy. Calculations made by a UNICEF observer in Bolivia suggest that desertion rates during the course of the school year rose in primary schools there from 2.2 per cent to 8.5 per cent from 1980 to 1983, due, he argues, to economic pressures which meant that parents could not afford clothes and equipment to send their children to school.[30] Enrolment figures also ignore the impact of family stress on children's performance in terms of rates of repetition of individual grades. Nonetheless, it is clear that Latin America's poor families are very conscious of the need for investment in human capital, and will do anything possible to secure education for their children if they can.

Governments have not shown anything like the same commitment. Since 1983, the majority of Latin American countries have been cutting the proportion of central government funds going on education, in spite of the pressure of growing school-age populations.[31] The cuts have not always been consistent, with one country after another attempting to put them into reverse. But over a four year period, they are significant. Between 1980 and 1985, educational expenditure was below 1980 levels by an average of 30 per cent every year in Costa Rica, 14.5 per cent every year in Argentina, 12 per cent in Mexico, and 8 per cent in Chile. Per capita expenditure in Bolivia declined by 7.4 per cent over the three years of the Siles Zuazo government, in spite of an effort to raise the real resources going to education by more than a third in 1984 (which collapsed again in 1985).[32]

Anecdotal evidence suggests that throughout Latin America the quality of educational service has been declining, particularly in the state primary sector, with staff ill-paid and forced to work at two or three different jobs in order to survive, and supplies of equipment, textbooks and even such basics as pencils and paper falling victim to the cuts.

Latin America's Horrorscope

In the 1970s when the dance of the millions was in full swing and many Latin American economies were superficially booming, Westerners of the Left and Right alike scoffed at earlier theories of the development of underdevelopment, associated with economists like Andre Gunder Frank.[33] Wasn't a great deal of new investment going into Latin

102

America (particularly Mexico and Brazil)? Wasn't the Brazilian working class growing by leaps and bounds? Wasn't Brazil, with plentiful reserves of cheap labour and a range of manufactured exports, emerging in the minds of the West and its military elite as a possible Great Power in long run competition with the UK and the US?

That picture was always unrealistic. It ignored the real cost of the Brazilian miracle to the poor — now visible in the relatively rapid deterioration of health standards there compared to those in countries which have objectively suffered more from the crisis of the 1980s. It ignored Latin America's generally inadequate performance in raising wage-earners' standards of living. It ignored the fact, obvious from statistics, that Brazilian and Mexican industry were booming as a result of a process of concentration whose other face was the deindustrialisation of Argentina, Chile and Peru; while at the other end of the scale, the sugar economies of the Caribbean were facing an increasingly closed world market, and beginning to crack under the strain. It ignored the extent to which local prosperity was built on paper mountains, recycled from the Middle East by the world's private banks.

Nonetheless, there was some truth in the vision. Real rates of investment generally continued to rise as they had done since the early 1960s, giving hopes of a greater prosperity which in future years might filter down to the poor. In Brazil, local capitalists were charmed into investing in Brazil rather than New York. The Brazilian working class was becoming better organised and more unwilling to let capitalists take the lion's share of the gains from the miracle. Increased oil revenues were buoying up hitherto backward economies like Ecuador's. There were signs of decreased investment and working class revival even in the deindustrialising countries of the Southern Cone. The notion that Latin America was on a royal road to success may have been ridiculous, but there was room for hope.

The crisis of the 1980s, with its debt burden, declining commodity prices, and prospects of a real world slump in reserve, faces Latin America with the possibility of a reversion to the kind of Frankian world which was common in the Peruvian *sierra*, before the 1968 military coup introduced a land reform.[34] A society whose landlord makes large profits essentially by ensuring that labour is extremely cheap, and then takes his profits *out* of the highlands, to invest in his house in Lima and his bank account in New York; a society where local farming techniques remain at a (picturesque) primitive level, because labour is so cheap that the landlord does not need to invest in capital equipment to ensure his high profits, and where the local poor are ignorant, conveniently ensuring that they do not get ideas above their station.

The landlord in this case may be a New York banker. He may be a Brazilian businessman who decides that after all, the developed world is a safer and more pleasant place to put one's capital and build one's principal place of residence. To the Latin American poor, it would not really matter. Businessmen are only useful to the poor if they invest their capital in *local* development. The 1980s have seen an enormous diversion of investment funds from Latin America to the industrial world. The challenge of the 1990s is to ensure that investment once again happens *within* Latin American countries, where it might be of some use.

6. The Debt Collectors

'Banks should be forbidden to report profits on any foreign loans on which the banks are lending borrowers the money to pay interest. This will not only reduce the rewards for loaning money to pay back loans; it will also give banks an incentive to lower their interest rates to levels that debtor nations can pay without taking out new loans.'
Congressman Charles Schumer, 23 June 1985.

Band-Aid at Work, 1982-85: Private Gains...

When Mexico declared itself unable to continue payments in 1982, the position of the US banks was not good. Due to the coincidence of the Third World debt crisis with parallel shocks in the US energy and farm sectors (also caused by the 1980s' downturn in commodity prices), they were particularly vulnerable to a crisis of confidence. In 1983, more US banks failed than in any year since 1940. In 1984, the weight of losses from energy sector loans caused the crash of one of the major US banks, Continental Illinois, and triggered rumours about the possible failure of three others — Manufacturers Hanover, Chase Manhattan, and Morgan Guaranty.[1] The banks were therefore under pressure to protect their reputation with shareholders and depositors.

In the face of the Mexican crisis, US banks were therefore in an anomalous positon. On the one hand, like the Europeans and the Japanese, they were keen to run down the overall proportion of their assets (i.e. loans) held in Third World countries. As already shown in chapter three, the next five years revealed just how reluctant they were to make new loans. On the other hand, they needed to preserve the flow of interest payments from Latin American debtors. Interest income from individual Latin American countries bulked large in their accounts. In 1976 Brazil already represented as much as 20 per cent of Citibank's global earnings.[2] By 1983 this reverse dependency had

105

Table 6.1
The Importance of Latin American Interest Payments to the
Four Major UK Banks, 1982-85*

	1982	1983	1984	1985
Total Loans (US$m)	17,400	17,600	18,883	19,494
Estimated Interest Rate (%)	13.60	9.50	10.80	9.40
Estimated Latin American				
Earnings (US$m)	2,366	1,672	2,039	1,833
As % Net Interest Income	25.6	18.4	25.5	17.1
As % Pre-Tax Profits	98.1	69.1	92.1	49.3

*Barclays, Lloyds, Midland, National Westminster.
Source: S. Griffith-Jones, M. Marcel, G. Palma, *Third World Debt and British Banks*, Fabian Society, London, 1987, based on authors' calculations from banks' and debtors' information.

spread much more widely: in the year after the Mexican crisis, the three largest Latin American debtors owed the nine largest US banks approximately US$3.4 billion in interest payments, equivalent to 62 per cent of their pre-tax profits in 1982. This state of affairs changed much more slowly than the decline in new bank lending to Latin American countries might suggest. As late as 1985, Citicorp, the leading US bank, was taking US$245 million in pre-tax profits from Latin America and the Caribbean — equivalent to about 25 per cent of its total pre-tax earnings, more than it made from Europe, the Middle East and Africa, and about half what it was earning in North America.[3]

The four major UK clearing banks were in a similar position. Between 1982 and 1985, their collective earnings from Latin America amounted to between 17 and 26 per cent of all their income from interest payments.(see table 6.1) For Lloyds and the Midland, Latin American earnings frequently amounted to more than the banks' total declared pre-tax profits — 122 per cent in the case of Lloyds' and a staggering 424 per cent of the Midland's.[4] Midland's exaggerated dependence on Latin American earnings matched the position of US banks because of its acquisition of Crocker International in 1981, a US regional bank weighed down both by Third World debt and bad loans to the energy and farm sectors.

Despite constant assurances from bankers and US government officials that the debt crisis was under control, the banks' overall vulnerability changed very little in the first five years of the crisis. In 1982, 42 US banks failed, more than four times those collapsing in 1981 (though most of these were small). In 1985, the number was 120, in 1986, 138. By 1987, the US government was keeping more than 100 insolvent savings and loans associations open at a cost of US$5 million a day; bad farm debts had pushed the government's own farm credit system to the brink of technical insolvency; and yet another major US bank, First City Bancorp of Texas, had followed Continental Illinois into the arms of the Federal Deposit Insurance Corporation as a result of bad energy sector loans. Total domestic debt in the US was US$7 trillion, an increase of US$1 trillion within the year, only a quarter of which was accounted for by the Federal deficit. Both US consumers and US corporations were burdened with the highest debt ratios seen since the Depression, and there were fears of widespread bankruptcies in the next recession.[5]

Nonetheless, the banks did a marvellous job of keeping up appearances. In 1983, three of the top six US banks were able to declare pre-tax profits of more than US$500 million, and so were all four of the British banks. Pre-tax profits for the nine biggest US banks amounted to US$5.2 billion, in spite of the difficulties of Chase Manhattan and Continental Illinois with loans to the energy sector.

The continuation of interest payments from developing countries was one important factor in preserving a comfortable safety margin. So too were the exceptional risk premiums charged on the first wave of band-aid reschedulings, with the cost of new loans to Latin American debtors now well over twice the equivalent cost of loans in the 1980-81 period.(see table 6.2) In Mexico, for instance, banks charged an additional half percentage point over Libor compared with pre-rescheduling loans, adding an extra US$500 million to their collective earnings. In Brazil, where the new risk premium was a full percentage point, the new loans thus earned the banks an extra US$1 billion.[6] These figures do not include the additional charges earned by lead banks for arranging a new syndicated loan (1-1.5 per cent of the total), or the 1 per cent commission fee earned by all participating banks.

Such exceptional profits could not last, if only because they worsened the long-term ability of debtors to keep up their payments. They duly began to be whittled away in negotiations for the second round, in 1983-84, as the average cost of new loans to the debtors came down to a mere 140 per cent of what it had been four years earlier. By the third round, bankers were suffering from negotiated conditions 10 per cent less profitable to them than pre-crisis levels, and residual enthusiasm for involuntary lending was all but dead.

While the profits were there, bankers made every attempt to defend them — even as they made the underlying logic of the band-aid solution unsustainable by slowly withdrawing funds for new loans. In May 1984, with an Argentine default looming, the chairman of the Federal Reserve Board suggested to a Senate Banking Committee that

Table 6.2
The Cost of Rescheduling:
Conditionality of post-1982 Loans Compared with Pre-crisis Terms, 1982-85
(US$m and Index of Conditionality*
1980-June 1981 = 100)

	First Round 1982/3			Second Round 1983/4			Third Round 1984/5		
	Amount	New Loans	Index of Cond'y	Amount	New Loans	Index of Cond'y	Amount	New Loans	Index of Cond'y
Mexico	23,700	5,000	281	12,000	3,800	160	48,700	000	83
Brazil	4,800	4,400	144	5,400	6,500	108	—	—	—
Argentina	13,000**	1,500	317	—	—	—	13,400	4,200	116
Chile	3,424	1,300	250	000	780	151	5,932	714 371†	89
Peru	400	450	197	662	000	133	—	—	—
Uruguay	630	240	349	—	—	—	—	—	—
Ecuador	1,970	431	342	900	000	191	4,811	200	109
Venezuela	—	—	—	—	—	—	21,200	000	68
Costa Rica	650	225	133	—	—	—	280	75	83
Cuba	130	000	148	103	000	93	94	000	—
Dominican Rep.	568**	000	235	—	—	—	868	—	—
Honduras	121	000	153	—	—	—	220	000	63
Panama	180	100	274	—	—	—	603	60	81

*Includes margin of interest rate charged over Libor, period of amortisation, commissions. Calculations from source.
**These loans were negotiated but never finally signed.
†1986. Includes US$150 million loan guaranteed by World Bank.
Source: Robert Devlin, *Financial Discipline vs. Economic Development*, ECLAC, 4 March 1986, *mimeo*, Tables 1, 3.

banks might solve the debt crisis by putting a cap on interest rates to debtor countries, charging less than the market rate in service payments and keeping their accountants happy by including unpaid interest in the principal of the debt (in order to avoid having to declare a loss). At the time, this proposed solution would presumably have been doubly unacceptable to the banks, as it both affected their short-term earnings and increased their build-up of long-term assets in countries from which they wanted to withdraw. The banks duly gave it a public burial, citing its possible effect on their accounts and profits. It was never revived again as a serious possible solution to the debt crisis, though the Federal Reserve Board made its own calculations of the cost to the banks of eliminating all the spread of interest rates above Libor being charged Latin American debtors in 1986. It came to the conclusion that the cost to the 24 largest US banks would have been a mere 6 per cent of their pre-tax earnings.[7]

...Public Losses

'We foreign bankers are for the free market system when we are out to make a buck and believe in the state when we're about to lose a buck [...] This thing [the negotiations with Argentina] will come down to a matter of muscle.'
Bank representative, quoted in *The Wall Street Journal*, 24 May 1985.

Besides increased financial gains, the banks walked away with another prize from the first round of negotiations: an acceptance on the part of the debtor countries of national, i.e. government, responsibility for all outstanding loans. In the halcyon days of the dance of the millions, governments and state companies were significant borrowers, but by no means the only ones. Overall, 34 per cent of the Latin American portfolios of US banks were government debt, 29 per cent took the form of credits to local banks and 37 per cent were loans made directly to private sector companies.[8] Multinationals often found it convenient to borrow abroad where interest rates were cheaper than could be had locally, and recent estimates suggest that in 1982 they accounted for about 8 per cent of the region's total long term debt.[9] Private banks were particularly important clients because, in the era of cheap money, fabulous money could be made by borrowing money at low interest rates on the international financial markets, and loaning it out locally at high interest rates made necessary by restrictive monetary policies and government efforts to prevent capital flight.

In spite of the fabled efficiency of the market, international banks were left chasing some very dubious debtors in the private sector when

109

the dance of the millions came to an end. Following the best interventionist traditions of Latin American development — so much deplored by the IMF and successive US governments — some governments almost automatically accepted responsibility for banks and other private debts. As early as 1976 the Brazilian state had introduced legislation allowing private sector debtors to off-load their debts on the Central Bank by pre-paying all or part of the nominal dollar value, leaving the Central Bank to assume any further foreign exchange costs of servicing the debt.[10] For all the nationalist rhetoric in which it was enveloped, the principles behind the nationalisation of the local Mexican banking system in 1982 were much the same.

But other governments were well satisfied with the official position shared by the financial markets, the IMF, the World Bank and the Reagan administration, according to which private investment was always better than public (because private firms have to be efficient or face bankruptcy). The Chilean government, nothing if not skilled in propagandising the ethics of the international business community, even mounted campaigns around the slogan, 'Bankruptcy is a positive good'.

Following the outbreak of the debt crisis, foreign bankers were keen to jettison this principle as quickly as possible. Their success can be measured in the growing weight of government debt as against that of the private sector.(see table 6.3) Sometimes the demand for the state to assume responsibility was indirect: governments had to provide the private sector with dollars in exchange for their freely offered local currency, to make the requisite dollar payments on their debts, even in countries where the private sector had used the dance of the millions to build up massive private accounts abroad out of which the debt could logically have been paid. Thus in 1984, faced with an attempt by the Venezuelan government to force private sector debtors to pay interest and amortisation on their foreign loans out of foreign deposits, the Wells Fargo bank publicly threatened to torpedo all negotiations on rescheduling of Venezuela's public sector debt. Similar pressures were brought to bear on another major victim of capital flight, Mexico — apparently with the backing of the IMF.[11]

Argentina provides an example of even more blatant blackmail: the pressure on local states to provide *post facto* guarantees for unguaranteed and otherwise uncollectable private sector debts. Foreign bankers refused to accept the liquidation of Argentina's eleventh largest bank, the Banco de Italia, which would have wiped out US$250 million of their assets. The Banking Advisory Committee telexed the Argentine government pointing out that unless the local state accepted responsibility for the debts, current negotiations on a

Table 6.3
Private Gains, Public Losses:
The Transfer of US Bank Claims to the Latin American Public Sector, 1982-84
(US$ billion in 1984 and % change over previous two years)

	Public Sector Loans		Loans to Banks		Loans to other Private Cos.	
Total Non-OPEC	$37.7	+48%	$19.2	−11%	$17.3	−22%
Argentina	$ 4.0	+32%	$ 1.8	−18%	$ 2.1	−28%
Brazil	$11.9	+63%	$ 8.1	−7%	$ 2.9	−14%
Chile	$ 2.6	+144%	$ 2.9	−10%	$ 1.1	−35%
Mexico	$13.5	+39%	$ 4.4	+11%*	$ 8.6	−19%
OPEC						
Venezuela	$ 5.4	+11%	$ 2.3	−21%	$ 3.2	−18%

*Mexican banks were nationalised in 1982.
Source: The Banker, September 1985, p.66.

US$4.2 billion loan would be jeopardised.[12] Even the Pinochet government in Chile, renown for its deficit-cutting and devotion to free market principles, was forced to intervene to pay for private sector debt. The Chilean government owed only 18 per cent of the foreign debt which accumulated during the 1970s and early 1980s. Of foreign banks' loans to Chile, half took the form of credits to private local banks, the other 30 per cent being loans directly to private companies. Nonetheless, when one Chilean bank after another began to fail in 1983, the Chilean government was forced to accept responsibility for their accumulated foreign debts.[13]

The behaviour of international banks in this quiet campaign for the nationalisation of bad Latin American debts, and the tacit approval which they enjoyed from the IMF and the Reagan administration, makes their well-aired views on the need for a reduction of the weight of the state in Latin American economies little more than fraud.[14] It also cast a very cold light on the repeated conviction of OECD governments that the debt was not a political issue, and that there could be no case for an OECD government plan to rescue both debtors and banks.

The real benefits to banks from nationalisation were matched by the damage wreaked on the financial position of local states. Government investment in bailing out foreign banks necessarily came at the expense of investment in infrastructure and production, as funds were diverted to buying dollars from the local private sector to pay off private sector debts. Where the impact of the crisis made it impossible

111

for governments to reduce expenditure sharply enough, the result was inflation and increasing local government debt.

Managing Withdrawal

The band-aid solution thus helped to preserve bank profitability, while the US and UK majors hastily looked round for new and safer sources of profits to ease their withdrawal from problem borrowers. The growing market for credit cards was a particularly attractive option, padding their pre-tax earnings through annual interest rates of almost 24 per cent. Mortgages were another favourite. Banks also began to campaign for the deregulation of local markets to enable them to compete with stockmarket firms and insurance companies.

Meanwhile, in spite of the new powers of the IMF to force through involuntary lending, the scale of the new loans from commercial banks to developing countries shrank drastically. The banks' retreat actually dates back to 1982, six months before Mexico announced its inability to repay its debts. Their withdrawal from a market with shaky foundations helped to trigger the Mexican crisis in the classic market pattern.[15] In the two year period before the debt crisis broke, total bank loans to Latin America rose by roughly US$60 billion. In the eighteen months which followed its public recognition, the increase was just about US$9 billion, less than the total involuntary funding demanded by the IMF in connection with individual country rescheduling programmes.[16]

Bankers simply refused to lend new money unless forced to do so: new money being their own contribution to their own interest bill, which could no longer be met from debtor countries' foreign exchange earnings alone. The stage was set for a slow but consistent pattern of bank withdrawal from the Third World, which the band-aid solution and the Baker Plan were at best only able to slow down. Table 6.4 shows the overall pattern of decline from 1982 to 1986. In 1985, on IMF figures, private banks managed to secure repayments on their outstanding loans to developing countries worth US$2.7 billion. In 1986, they pushed this figure up to US$7.2 billion. Bank loans outstanding to the Baker fifteen also began to fall, from US$281.6 billion in 1985 to US$280.3 billion in 1986.[17]

In this new game, differences of interest and commitment to Latin America quickly emerged between the US major banks tied to the fate of the biggest Latin American debtors by heavy commitments in overall loans, and the smaller regional banks whose share of Latin American assets was tiny and whose willingness to throw good money after bad accordingly less secure. Differences also began to emerge

112

Table 6.4
The Slowdown in Bank Lending, 1980-86 (US$ billion)

	1980	1981	1982	1983	1984	1985	1986
New Net Flows from banks to:							
Latin America	27.3	30.5	12.1	7.8	5.7	1.3	−0.5
Africa	2.0	2.2	1.7	0.3	0.1	0.4	−0.4
Asia & Middle East	9.7	7.4	5.9	3.5	4.6	6.8	−0.9
All non-OPEC LDCs	39.0	39.9	19.8	12.2	10.4	8.5	−1.8

Source: S. Griffith-Jones, *The Banker*, September 1987, from BIS 1986 annual report. B.A. Kettell and G.A. Magnus, *The International Debt Game*, Graham and Trotman, London, 1986, Table 5.6, p.57, from BIS data.

between US and UK banks and their less heavily committed European partners, whose willingness to sell off portions of their Latin American portfolios was largely responsible for the growth in a secondary market from 1983 onwards. These pressures accelerated the process of withdrawal as each segment of the banking community strained to look after its own interests and defend itself against the possibility of rivals getting a free ride, i.e. using the new money provided by other banks to cover their own withdrawal, interest payments in hand.

1987 — The New View of the Banks

In private, bankers must have entertained some doubts about the viability of the band-aid and Baker Plan solutions, which apparently committed them to rescheduling loans to Latin America in a fashion which assumed growing regional indebtedness far into the future. Nonetheless, they continued to give the Reagan administration's solutions open support until the fourth round of negotiations with Latin American countries in 1986-87. Officially, they supported the US belief that the debt crisis would be solved when involuntary lending came to an end, and the main Latin American debtors could once again return to international financial markets and obtain voluntary commercial loans. This carrot was still being waved by bankers in front of their Latin American negotiating partners as late as April 1987.

But in practice, bankers supported the official solution essentially because it protected their interest payments and gave them cover for a slow strategic retreat. They showed no similar commitment to the principle that debtor countries should be allowed to grow to contain any possibilities of a social explosion, supposedly inherent in the band-aid and Baker solutions. When this principle began to figure in the negotiations with debtors, support for the official position evaporated

Mexico's Debt Strategy: So Far From God, So Near to the US...

For the US, Mexico is the key country in Latin America. The two countries share a 2,000 mile-long border: in 1985, US border patrols arrested 1.3 million Mexican illegal entrants. 2,900 US companies have major direct investments in Mexico, and two-thirds of what they produce crosses the border to service US markets. Mexico is the US's third largest trading partner (after Japan and Canada), and in 1981, US exports to Mexico amounted to US$17 billion. The US thus has a paramount interest in preserving the Mexican economy, and while it does so, Mexico has every reason not to break with the US.

Throughout the debt crisis, the Mexicans have therefore played a double game. On the one hand, they have pioneered Latin American debt renegotiating strategies and played a key role in setting up coordinating bodies of Latin American debtors — not debtors' cartels but payers' clubs, as Mexico's former Finance Minister, Jesús Silva Herzog all too accurately described them. On the other hand, they have used the threat of a unilateral Latin American default to gain new concessions from the US at crucial moments. Undermining the organisation of joint responses in the wake of each new negotiating success, they have assured other Latin American countries that the concessions can be generalised.

In practice, the Mexicans have weakened the possibility of other countries taking unilateral action. In March 1984 Silva Herzog organised an emergency loan from other Latin American debtors, to prevent Argentina from defaulting. At the time, it was strongly rumoured that the funds originally came from the US. In March 1985, Mexico repeated the process with Costa Rica and the Dominican Republic.

The 1982 Mexican negotiations provided the model for the band-aid solution, accepting both IMF supervision and negotiations with a bankers' cartel (seven US banks and six from other countries) as key parts of the rescheduling process. In return, they secured a bridging loan from the US Treasury, advance payment for increased sales of oil to the US (paid at below-market prices — the deal is supposed to have been the equivalent of an annual interest rate of 30 per cent). The banks were slightly less extortionate. In return for Mexico's agreement that everything possible should be done to preserve the international banking system, they rescheduled US$23 billion in principal payments falling due over the next two years, charging Mexico more than the cost of previous loans, but less than Brazil would pay. The agreements cost Mexico one year of economic contraction, but the social cost of IMF policies was severe and prolonged. (see box p.85, chapter five)

During 1984, after helping the US government to head off confrontation with Argentina and ensuring that the Cartagena Group avoided radical positions, Mexico negotiated its own second rescheduling agreement, signed in the following March. The new package secured Mexico a lower rate of interest (1.13 per cent over Libor), and a formal commitment by the banks to multi-year rescheduling (MYRA). ▶

In theory, MYRA pre-empted any further need on Mexico's part for new money. In practice, falling oil revenues had begun to undermine the 14-year agreement even before it came into effect. By mid-1985, the Mexican economy was seen by the IMF and its creditors to be slipping. Mexico now took advantage of Alan García's July call for united Latin American action, letting it be known that they might follow Peru's example. In August, they told bankers that MYRA was no longer a solution to Mexico's debt problems. In September, this delicate political pressure was boosted by the Mexican earthquake. The result was the Baker Plan.

In January 1986, oil prices collapsed. Mexico and Venezuela called an emergency meeting of the Cartagena Group, pushing for a committee to monitor the effects of lower oil revenues, and 'establishing the principle that the Consensus would support unilateral action' while failing to provide real support either for Peru's initiative or for possible action on the part of Argentina.

The Mexican cabinet then threatened an indefinite suspension of all debt service payments to commercial banks. The situation provoked a personal visit from Paul Volker, Chairman of the US Federal Reserve Board. Volker in turn threatened an immediate suspension of all bank credits the moment Mexico took unilateral action, but he also held out the possibility of new loans. In June, Mexico's Finance Minister was dismissed: a move seen as toughening Mexico's negotiating stance. In July, Mexico reached an agreement with the IMF, which for the first time recognised the need for compensatory finance.

Despite Mexico's best negotiating powers and privileged treatment, by the end of 1987, after five years of austerity, Mexico was once again facing economic difficulties. In the wake of Black Monday, its stock market suffered losses of 75 per cent on existing share values. By January 1988, after a 40 per cent devaluation, Mexico was facing a new round of austerity policies, including further cuts in the government budget, additional sell-offs of state companies, and wage controls.

very quickly. The turning-point came in 1986, when Mexico again tried to use its relatively strong negotiating position to shift the parameters of debt negotiations towards repayment with growth.

The Mexican Watershed

Mexico has always acted as a pioneer in the debt crisis, largely because of the extraordinary political leverage it enjoys as a result of its 2000-mile long frontier with the US and its position as the most significant importer of US goods in the Third World.[18] (see box p.114) In 1984 the Mexicans pioneered multi-year rescheduling. In return for this concession to the banks, they offered a programme of restructuring

Structural Changes in Mexico

By the time that the Mexicans had struck a new deal with the IMF and the Reagan administration, they had agreed to make a number of fundamental, structural changes in their economy:

- Mexico is ignoring its investment law forbidding foreign control of more than 49 per cent of a company, despite the fact that this law is enshrined in the constitution.
- Mexico has agreed to dismantle or sell over 300 state-owned companies to the private sector, including airlines and steel mills.
- Mexico has allowed foreign creditors to take effective control of the Alfa group, the country's largest private conglomerate, through a debt-equity swap. (The steel and petrochemical giant had suspended debt payments during tie 1982 crisis.)
- Mexico is facilitating the expansion of foreign corporations such as Ford, Chrysler, General Motors and Nissan by cooperating with lucrative debt-equity swaps and offering tax concessions in border zones.
- Mexico has acceded to the longstanding US demand to join the General Agreement on Tariffs and Trade (GATT). Mexico promised to speed up the tariff reductions and elimination of import quotas and licenses when it signed its new deal with the IMF. Mexico has thus capitulated to the Reagan administration's strategy to use the GATT to win new access to markets and safeguards for its financial, pharmaceutical and other corporations under the guise of GATT codes covering trade in services and 'intellectual property rights'.
- Mexico has promised to promote foreign investment in export industries.

Source: *GATT-Fly Report*, November 1986, p.9.

which promised the privatisation of state enterprises and a considerable relaxation in Mexico's rules on direct foreign investment. (see box above) The formula was essentially adopted by Baker himself in his Plan. Subsequently, Mexico was one of the first countries to organise a programme of debt-equity swaps. (see box p.122)

In mid-1985, another collapse in world oil prices made it impossible for Mexico to keep to the terms of the 1984 agreement. Mexican negotiators campaigned to tie the package of government, multilateral and commercial loans involved in its rescheduling agreement to the principle of the need to secure a minimum rate of growth: if growth rates fell, then Mexico would receive more credit. A deterioration in the country's export markets would thus trigger larger, not smaller, flows of credit. Interest rates were also to be forced further down. In its attempt to impose these new conditions on financial markets, the

Mexican negotiating team had more or less explicit support from the US government. The basic principles of this package were also accepted by the IMF and the Paris Club.

Securing the acceptance of the private banks to an agreement which committed them to underwrite an explicit link between Mexico's growth rate and the amount of money they were willing to loan took much longer and was much more fraught. Technically, the deal was concluded in October, with the Banking Advisory Committee agreeing to a contingency fund of US$1.2 billion to be disbursed when the IMF saw fit, and a further US$0.5 billion, half of it guaranteed by the World Bank, which would be made available if Mexico failed to achieve a 3-4 per cent growth rate in 1987. In addition to this major concession, Mexico also achieved lower interest rates than any hitherto charged to developing countries — less than 1 per cent over Libor. In practice, US regional banks rebelled, together with the British and European. The negotiated Mexican agreement was only finally signed in the wake of Brazil's declaration of a moratorium in February 1987, and with it the emergence of a new threat to take the entire debt question to a higher political court.

The ill-feeling generated by these battles was clearly in evidence when bankers met with Brazilian negotiators in January 1987. Bankers saw the upcoming Brazil negotiations as a vital test case — Brazil was the Third World's largest debtor — and they were determined that there would be no extension of the concessions made to Mexico. The US financial press was informed that the Mexican agreement had only been reached because of exceptional pressures from the US government and had been presented to them by the US administration, the IMF and the World Bank as a *fait accompli*. John Reed, chairman of Citicorp, gave a public interview to the *Wall Street Journal* complaining that an extension of the Mexican terms to other big developing countries (he mentioned Brazil, Argentina, Venezuela, Chile, and the Philippines) would cut Citicorp's revenue from loans to these countries by a third, which was unacceptable. US government officials countered that Citicorp had taken a corporate decision to block efforts by the Federal Reserve Board and the US government to secure lower interest rates for debtor countries, jeopardising ongoing negotiations in the Philippines and Chile as a result. They also complained that banks were now charging spreads for new loans higher than those they had received in 1982 and 1983, at the height of the original Mexican panic.[19] Bankers, for their part, made public their doubts about the ability of the existing Banking Advisory Committee to survive without a sea-change in the rules of the game.

By early 1987, it was clear that the marriage of interests between the

US administration and the world's leading international banks over the debt issue was coming apart at the seams. Citicorp's strategy seems to have been to take advantage of the overall optimism generated by the Baker Plan in 1986 to chalk up profits as high as possible against the day of the inevitable breakdown. Meanwhile, it had begun to prepare an alternative plan of its own. The breakdown perhaps came a little earlier than expected, essentially because of a new growth crisis in the world's second largest debtor, Brazil.

The Brazilian Watershed

Brazil's moratorium had not yet reached the 90-day mark (after which US loans have to be declared non-performing) when Citicorp suddenly announced that it was adding US$3 billion to its loan loss reserves, taking them to three times the level of the previous year, in order to cover itself against the risk that Brazil and other major Third World debtors might not pay their debts at all.

The move took other banks by surprise, but in a competitive market, they had little choice but to follow suit. Within two months, all the major US and British banks made similar provision, raising their insurance against losses to between 25 and 30 per cent of total loans to Third World. The immediate consequence was a spate of declared losses on the six-month accounting period to the end of June. Citicorp's move implied a willingness to accept short-term losses (US$2.3 billion in its income over six months) in the search for medium-term security. The next five leading US banks, apart from Manufacturers Hanover, set aside more than US$1 billion each. In Britain, the losses ranged from £700 million at Lloyds and Midland, and £40 million at Barclays, to a declared profit of £250 million at National Westminster. In any case, banks could expect a profitable second quarter to allow them to make good this extraordinary loss; and in some cases such as Lloyds, they even increased their dividends in anticipation. Losses in Britain were sweetened by the UK Chancellor's decision to offer 35 per cent tax relief on bad debts. Stock markets in both countries reacted enthusiastically.

Whether this acceleration in the very slow pace at which banks prepared themselves against a possible default was sufficient, is another question. By some European standards, even the June measures left Anglo-Saxon banks relatively underprovisioned. West German and Swiss banks' loan loss provisions already amounted to between 30 and 50 per cent of their exposure in underdeveloped countries. Swedish banks averaged 50 per cent.[20]

Citicorp's forcing of the pace on increased loan loss provision

Table 6.5
Loan Loss Provision after Citicorp's US$3 billion, 1987 (US$ billion)

	Total Assets	Second Quarter Loan Loss Provisions	Total Loan Loss Reserves	As % Total Assets	Non-performing loans	As % Total Assets
US Banks						
Citicorp	194.4	3.4	4.9	3.68	6.3	4.9
Chase						
Manhattan	98.9	1.7	2.7	4.00	4.6	4.5
Bank of						
America	97.0	1.3	3.2	4.91	5.1	7.7
Chemical						
New York	78.4	1.2	2.1	4.15	3.0	5.9
J.P. Morgan	74.7	0.8	1.8	5.35	1.7	5.2
Manufacturers						
Han.	73.8	1.8	2.7	4.88	3.5	6.2
UK Banks						
Nat. West-						
minster	138.9	0.9	2.5	3.0	0.8	n.a.
Barclays	134.7	1.2	2.9	n.a.	n.a.	n.a.
Midland	82.3	1.7	3.1	5.5	n.a.	n.a.
Lloyds	77.8	1.8	3.0	n.a.	n.a.	n.a.

Source: The Banker, September 1987, p.31.

created severe difficulties for the Bank of America in the US and Midland in Britain. Midland was forced to dispose of its Scottish and Irish assets and was left open to the threat of a takeover by other local and foreign firms. However, neither bank was precipitated into liquidation, nor were there any rumours of government intervention. Citicorp itself was sufficiently encouraged by the stock market's reaction to take another major step in August designed to improve its capital:assets ratio to 3.6 per cent. Once again the rest of the banking world felt compelled to follow suit.

In the short run, secure in the belief that after five years no debtors' cartel would be forthcoming, the Western financial press saw the new loan provision as strengthening the hand of the banks in negotiating with recalcitrant debtors such as Brazil, by ending their vulnerability to a debtor's declaration of default. As yet, banks were still unwilling to offer any concessions on the absolute size of the debts owed by their Third World debtors. Latin Americans drew the opposite conclusion:

if the banks were now in a better position to survive default, more could be done to relieve the pressure on the debtors in terms of interest relief and other measures.

Both sides were wrong. Debtors were beginning to reach a position in which tough talk from the banks made little or no difference to their willingness to pay. In spite of a change in the Finance Minister (organised with the vocal encouragement of the US administration and the banks) Brazil did not resume interest payments until late 1987, and the *de facto* moratoriums in Brazil and Peru spread to Ecuador (suffering the effects of the earthquake) and Zambia. More significantly, as table 6.5 shows, total loan loss provision by the major US banks was still generally smaller in each case than the quota of non-performing loans, let alone to the total of all outstanding loans. A reasonable assumption, then, was that after May and June 1987, US and perhaps UK banks could expect to survive the default of one major Third World debtor, but not a debtors' cartel, still less the combination of a series of Third World defaults with others in their domestic or OECD loan portfolios, such as might be provoked by a world slump.

This vulnerability was underlined in September 1987 by James Baker's dramatic public repudiation of a preferred Brazilian solution to the debt crisis. Brazil had suggested that half of its existing commercial debt of US$68 billion should be converted into long-term securities, repayable over 35 years, with an interest rate of perhaps six per cent, selling at a discount to take into account the prevailing price of Brazilian debt on the secondary market. Assuming that Citicorp's May provision had signalled bank acceptance of the uncollectable nature of existing debts, Brazil's negotiators argued that some relief on the interest burden was overdue. The banks charged that the Brazilian plan would cost them immediate losses of US$16.5 billion, with more to come as other debtor countries sought to follow the Brazilian example. These loans, they said, would overwhelm many large US banks, in spite of the US$22 billion 'and more' added to US and UK loans loss reserves since May. Despite the stock market's belief that banks were less vulnerable to Third World problems after the May provision, Secretary Baker took the side of the banks.[21] Brazil was not even allowed to bring its proposal to the negotiating table for discussion.

A Menu of Options: the Banks' Solution?

'The latest restructuring gives us 20 years to repay principal, with no principal payments for nine years. So why are we giving money away? Why pay 88 cents for debt worth 60 cents?'

Mexican negotiator, Angel Gurria, quoted in *Fortune*, 3 August 1987.

By April 1987, a new piece of jargon had begun to appear in the financial press: a menu of options. The US Treasury lent its weight to the notion that such a menu could cope with the debt crisis, its appetising contents to be sampled by bank negotiators and debtor countries. The idea of the menu was to reduce debtors' needs for new bank credits, by transforming existing debt in the portfolio of New York and London bankers into something else. This could take the form of new equity capital in the debtor countries for the banks or other foreign investors, through what were known as debt-equity swaps (see box p.122); or new trade loans, in which banks accepted export goods for sale in OECD markets in lieu of interest payments; on lending, which was the transfer of debt from one borrower to another; bank loans guaranteed by the World Bank; and even exit bonds, which converted debt into long-term securities at low interest rates which could be sold to non-bank investors, along lines not dissimilar to those suggested in the Brazilian plan of September 1987. Once again Citicorp was in the vanguard, announcing that in addition to its US$3 billion in loan loss reserves, it planned to reduce Latin American exposure by US$5 billion over the next five years, essentially through debt-equity swaps and loan sales.[22]

In practice, the six months between April and October 1987 revealed clear limitations to this menu. Early in the year Argentina offered exit bonds to its creditors, but there were very few takers. Two banks, including the Midland, took up a Peruvian offer to negotiate payment of interest otherwise blocked by García's debt policies, if banks undertook to sell Peruvian goods in foreign markets. But it was quite clear that Western bank and financial markets, like Citicorp, reserved their real enthusiasm for debt-equity schemes and loan sales, which held out the hope for banks of accelerating the existing policy of withdrawal from Third World loans.

With the powerful support of James Baker, debt-equity swaps gained enormous respectability, and many extravagant claims were made for them. They would solve the problem for the banks and the debtors, as banks would rid themselves of dubious bank loans and debtors would reduce their debt repayments. They would also end existing investment famines in debtor countries as multinationals and other investors would be attracted into the country. But economists and governments were soon expressing doubts, and not only because, as one economist pointed out, the debt-equity exchange committed debtors to swap 'good assets (why else would foreigners buy them?) for bad assets (why else would creditor banks sell them at a discount?)'.[23]

There were many justifications for such doubts. Preliminary sums suggested that the entire secondary loan market only covered a small

Debt-Equity Swaps

A debt-equity swap can take one of two forms: either the creditor bank can swap its bank loans in US dollars for the equivalent face value of the loan in local currency, to be invested in local capital markets or in an extension of the banks' own local subsidiaries; or it can sell off its loans to a third party interested in investing in the debtor country such as a foreign company, or even a national of the debtor country who has built up a personal stock of dollars abroad through capital flight, and for some reason wants to take those dollars back home. For example, a US bank wants to rid its portfolio of a US$10 million loan it originally made to Mexico. A major multinational wants to expand its Mexican subsidiary. The bank sells the US$10 million loan to the multinational on the secondary market for US$6 million (its value on the secondary market). The company in turn sells the loan back to Mexico for US$8 million worth of investment in its subsidiary. For the private investor or company, debt-equity swaps thus offer large amounts of local currency on the cheap.

Essentially debt-equity swaps are possible because of the difference between the face value of bank debt and its real market value as measured in the secondary market, which takes into account such factors as the likelihood of default and the pressures capable of pushing countries towards moratoriums on interest payments. On the whole, the secondary market has been cynical about the value of Latin American debt. For example, in September 1987 Brazilian debt was trading at 42 per cent of its face value, and Mexican debt at 46 per cent.(see table below) The difference between the face value of the debt and its value on the secondary market provides the margin for third party profit, mainly because the banks are prepared to take a loss on the face value of their debt and because the debtor countries are prepared to waive most, or all, of the relief to which they might feel entitled from discounted secondary market debt, and honour debt paper at close to its full face value.

Banks can minimise losses under this system by becoming investors themselves, although they then exchange high interest payments in the short-term for the longer-term vicissitudes of an investor in the real economy. Chile has been a path-breaker in this field, as in many other free market ideas. In early 1986, it allowed the US Bankers Trust to trade US$43 million in loans for a controlling interest in the country's largest pension fund and largest life insurance company. In Brazil, the Bank of Scotland has used a debt-equity swap to purchase a stake in a Brazilian paper and cellulose company.

The real rub is the disproportion in size between existing Latin American debts with foreign banks and existing stocks of local capital. Citicorp alone has US$10.6 billion worth of debts in Brazil, Argentina, Mexico, Venezuela and Chile. But Latin America's capital markets are relatively small. In January 1987, Sergio Barcellos, the president of the Rio Stock Exchange, estimated that US$20 billion would buy all the firms with listings on Brazil's stock market. Even in the unlikely event of Brazil allowing a total transfer of its local stock of private capital to foreigners, local capital markets could not mop up the debts.

Private companies have already made some deals. The New Zealand timber company, Carter Holt, bought up the forestry operations of a bankrupt Chilean conglomerate, using the US$161 million's worth of Chilean loans which it bought for US$114 million on the secondary market. Chrysler has used debt-equity swaps to boost its export capacity in Mexico by 40 per cent, as well as paying off local debts, reputedly securing a US$100 million investment for US$65 million.

But the potential for trading old bank debt for new foreign investment faces the problem of too little foreign investment, too much bank debt. In 1984, total flows of new foreign direct investment into Latin America were only US$3.3 billion, having declined from a peak of US$7.6 billion in 1981. Even with the additional incentive offered by debt-equity swaps in the form of investment on the cheap worth a possible US$5 billion a year, foreign direct investment was clearly incapable of mopping up the vast sea of Latin American debt.

Decline in Secondary Market after Citicorp's Loss Provision, 1987
(US cents per US$1 of debt)

	Mid-April	Mid-September
Argentina	61	38
Bolivia*	9*	9*
Brazil	65	42
Chile	70	57
Colombia	89	80
Ecuador	55	33
Mexico	60	46
Panama	68	60
Peru	16	12
Venezuela	75	55

*May figure, taken from Salomon Brothers, quoted in the *Financial Times*, 21 May 1987.
Source: *South*, London, November 1987.

---

proportion of the Latin American debt. Loan sales in 1986 amounted to US$5 billion, half Citicorp's exposure in the five biggest Latin American debtors. In 1986 roughly 40 per cent of these sales were going to finance debt-equity swaps. Although banks frequently and loudly claimed that prices on the secondary market were too cheap (giving buyers too large a discount on the face value of country debt), the most striking characteristic of the market was its artificially limited number of sellers. Most of the debt traded in the market had its origins in European banks, either because US banks were unwilling to admit a loss on the face of their debts, or because US auditing relations made it relatively expensive for them to do so.[24]

For Latin Americans there were much clearer drawbacks. The debt-equity swaps implied a massive flight of locally-controlled capital into foreign hands. Moreover, in the short-term, when a government redeemed existing debt paper at face value, or close to it, local resources had to be mobilised on precisely the same scale as if it had repaid the bank in local currency in full. Simply printing money to cover these new costs was not an attractive policy given the high rates of inflation in Latin America and the IMF's opposition to it. Governments would thus have to borrow money again on their local financial markets, usually at high rates of interest, and could end up swapping debt denominated in dollars at an interest rate of 12 per cent every six months, for debt denominated in *pesos* at 600 per cent a year. In the long-term, debt swaps also involved Latin American countries in a tricky calculation of priorities. They purported to save countries an outflow of dollars in the short-term on interest payments. But in so far as debt-equity swaps attract investors who would come anyway, the debtor country would simply lose the stock of dollars they would have brought in their own right, for the benefits of cancelling a small proportion of its interest repayments.

As these and other problems with the debt-equity swaps emerged for debtor countries, not surprisingly the reaction of Latin American governments was unenthusiastic. Brazil, with the largest capital market in the region, was cautious, and even in Chile and Mexico, the countries most enthusiastic about debt-equity swaps, the total sums involved were relatively small, amounting to US$2.5 billion and US$1.7 billion respectively. In the case of Chile, they just about offset the growth in new debt.[25] Mexican negotiators saw the programme as a form of subsidy for investors. There were clear signs that both governments would set ceilings on the programme. Banks also wanted a reasonable assurance of the profitability of their new equity investments before they traded their all-important earnings from interest payments, and the real opportunities available for profitable investment in Latin American countries were limited after five years of shock.

Summary

In retrospect, the extraordinary reluctance of US banks to admit that the position of Latin American debtors was unsustainable can be measured in three parallel political decisions. It has been clearly visible in their long term abstention from secondary markets in Latin American debt, even while they acted as intermediaries for European banks in this market. As consistently — and with the backing of the US government — they have refused to let Latin American debtors themselves take any advantage of the discount on their debts available in such markets. Their response to the Pereira solution of transforming debt into long-term bonds at the discount implicit in the secondary market fits this pattern perfectly. Thus by 1987, Latin America countries were being forced to service in full debts which the judgement of the market were only worth 60, 30 or sometimes 15 per cent of their face value.

When the banks came to consider the possibility that they themselves might have to trade off debt for equity — Latin American debt as against local investment, along the lines contemplated in the menu of options — the implicit assumption in their proposals was always that Latin American countries would convert the debt at its face value. If the banks themselves could not make the investments, the benefits of their loss would fall to Western corporations, who were allowed to buy debt cheaply on the secondary market and trade it in for local currency at face value — specifically what the debtors were not allowed to do.

Equally clear has been the refusal of the banks to accept an interest rate cap on their problem loans. The chairman of the New York Federal Reserve Board, Arthur Salomon, proposed this solution in 1984. In his formula, which entailed capitalising the foregone interest and amortisation payments in the overall total of the debt, an interest rate cap would have postponed the debt problem rather than solving it, but it would have alleviated the pressure on the Latin American debtors and done something to correct the US's own growing trade deficit with the region.

Bankers' determination not to allow any generalisation of the concessions made to Mexico in 1986 effectively killed the Baker Plan as a feasible strategy for reconciling Western interests with those of the Third World. It was a second Mexican crisis in 1985 which helped trigger the introduction of the Baker Plan: the Mexican package of 1986 was the Baker strategy made flesh, the very model of a compromise designed to keep debtor countries paying their debts, with just sufficient finance to make it possible for them to contain internal tensions and continue to grow.

Over the years of the debt crisis, Western banks emerged as a key obstacle to the search for any solution which reconciled the needs of creditors and debtors. Like vampires, they claimed at every key conjuncture in negotiations that they could not survive without a transfusion of Latin American interest. It may be that there was a great deal of truth in the claim. Successive bad judgements on loans made elsewhere left the West's greatest financial institutions with no alternative but to live off their ill-gotten gains from the Reagan-inspired interest rate rise after 1980 and thus ensure their own survival at the expense of the poor. Perhaps without that transfusion, civilisation as we know it would have been fundamentally changed with the collapse of international trade and capital flows. Possibly of course, the risks they were facing were less awesome: a cut in profits, a series of forced mergers, the loss of some of the salaries and privileges associated with the spread of international banking and financial deregulation around the world.

In either case, the picture the debt crisis presents of the world's international institutions is hardly reassuring. Vampires have never been considered trustworthy in Western folklore, nor have authors wasted much sympathy on their explanation that, in the end, blood-sucking is good for the victim. Equally, they are hardly the sort of person you would want in charge of your local castle or your local Barclays, still less at the head of the largest financial institutions in the world. The banks' behaviour in the debt crisis suggests that something was strangely awry in the gloriously free international financial markets out of which they grew.

7. Brazil

As it has the largest foreign debt in Latin America in absolute (though not per capita) terms (see table 7.1), Brazil has received considerable attention from the bankers. Each stage of Brazil's increasingly desperate attempts to cope with this burden has been well covered in the Western press, better than most events in Latin America.

The stories have been dramatic. Between 1983 and 1985, the last military government failed no less than seven times to meet the economic targets it had previously agreed with the IMF, making nonsense of IMF policies, but building up vast trade surpluses which pleased the bankers, guaranteeing them their interest payments — and displeased both the poor (who paid the cost of those trade surpluses in drastic cuts in their consumption) and local industrialists in São Paulo, who watched their local markets disappear. Local dissatisfaction with IMF-induced recession, and with Brazil's humiliation at the hands of IMF missions, helped forge the protest movement for 'Direct Elections Now' which finally put an end to military rule.

In late 1985, after just five months of civilian government, Finance Minister Funaro took a decision to break with IMF adjustment policies entirely. He rejected IMF loans and decided to go it alone, in deference to the public outcry over IMF policies during the past two years. His alternative was a bold experiment with heterodox economic policies (involving increased state controls), known as the Cruzado Plan, and for several months this appeared to be the answer to the country's problems. But a by-product was the disappearance of the trade surpluses which had made interest payments possible, as the local population consumed more and more of what Brazil produced.

In late 1986, the Cruzado Plan collapsed in a renewed spurt of hyperinflation, and Funaro took action on the debt, announcing a four-month long suspension of interest payments while he paid a formal visit to Washington and to European capitals, vainly looking

Table 7.1
Brazil's Debt Burden, 1978-86

	Gross Foreign Debt (US$ million)	Debt as % of Export Earnings	Service of Debt as % of Export Earnings
1978	52,187	391	24.5
1979	55,803	359	31.5
1980	64,244	320	34.1
1981	73,963	313	40.4
1982	85,364	414	57.1
1983	93,556	404	43.5
1984	102,039	353	39.7
1985	103,283	368	40.0
1986	110,572	386	37.7

Source: Boletin do Banco Central do Brazil.

for government-to-government negotiations on the debt issue. As a bargaining tactic this failed, and after much pressure from Western governments, Funaro was dismissed.

Funaro was replaced by a new Finance Minister, Bresser Pereira, who introduced IMF-style policies in a drive to restore Brazil's trade surplus and control hyperinflation, but preserved the suspension of interest payments until the end of 1987, in an attempt to drive a tough bargain with Brazil's commercial creditors. The Pereira solution to the debt crisis was in turn publicly rejected by US Treasury Secretary James Baker in October 1987.

If all these events in Brazil's debt crisis have received due coverage, however, far less attention has been paid to the reasons why Brazil accumulated such an enormous foreign debt in the first place. Less attention still has been paid to the social cost that the servicing of this debt imposed on the Brazilian people between 1982 and 1985, and once again, as Brazil returned to orthodox economic policies in the second half of 1987. Nor has the Western press devoted much attention to the deeply conservative nature of the Sarney government, which has been the fundamental factor behind the failure of Brazil's attempts to find its own, non-negotiated solution.

The key to understanding the particular form that the debt crisis has assumed in Brazil, is an understanding of the previous two decades of military rule. Military governments first sent Brazil down the path of increased reliance on foreign borrowing, in the course of a series of economic experiments which largely shaped the structure of economic and civil power in today's Brazil, and its immense problems with income distribution. Military priorities during the transition to civilian rule in the 1980s determined the early fumbling of debt negotiations, as the armed forces sacrificed the economy to preserve a political structure over which they would have some control. This multi-faceted inheritance explains how Brazil acquired its debt, and also why the holder of the world's second largest foreign debt (after the US itself), has had so much difficulty in wielding the very considerable power which the threat of a Brazilian default should bring in its train.

The Early Military Years: Cheap Wages and Debt

In 1964, nationalist military chiefs joined forces with a tiny civilian elite, mainly technocrats, and set out to forge a new Brazil. They dreamed of turning Brazil into a world power, commensurate with its huge territory and its abundant natural resources. The government put all its energy into the expansion and modernisation of the economy, making little attempt to hide its determination not to hand over real power to civilians, who, they believed, would only be a hindrance, preventing Brazil from achieving its true destiny. Nonetheless, the early years of military rule were characterised by relative political freedom, with Congress functioning, if with very limited powers. Though the middle classes had been excluded from power, they initially supported the new government, largely because they had been thoroughly scared by the political turbulence in 1962 and 1963.

Tough fiscal policies were imposed, with a severe cutback in public spending, particularly in social services, and strict controls over wage rises. Though the military government claimed to be a firm defender of private enterprise, state intervention increased significantly, principally because it was the only sector with resources available for investment. Brazil thus preserved its pre-coup traditions as an economy in which state firms and government policies played the crucial role in directing private-sector activity, subsidising the private sector (local and foreign) at every turn. However, in the early years, the state played a secondary role in foreign borrowing. In 1973, private firms and banks were responsible for 60.3 per cent of all foreign debt. Government measures which introduced the principle that the value of old contracts would be automatically adjusted in line with inflation, gave companies which contracted loans abroad a guarantee that they would not lose out from the country's successive mini-devaluations, introduced to keep its exports competitive abroad.

After several years of stagnation, during which the government's economic policies were widely regarded as a failure, the economy unexpectedly began to expand vigorously. The average annual growth rate reached 9-10 per cent in the late 1960s and early 1970s. With hindsight, it now seems clear that the policies carried out in the first stage of military rule, had indirectly and almost inadvertently paved the way for the boom: by holding down wages and thus transferring income from wage-earners to businessmen, money had been freed for investment; and, by moving public expenditure away from social services into productive sectors, such as the steel industry, the basic industrial infrastructure had been strengthened.

The features of savage capitalism for which the Brazilian model was to become famous were generated in the late 1960s; ever-increasing state power, contempt for the problems of the poor and the violent suppression of opposition. Popular discontent over slashed wages and the prolonged recession, generated considerable political mobilisation, with trade unions and students organising large protest demonstrations in 1968-69. A new military President, General Medici, responded by increasing the repressive powers of the state, a trend already visible in late 1968, with the closing down of Congress and the declaration of an extremely powerful repressive law, Institutional Act no. 5. President Medici conveniently forgot that the earlier economic reforms had taken place in a climate of relative freedom. He and his military successors repeatedly claimed that 'law and order' — which became their code name for repression — had been an essential factor behind the growth.

In the economic field, a rising new star, the economist Antonio Delfim Netto, took control, dominating all the other economic ministers. An extraordinary cynic, who freely admitted that he favoured savage capitalism, Delfim Netto openly used his unprecedented authority to strengthen his own position. The power of the state, which under the previous administration had been increased almost inadvertently, was further strengthened, this time quite deliberately. By the end of his term of office, Delfim headed an enormous empire of patronage and privilege, which benefited greatly big economic groups, both Brazilian and foreign. Delfim took no care to hide his cynical, opportunistic views, and apparently delighted in shocking his critics. Many of his throwaway remarks, such as 'Give me a year and let the decades look after themselves', and 'I can only work for 60 per cent of the population; the other 40 per cent (the very poor) are no concern of mine', have become part of Brazilian folklore.

During the Medici years, the gross foreign debt began to grow in a big way, increasing by an unprecedented US$10 billion from 1969 to 1973. It is important to stress that there was no real economic need for foreign borrowing at this time, as Brazil's foreign trade was balanced. As a result, about US$6 billion of the borrowing had to be deposited

130

abroad, as no use whatsoever could be found for it at home.

At first sight, the government's decision to authorise — let alone encourage — this debt seems perplexing, particularly as with hindsight it is clear that it was this initial debt, limited as it was, that sent Brazil careering down the slippery slope of excessive indebtedness. But two factors seem to have been at play. First of all, the Brazilian economy was growing fast, overtaxing the resources of the local banking system. It was easy for the government to authorise the foreign borrowing, change the dollars for the equivalent in local currency, the *cruzeiro*, and then deposit the dollars abroad. It would have been more difficult and expensive — though far more satisfactory in the long term — to develop and modernise the local banking system.

Secondly, borrowing abroad suited the interests of the multinationals, who were responsible for 60 per cent of the foreign borrowing during this period. By financing themselves with foreign loans, rather than borrowing locally or bringing in capital as equity (that is, as an investment in the capital of their subsidiary), the multinationals gained two key advantages: they provided themselves with an easy way of both repatriating profits without paying tax to the Brazilian government, and of avoiding tax in their country of origin as well, by making the debt repayments to paper companies in the so-called tax havens, such as the Cayman Islands and the Bahamas. This type of across-frontier indebtedness also gave them much leeway for book-keeping tricks, such as under-billing or over-billing. In 1980-81, half the funds flowing into Brazil for foreign direct investment took the form of inter-company debt.

Reacting to the Rise in Oil Prices

The worldwide rise in oil prices coincided with the succession of General Ernesto Geisel to the presidency. Despite the world recession the government was determined that the Brazilian economy should keep on growing. In the words of President Geisel, it was to be 'an island of tranquillity in a sea of storms'. So Brazil did not follow the example of almost all other oil-importing nations and impose recession to cut down the oil bill. Instead, the government chose to run an uncharacteristically high trade deficit — of about US$10 billion — over the three year period 1974 to 1976. It covered the deficit with additional foreign borrowing, an option that was very easy, given the vast quantities of petro-dollars sloshing around in the commercial banks' accounts.

But this much-repeated explanation for the origin of Brazil's huge debt does not tell the whole tale. Most of the trade deficit in this period

Table 7.2

Debt Service Charges as percentage of Gross Borrowing, 1973-81

(US$ billion)

Year	Gross Interest Charges (1)	Amortisa-tion* (2)	Total (1)+(2) = (3)	Gross New Borrowings**	Debt Service as % Gross New Borrowing
1973	0.8	1.7	2.5	4.3	58.4
1974	1.4	1.9	3.3	7.5	44.1
1975	1.9	2.2	4.0	7.2	52.8
1976	2.1	3.0	5.1	9.1	56.0
1977	2.5	4.1	6.6	8.9	74.4
1978	3.3	5.4	8.8	15.6	56.2
1979	5.3	6.5	11.9	12.6	94.4
1980	7.5	6.7	14.1	14.9	95.2
1981	10.3	7.5	17.8	18.9	94.4

*Long and medium term loans.
**Long and medium term loans and other liquid capital.
Source: P. Nogueira Batista Jr., *Mito e Realidade na Dívida Externa Brasileira,* Editora Paz e Terra, Rio, 1983, p.102.

could have been covered by a combination of direct investment — which reached the sizeable sum of US$3 billion in the period — and by trade-related credits, which increased to US$5.3 billion. But, if the trade deficit alone does not explain why Brazil borrowed almost US$16 billion during the three years, what does? The fact is that, even in this early period, Brazil was sometimes spending 70 per cent of its gross borrowing in the servicing of its old debt. The debt was already becoming a monster whose enormous appetite could only be satisfied by more and more foreign borrowing.(see table 7.2) In 1987 Brazilian trade unions estimated that over two-thirds of Brazil's US$110 billion debt represented payments on interest charges. (see box p.133)

The change in the use of the foreign borrowing led to a change in the composition of the borrowers. This is clear from the statistics covering loans contracted under law 4,131, the main Central Bank mechanism through which foreign loans entered the country. Whereas the public sector was responsible for only 25 per cent of the loans entering the country under law 4,131 in 1972, their share increased to 50 per cent in 1975 and 77 per cent in 1979.

There is no doubt that in the early 1970s state companies turned to foreign borrowing as an attractive source of cheap and abundant long-

US$110 Billion — The Union View of Where the Money Went

Opposition economists (and some who are now in government) have had five years to work out the accounts for the dance of the millions. According to the CUT *(Central Unica dos Trabalhadores)*,

● *13 per cent of it went in capital flight*:

These are Morgan Guaranty Trust figures, which gives a total of about US$14 billion. The Central Bank puts the figure higher at 18 per cent.

● *35 per cent was originally borrowed by private companies*:

Most of these were multinationals, who were responsible for US$16.6 billion contracted between 1973-81. About one dollar in six of their original debt represents loans borrowed by a subsidiary from its home office — essentially, a handy way of evading government restrictions on profit repatriation. Nonetheless, pressure on the Brazilian state to nationalise private debts had reduced the weight of private debt to a mere 20 per cent by 1986.

● *the other 65 per cent was borrowed by state companies*:

Four of these were particularly important: the nuclear industry, Electrobras (which produces electricity), Siderbras (steel) and Petrobras (oil). But funds were not always borrowed to finance real projects in these sectors. The government sometimes used the companies as intermediaries, borrowing funds through Petrobras which actually went on building the São Paulo Metro, giant hydroelectric plants at Itaipu and Tucurui, highways, ports and a railway (the Ferrovia do Aco) which was never actually constructed. Corruption also raised the costs of these pharaonic projects enormously, as construction firms made the best possible use of their political contacts. In 1973, Itaipu was meant to cost US$2 billion — in 1986 the new civilian regime calculated its final cost to be US$25 billion.

● *70 per cent of all the present debt represents interest charges*:

Some of this 70 per cent is the result of decisions by military governments and private companies to roll over existing debt when international funds were easy to come by, using new debts to pay off old debt and old interest together. But the extordinary rises in interest rates in the late 1970s and early 1980s accounts for almost one third of Brazil's total debt. In 1973, interest rates stood at 6.66 per cent. According to CUT economists, if they had remained at that level, Brazil would have a debt burden lighter by US$34.6 billion.

term investment capital. Though they used some of the money to import equipment, they mainly converted the foreign currency into *cruzeiros* and invested it locally. It was the kind of capital that the country's investment banks should have been able to provide, but never did so adequately.

But, as the country's balance of payments crisis deepened, so the rationale behind the borrowing changed. Two public sectors — energy and steel — became particularly active on the Euromarket. In 1972, their foreign borrowings were worth only US$89.9 million and US$3.9 million respectively, accounting for 3.6 and 0.2 per cent of foreign borrowings entering the country through law 4,131. But, by 1979, their borrowings had grown enormously, in both absolute and relative terms, reaching a staggering US$1,599 million and US$913 million respectively, with their share increasing to 18.5 and 10.6 per cent.

It is evident that neither company required such huge amounts of money as investment capital. Under government instructions, they had started borrowing more than they needed to make sure that the country obtained the enormous — and increasing — number of dollars required for debt-servicing. But, by doing so, the two sectors became caught inextricably in the debt trap. Though the dollars were deposited with the Central Bank, the sectors were left with the responsibility in the future of finding the dollars for paying the interest on these loans. By 1979, the two sectors were heavily dependent on foreign loans for their financial viability. And, once enmeshed, escape, unaided by the government, became virtually impossible: even today, almost a decade later, the future of these two sectors, of vital importance for Brazilian development, is seriously compromised by their excessive foreign indebtedness.

The Legacy of the Miracle Years

During the 1960-80 period, Brazil undoubtedly experienced rapid economic growth, most of it under military rule. Its economic output quadrupled, from US$55 billion in 1960 to US$229 billion in 1980. It was the fastest economic growth in the region and Brazil was widely proclaimed as the Latin American economic miracle. There has been a heated controversy in Brazil over the nature of this growth. Some left-wing economists have claimed that it brought no benefits at all to the mass of the people, while government officials have claimed that everyone prospered. Detailed research carried out recently suggests that absolute incomes rose during the boom years for every section of the social scale, but the rich, nonetheless, took the lion's share of the benefits, and Brazil's unequal income distribution grew steadily worse.

In constant 1970 dollars, the average annual income of the poorest 10 per cent of the population increased from US$102 in 1960 to US$138 in 1976, a modest rise of 35 per cent. In contrast, the average annual income of the richest 1 per cent, which was already US$6,631 in 1960, increased dramatically, by 267 per cent, to US$24,328 by 1976. The share of national income in the hands of the poorest 10 per cent fell from 1.9 per cent to 1 per cent over the period, while the proportion going to the richest 1 per cent rose from 11.9 per cent to 17.4 per cent. The national standard of living improved over the miracle years, adding six years to the life expectancy of a male child, cutting infant mortality by a third, and reducing the number of children dying between the first and fourth years of life by 57 per cent, between 1965 and 1983. But Brazilian achievements here were less impressive than those of Argentina, Colombia and Mexico, not all of them doing as well as Brazil economically. Compared with the performance of its rival South Korea — which added nine years to the life expectancy of a male child, cut infant mortality by 55 per cent and mortality in early childhood by 67 per cent — Brazil did even less well.

That the Brazilian economy grew, albeit in a socially unjust way, seems indisputable. What is far more dubious is to claim, as some military apologists still do, that heavy foreign borrowing was necessary to finance this growth. Measured purely in terms of the accumulated trade deficits of 1974-80, Brazil needed to borrow just US$17.5 billion. (see table 7.3) The dollars were contracted abroad and, except for those needed for debt-servicing, were deposited with the Central Bank which paid the borrower the equivalent in *cruzeiros*. These *cruzeiros*, which as the years went by became a smaller and smaller residue after the heavy debt-servicing payments were made, were then used for investment projects. If the government had developed properly the local banking system, these *cruzeiros* could have been provided by the local development banks. In any case, whether backed up by dollars or not, the *cruzeiros* had to be issued by the government. Servicing problems could have still arisen if the resources had been provided by local development banks, but, as the repayments would have been in *cruzeiros*, they would have been far more manageable.

The risks inherent in foreign borrowing became far more apparent during the government of General João Figueiredo (1979-85), the last of the military presidents. The rapid increase in world interest rates, that stemmed from the financial policies adopted by the government of Ronald Reagan in the US, created a real nightmare for the Brazilian government (though Delfim Netto continually denied that he was

Table 7.3
Trade Deficits and Surpluses
From the Oil Crisis to the Debt Crisis, 1970-86 (US$ billion)

	Exports	Imports	Merchandise Trade Balance
1970	2.7	2.5	+ 0.2
1972	3.9	4.2	− 0.3
1973	6.1	6.2	− 0.1
1974	7.8	12.6	− 4.7
1975	8.5	12.1	− 3.5
1976	10.0	12.4	− 2.4
1977	11.9	12.0	− 0.1
1978	12.5	13.6	− 1.2
1979	15.2	17.9	− 2.7
1980	20.1	23.0	− 2.8
1981	23.3	22.1	+ 1.2
1982	19.0	19.4	+ 0.7
1983	21.9	15.4	+ 6.5
1984	27.1	18.3	+13.1
1985	25.5	15.4	+12.4
1986*	22.4	13.9	+ 9.5

*Preliminary estimate.
Source: IDB Annual Reports 1975 (Table 35), 1982 (Table 42), 1985 (Brazil and Table 43), 1987 (Brazil).

facing more than passing, minor problems). To pay the enormous interest bill, the country had to borrow more and more, and the debt snowballed, completely out of control. Many of the country's leading economists became seriously worried. In January 1980, Karlos Rischbieter, the Finance Minister, tired of his repeated, ineffectual attempts to influence the government from within and issued a 29-page document in which he publicly challenged Delfim Netto's optimistic views. He warned that the country was facing 'an intolerable resource gap' that could not be sustained indefinitely. As Rischbieter must have predicted, this act of defiance cost him his job: just a few days after issuing the document, he was asked to resign by Figueiredo and Delfim Netto was left in absolute control.

Nonetheless, in November 1980, the Brazilian government introduced IMF-style policies on its own initiative, in an effort to avoid being forced into the IMF's arms. This stabilisation programme was successful, from the government's point of view, on both key fronts. It transformed the trade deficit of US$2.8 billion in 1980, to a surplus of US$1.2 billion in 1981; and the banks agreed to offer the country new loans. The cost of this pre-IMF version of 'adjustment'

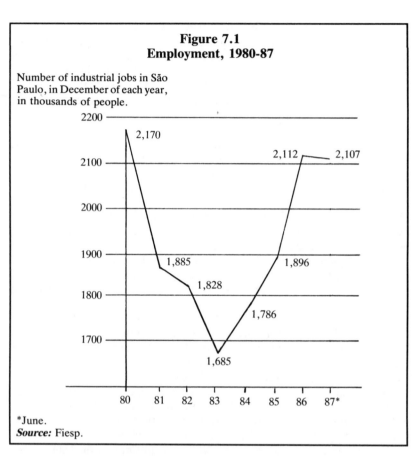

Figure 7.1
Employment, 1980-87

Number of industrial jobs in São Paulo, in December of each year, in thousands of people.

*June.
Source: Fiesp.

was a decline in GDP of 2 per cent in 1981, and the biggest fall in GDP per capita in two decades, over 4 per cent. Manufacturing suffered badly, and industrial unemployment in São Paulo became a source of real concern. For workers in São Paulo industries, this is the real moment at which the debt crisis began: employment in São Paulo factories would not reach the same level even during the fabled year of the Cruzado Plan.(see figure 7.1)

But in spite of these efforts the fears continued, even within the upper echelons of government. In early 1981, a government study on the country's financing requirements in the 1983-85 period warned that, even if exports grew as rapidly as Delfim Netto hoped, each year the country would run a current account deficit of about US$11 billion, which, it said, was 'intolerably high'. It became evident to many of the country's leaders that Brazil would be forced, sooner or later, to renegotiate its ever-bigger debt. And many began to believe that Brazil should act immediately, while it still had bargaining power: in a survey carried out in May 1981 — a full 18 months before the government took any action — the *Gazeta Mercantil*, the country's leading financial newspaper, discovered that 68 per cent of the country's leading businessmen wanted to start rescheduling talks with the country's creditors.

But, under a military government, these businessmen found it difficult to express their views, let alone lobby openly in favour of a change in policy. Figueiredo wanted to remain in charge of the tortuous and protracted process of redemocratisation, and knew that, in order to do so, the pro-military political party, the Social Democratic Party (PDS), had to perform well in the congressional elections in November 1982. If he were to renegotiate the debt, he would have to agree to an IMF austerity package — a move which would undoubtedly wreck the PDS's already slim chances in the elections. At the same time, Figueiredo was unable, ideologically, to contemplate the only other alternative: confrontation with the foreign creditors.

So he sought to postpone for as long as possible the day of reckoning by additional foreign borrowing, even though none of the new loans brought Brazil any real benefit. Gross foreign borrowings were worth US$13.1 billion in 1979, US$16.3 billion in 1980, US$17.7 billion in 1981 and US$16.3 billion in 1982. In other words, Brazil borrowed US$63.4 billion, well over half of its total gross foreign debt, in these four years, in a frenzied, and eventually useless attempt to avoid default. Almost all of this money did not even enter Brazil, but stayed with the foreign banks (US$60.9 billion, of which US$27.9 billion was in debt repayments and another US$33.0 billion in interest). After Brazil's other, comparatively modest, foreign currency requirements, such as royalties, dividends and freight, were satisifed, the country actually had a shortage of dollars, despite the massive loans it was contracting. It had to dip heavily into its foreign reserves just to remain solvent.

Paradoxically, Brazil was throughout this four year period actually sending back to the banks more dollars than it was receiving, while, at the same time, more than doubling its foreign debt. Though the full implications of what was happening were not apparent to most Brazilians, who were lulled into acquiescence by the artificial boom that the economy was still experiencing, the country was, in practice, being double-crossed. The high interest rates in the world market — which were created by an artifical, financial decision in Washington —

led Brazil to contract a huge paper debt that it would later be forced to honour through the export of real goods. It was a financial con trick on an unprecedented scale.

Paying Off the Debt, 1982-85

However, it was not long before the Brazilian people were abruptly expelled from their fool's paradise. Brazil ran out of foreign reserves in September 1982, shortly after the Mexican crash that made foreign banks extremely wary of all Latin American borrowers. Because of Figueiredo's insistence that the IMF could not be called in before the November elections, Brazil stumbled on for another couple of months. There was one period in September — which earned the nickname of the 'black week' — in which the New York subsidiary of the Banco do Brasil actually ran out of funds and had to be bailed out by the Federal Reserve Board.

The government clearly should have taken action while it still had some foreign reserves and thus considerable bargaining power. Its refusal to do anything until the country was absolutely insolvent was a blatant example of short-sighted, political opportunism, an attitude that, unfortunately, was to be copied, with equally disastrous effects, four years later by the civilian President, José Sarney.

No sooner were the ballot stations closed than Delfim Netto flew to the US to start talks with the IMF and the creditor banks. A rescue package, in which Brazil rescheduled US$4.7 billion of overdue debts and was given US$4.4 billion in fresh money, was rapidly negotiated. Brazil, which was as close to bankruptcy as a country can get, was in no position to demand fair conditions. The deal, of which even some bankers seem ashamed today, was pure extortion. As well as being charged a record spread — 2.125 per cent over Libor for public debts and 2.5 per cent over Libor for private debts — Brazil was made to pay a variety of different fees and commissions. These included a front-end fee of 1.5 per cent, which was deducted from the disbursement, (which meant that, while it had to pay back US$100 and pay interest on US$100, Brazil only received US$98.5), and agreement to pay an additional 1 per cent interest on any part of the loan that was paid back late.

It also had to sign an extraordinary document, which placed all kinds of rights, including that of determining the floating interest rate, in the hands of the creditor banks. The whole deal was masterminded by Anthony Gebauer, from Morgan Guaranty Trust (who, significantly, was to be charged three years later in the New York courts for fraudulent dealings involving Brazilian clients). It was the banks that clearly gained most from the rescheduling, but it was Brazil that had to promise to carry out painful, internal reforms in order to qualify for it. For, as elsewhere in Latin America, the IMF's seal of approval was required before any of the new money was released.

On 3 January 1983, the government officially declared a moratorium on its debt, though in practice it had been unable to make proper service payments for the previous three months. And then it started extremely hasty negotiations with the IMF, which was anxious to conclude a deal quickly so that fresh funds could be disbursed before the international banks faced really serious problems of insolvency. The talks were concluded in record time and, on 28 February 1983, Brazil signed its first letter of intent and the anxiously-awaited funds were disbursed. None of the money actually entered Brazil: it was all immediately deposited with the international banks, which were thus saved in the nick of time from having to register the country's failure to pay interest in their accounts, and classify the loans as non-performing.

To secure the banks against such a fate, Brazil promised the IMF to generate a trade surplus equivalent to US$6 billion, boosting its exports by 12 per cent and cutting imports by US$2.4 billion over the 1982 levels. As the very premise of the programme, it was assumed that, within three years, the Brazilian economy would have to be adjusted, that is, paying full debt service. If this meant that Brazil had to run enormous trade surpluses, of US$12-13 billion, maladjusting the local economy, leading to serious shortages in industry and a marked decline in living standards — then so be it. Adjustment was seen from the point of view of the creditors, not the debtors.

With this aim in mind, Brazil was constrained to make other promises. Government expenditure was to be cut, halving the government deficit (from 16.6 per cent of GDP in 1982 to 8.8 per cent in 1983). The salaries of government employees were effectively cut by a government refusal to readjust them in line with inflation (standing at 100 per cent a year in 1982), which was supposed to fall by 10-20 per cent, a modest target which reflected the IMF mission's awareness that some of its other policies were highly inflationary.

Many economists in Brazil pointed out at the time that the austerity programme was ill-conceived — including Central Bank President Carlos Langoni, who resigned in protest over it in September 1983. The first IMF agreement contained a few sound reforms, such as the setting up for the first time ever of a consolidated budgetary system, which at last provided the government with an overall framework within which priorities could be assigned. But these good points were rare, and largely rendered ineffective by the incoherence and inconsistency of many of the other policies. Proposals to cut drastically

140

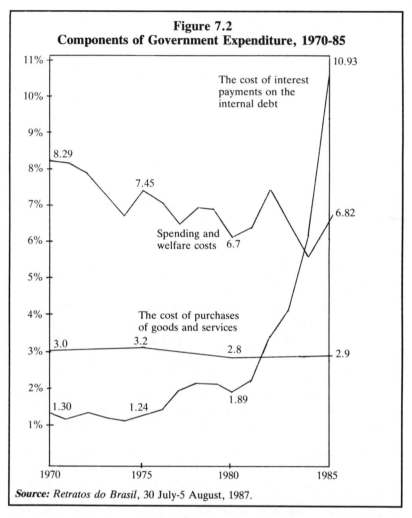

Figure 7.2
Components of Government Expenditure, 1970-85

The cost of interest
payments on the
internal debt

8.29

7.45

Spending and
welfare costs   6.7

10.93

6.82

The cost of purchases
of goods and services

3.0   3.2

2.8   2.9

1.30   1.24   1.89

1970   1975   1980   1985

Source: *Retratos do Brasil*, 30 July-5 August, 1987.

government subsidies on the domestic price of wheat, petrol and diesel
oil, were bound to have an enormous impact on the general level of
prices. So would proposals for accelerated devaluation of the *cruzeiro*
and higher interest rates. Some of the liberalisation measures on which
the IMF insisted as a matter of principle — removal of export duties
and import controls, a relaxation of government regulations restricting
multinationals ability to repatriate profits — were clearly going to
worsen Brazil's foreign exchange famine. IMF insistence on wage cuts,

141

and the prospects of yet further increases in unemployment, led to immediate political tensions.

By May, it was clear that Brazil would not reach its targets, and the IMF suspended disbursements, an action immediately copied by the international banks. Soon Brazil was back in the throes of a serious balance of payments crisis. Negotiations with the IMF over a new programme proved difficult, partly because of political resistance. The IMF demanded an end to all indexation of wages, leaving workers to carry the entire cost of inflation — half the value of their salaries, if inflation were to remain at 1982 levels. In the end, it achieved something more modest: a decree limiting wage rises to 80 per cent of the rate of inflation, which Congress finally passed in November adding some marginal concessions for low-wage earners; and an unofficial agreement between the IMF and the government that the official consumer price index would not reflect the real rises in inflation in wage goods. In November, a new deal with the IMF was signed.

The November 1983 IMF package was no more successful in economic terms than the previous ones, and the Figueiredo government was forced back to the IMF to renegotiate its target figures a further six times before finally handing over to a civilian regime in 1985. The consumer price index rose by an official 197 per cent in 1983, accelerating in the final months and reaching 227 per cent by the end of 1984. The money supply expanded, instead of contracting. Rising interest rates, combined with Brazil's system of indexing all contracts increased government costs, in the face of a parallel decline in tax revenues as the economy contracted: making nonsense of IMF demands for a reduction in the public sector deficit, 15.9 per cent in 1983 and 20.7 per cent in 1984. The government now found itself suffering from an internal debt crisis as well as an external one.

But this chapter of disasters failed to affect Brazil's achievement of the much-desired trade surplus out of which its creditors could be paid. Helped by expanding markets in the US, in 1983, the trade surplus reached US$6.5 billion.(see table 7.3) In 1984, it was double this figure. Many of the IMF's cherished principles had to be broken to achieve these results (direct government controls over imports, for example, contributed substantially to the reduction in Brazil's import bill from US$22 billion in 1981 to US$15 billion in 1983). Whatever the IMF's loss of face, however, foreign bankers were content.

Internally, however, popular mobilisation against the IMF was growing. By the end of 1983, the average wage had fallen by about 15 per cent since the beginning of 1980. By December 1983, São Paulo industry was employing nearly one worker in four less than it had done

142

three years earlier. Nationally, there were about four million people unemployed, and another eight million under-employed, none of them receiving unemployment benefit or social welfare payments of any kind. These people together made up about a third of the country's economically active population. Not all of those in work were much better-off. One out of every four workers earned the official minimum wage, equivalent to US$50 a month at the official exchange rate or US$25 at the more realistic black market rate. At the same time, food prices had risen disproportionately, the result of the combined impact of the abolition of the wheat subsidy and poor harvests. For anyone on the minimum wage, it took a whole day's work to earn enough to buy one kilo of beans, a staple food in Brazil. People began to joke that the true 'Brazilian miracle' was not the period of rapid growth in the late 1970s, but how an ordinary family was managing to survive.(see box p.144)

The fall in real wages among poorly-paid workers was soon reflected in a deterioration in health levels, particularly among the most vulnerable age group — children. The incidence of anaemia among children under five in the state of São Paulo rose from 11.3 per cent in 1980 to 16.3 per cent in 1984. The percentage of newly-born babies with a weight of less than 2.5 kilos — the minimum for a healthy baby — rose from 14.5 per cent in 1980 to 16.1 per cent in 1984. The proportion of children in São Paulo's hospitals suffering from malnutrition rose from 31.8 per cent in 1980 to 35.2 per cent in 1984. The increase in malnutrition was all the more serious because it occurred after decades in which, despite the 'economic miracle', the average nutritional intake had grown very slowly, or even dropped in some years. By 1984, there were signs that on average Brazil's children were suffering from more serious nutritional deficiencies than they had been 30 years earlier.

Quite apart from poor nutrition, many of the children from the poorer sectors were being excluded from the educational system. It was calculated in 1985 that 26 out of 100 children of school age had not stepped inside a school. In absolute terms, this meant that three million children were left completely outside the educational system. Moreover, poorly paid teachers and poor facilities meant that the failure rates were high. Many of the children gave up halfway through the course, often to begin working. Only 12 of the 74 who began school reached the end of the primary cycle. It was estimated that about 30 million people, 28 per cent of the population over five years old, were illiterate.

At the same time, a large number of children were not being properly cared for at home. Government officials spoke of an

Debt and the Minimum Wage

Brazil's minimum wage was first created in 1947, supposedly to cover the essential needs of a worker and his or her family for food, transport, clothing, health and education, which the 1946 Constitution promised to guarantee. It has never been the real minimum salary in the labour market. Domestic servants, rural workers, and temporary labour (particularly in the informal sector) rarely make as much as a minimum wage, and nationally they account for more than a third of the labour market. Even in the Greater São Paulo area, one worker in ten is earning less than the minimum wage. In June 1987, the cleaning staff in the National Congress were being paid less than the minimum (though they were employed not by the government, but by a private firm). Even officially, 15.5 per cent of government workers earn below the minimum wage.

During the early 1950s, the real value of the minimum wage doubled, but after the 1964 military coup and the severe cuts in wage levels, it fell. By 1979 it was worth about 20 per cent more than its 1947 value, but the effect of the debt crisis and the IMF adjustment programmes of 1983-84 was to reduce it dramatically. By June 1987, a worker on a minimum wage would spend more than a third of it on buying one litre of milk and two small rolls a day. According to Ministry of Labour data, in real terms, the minimum wage was worth 37 per cent less than in 1947, forty years previously.

Measured against the promises of 1946, Brazilian unions argue, the miracle years did very little for Brazilian workers. In 1965, it took 65 hours' work to earn enough to pay for the basic basket of goods, written into the 1946 Constitution. In 1986, in the heyday of the Cruzado Plan, an average labourer would have to work 117 hours to earn the right to survive at the same standard of living. Brazilians were also doing badly compared to other Latin American workers. The equivalent of Brazil's minimum wage was worth US$42 in July 1986, compared to US$140 in Argentina and US$53 in Peru.

enormous 36 million abandoned children, or about half of the population under 18 years old. This figure was misleading, for it included a wide range of children with problems, from those in one-parent families, who were not necessarily being seriously neglected, to those who had been genuinely abandoned. But there were clearly a large group of children who were suffering real hardship. Some worked in street markets during the day, but lived at home. Others roamed the streets, robbing — or carrying out a 'job', as they called it — when they needed money. They were often maltreated by the corrupt police, who tended to work with one gang, while pursuing another.

Well before social scientists were able to produce empirical evidence to demonstrate the deterioration in living standards, ordinary people were feeling it in their day-to-day lives and starting to protest. In April 1983, an early morning meeting of a few unemployed workers in São Paulo sparked off three days of rioting. Supermarkets were plundered, and a violent demonstration held outside the governor's palace. The wealthy classes began to fear a breakdown in social order. The alarming spectacle of rioting by the poorest of the poor revived old fears, never entirely allayed, that the real threat to the country's stability did not come from unionised workers — despite their sporadic militancy, they already had a big stake in the system through having a job — but from the mass of unemployed and under-employed, who were becoming desperate by their poverty and had little to lose by resorting to rioting and looting. The emergence of these fears was one important reason why, in the following year, the established elites were to abandon the military and forge a new alliance with opposition groups. Another was the preoccupation of local industrialists in São Paulo with the impact of three years of recession on the internal market, with no relief in sight.

However, the main reason for the elite's change of tactics was the enormous wave of political mobilisation in early 1984. In late 1983, the Workers' Party (PT) began a modest campaign to urge Figueiredo to allow direct elections to choose his successor. The proposal was taken up by the largest opposition party, the Brazilian Democratic Movement Party (PMDB), and the popular response was over-whelming, far greater than anything that the politicians could have imagined. Huge demonstrations, some involving over a million people, were held all over the country. Politicians came under enormous pressure to vote in favour of the amendment, proposed by the PMDB federal deputy, Dante de Oliveira, to reinstate direct elections. In the event, the government managed, by a meagre 22 votes, to prevent the opposition from obtaining the required two-thirds majority, but it was a near thing, far too close for the government's comfort.

Debt and the Civilian Regime

From that moment on, the country's main economic groups began to forge an alliance with the opposition to ease the generals out of government. After much behind-the-scenes plotting, the new allies planned, not to challenge the military rules by which the new president would be selected by an electoral college, but to beat the generals at their own game. They decided to put forward as presidential candidate Tancredo Neves, an elderly civilian politician, who was much respected in the country, partly because of his persistent refusal to work with the military governments. And, to represent the interests of conservative groups, who were only then breaking ranks with the military, they proposed, as candidate for vice-president, senator José Sarney, President of the pro-military PDS party. To comply with the constitutional requirement that candidates for both president and vice-president should belong to the same party, Sarney resigned from the PDS and joined the PMDB in June 1983.

The military leaders gradually accepted the new alignment of forces, particularly after they had received confidential reassurances from Tancredo Neves that he planned to head a transitional government and that that he would respect many of their privileges and prerogatives. In any case, many military leaders had less than lukewarm support for Paulo Salim Maluf, former governor of São Paulo, who had emerged as the PDS's presidential candidate, unexpectedly defeating the military's own candidate.

The key developments in 1984 were political. New alliances were forged that would shape the country's future for several years at least. Management of the domestic economy and the foreign debt lost the importance that they had enjoyed in previous years. Indeed, the IMF itself seems to have realised this, for it was exceptionally lenient, apparently anxious not to create intolerable difficulties for the elites as they adapted to the new circumstances and co-opted popular movements.

Though the government was clearly incapable of achieving the economic goals to which it committed itself time after time, the IMF carried on negotiating. By September 1984, Brazil had signed six letters of intent with the IMF, each of which had had to be torn up, after the government had shown itself incapable of carrying out the agreed objectives. By then, it had became clear that the Figueiredo government was a lame duck administration and that nothing would be achieved until the new government took over. In January 1985, Tancredo Neves and José Sarney were selected by the electoral college. This meant that in March 1985, Brazil would have its first civilian government for 21 years. The hopes of most Brazilians were riding high.

But nothing turned out as expected. In a dramatic turn of events, that for a while captured the imagination of the world's mass media, Tancredo Neves was taken seriously ill on the very eve of taking office. For a few weeks, Brazil held its breathe, with millions hoping against hope that 'Doutor Tancredo' would recover. But he died, and the presidency went to José Sarney, who had little popular support in the country and was intensely disliked by most people on the Left, who

146

remembered his active opposition to the campaign for direct elections.

It was a bizarre return to civilian rule: the new democratic goverment, which should have represented a clear break with the old authoritarian regime, was headed by a man who embodied the values of the 21 years of military rule. Most of Sarney's political experience had been gained under the military and, unlike Tancredo Neves, he had adopted military reflexes. He was a skilled operator in the corrupt system of patronage and political favouritism that had been built up by the military, particularly within the huge and sprawling state sector. Moreover, he was highly intolerant of all opposition and, as he was to demonstrate repeatedly during his term of office, his instinctive reaction was to resort to repression whenever seriously challenged, be it by trade unions or fellow politicians. He clearly belonged to the established ruling elite, and was one of the very last politicians from whom radical social, economic or political change could be expected.

On taking office, Sarney found himself with a ready-made cabinet that he had little option but to confirm in office, given the groundswell of support in the country for the legacy left by Tancredo Neves. As his Finance Minister, Tancredo Neves had selected his nephew, Francisco Dornelles, an uninspiring, orthodox civil servant who had previously headed the department of inland revenue. It seems that Tancredo Neves had hoped that, as a demonstration of support for the new civilian regime, both the IMF and the country's foreign creditors would relax their conditionality and agree to a multi-year rescheduling of the debt under generous conditions. But, if this is what Tancredo Neves had expected, he, like President Raúl Alfonsín in neighbouring Argentina and Siles Zuazo in Bolivia, would have been disappointed. From the outset of the government, both the IMF and the foreign creditors were cautious, but firm. They did not relax their conditionality in any way as an expression of support for the new government.

During his short term in office, Dornelles attempted to draw up a conventional economic programme, which would guarantee a US$10-12 billion trade surplus, hold down inflation and restrict growth. But Dornelles, with his limited experience, had neither the economic expertise to put together such a package, nor, even more crucially, the political skill to sell it to the PMDB, the dominant party in the ruling coalition. Most federal deputies and senators were remarkably ignorant of economic matters, partly because under the military, Congress had been forbidden from playing any role at all in economic policy-making. But the politicians were well aware of the high expectations of most Brazilians, who were confident that the return to democracy meant an end to recession and the resumption of full

147

economic growth. When it became evident that Dornelles could not satisfy these hopes, he lost crucial political support. His demise became inevitable.

He was replaced in August 1985 by Dilson Funaro, a São Paulo businessman who had first attracted public attention in early 1984, when he had courageously appeared at mass demonstrations in favour of a return to full democratic rule. Though Funaro himself did not have left-wing political views, he was genuinely distressed by the absolute poverty in which millions of Brazilians lived. He repeatedly said that his main political objective was to improve the living standards of the poor. In a political message that was well received throughout the country, he stated repeatedly that foreign debt payments would only be made when they were compatible with the government's social objectives, to which he attributed great importance.

To help him implement his policies, he collected around him a group of young economic aides, such as Luiz Gonzaga de Mello Belluzzo and José São Manuel Cardoso de Mello, many of whom had studied at Campinas University in the state of São Paulo under the Portuguese economist, María de Conceiçao Tavares, a PMDB activist known for her concern with the 'social debt' left by the miracle years, and her indignant repudiation of all debt associated with the post-1979 rise in interest rates.

From the outset, the young economists faced an uphill struggle. Not only in his style of government but also in his political practice, Sarney had strong links with the past, as did many other politicians within the governing PMBD, which had begun to inherit dissenters from the old military party as soon as this could no longer guarantee them a political career. Accordingly, the Sarney government left vast areas of crucial political and economic importance outside the scope of its economic reforms. The power of the military could not be infringed. Expensive military-backed development projects, such as the construction of the Calha Norte highway along Brazil's northern frontier, had to be preserved, even if they were economic nonsense. Nothing was to be done to upset the traditional sources of patronage and political influence, upon which Sarney was highly dependent. This meant that only modest reforms could be carried out in the huge state companies, though many were absurdly over-staffed and badly-managed. Little was to be done to diminish the power of the big landowning groups, to whom Sarney, and many PMDB politicians, were closely linked. This meant that the ambitious land reform programme, which many members of Funaro's team believed to be essential to reduce social tension in the countryside, was from the beginning doomed to failure.

Table 7.4
Index of Real Annual Income by Sector, 1986-87

	Wage-earners	Employers	Self-Employed
Jan-Dec 1986*	104.9**	122.8	126.7
Feb '86-Jan '87	104.2	124.2	130.0
Mar '86-Feb '87	103.9	124.2	131.8
Apr '86-Mar '87	102.8	123.8	133.2
May '86-Apr '87	100.7	121.8	131.8
Jun '86-May '87	98.2	118.0	129.5

*12-month period over which total income is averaged.
**June 1985 = 100.
Source: DIESSE (using ICV-DIESSE inflator) quoted in *Quinzena*, No.30, São Paulo, Central Pastoral Vergara, 1987.

The Cruzado Plan

In practice, the Funaro team was thus limited to achieving what they could within the restraints of the established economic and social order, without resort to structural reforms. They turned for inspiration to the so-called heterodox models of controlling inflation, heterodox because unlike the IMF proposals, they relied heavily on government intervention in the economy, particularly in the field of price controls. The new plan combined the best elements of contemporary experiments in Argentina and Israel, and added new features, designed both to maintain economic growth at a high level and to protect the living standards of the poorer sectors. The so-called Cruzado Plan was drawn up in complete secrecy (to forestall pre-emptive price increases by businessmen) and announced to an amazed nation at the end of February 1986.

Replacing old *cruzeiros* with new *cruzados*, the Cruzado Plan offered Brazilians the seductive prospect of zero inflation through a government freeze on retail prices. In the minds of the economic team, this was intended to be a temporary measure, to be followed by a controlled liberalisation. President Sarney took the slogan literally, making it the axis of the Plan's popularity and the basis of his own bid for an increased PMDB majority in the Congressional elections in mid-November. Consumers were mobilised to police the new, non-inflationary world, denouncing shopkeepers who brought in price increases in defiance of the law: they became *fiscais de Sarney*, or Sarney's inspectors.

Indexation was eliminated, though workers were offered the prospect of a built-in trigger for wage rises should it again reach 20 per cent. Local banks were offered compensation for this step, seen as a major attack on their sources of revenue. Workers, many of whom felt that the process by which their salaries had been frozen left them with real losses, were deliberately wooed with a special bonus of 8 per cent, and the offer of Brazil's first ever unemployment insurance. The programme was mildly expansionary: the heterodox economic theories of the Cruzado team suggested that the end of the indexation itself would prove deflationary, and they were anxious to avoid another recession.

For several months, the plan was a huge popular success. Zero inflation was seen as a godsend. Those with savings kept as a hedge against inflation now withdrew them to spend on goods while the bargains continued — thus dramatically increasing popular demand. Workers in the informal sector raised the prices (regardless of the government) and spent the proceeds on increased consumption of their own. Salesmen and women saw their take-home pay rise in line with rising purchases. These sectors and employers did the best out of the Cruzado bonanza, and were able to protect their increased real income the longest.(see table 7.4) Wage-earners as a whole did less well, but employment nonetheless rose again in local industry as demand for wage goods increased (see figure 7.1), and newly re-employed workers contributed to it in their turn. Skilled workers took advantage of the boom to demand an increase in their own pay, and strikes increased.

Thus, although its expansionary elements were small, the Cruzado Plan quickly ran into the classic problem of any redistributive policy in a Third World country, this time made much worse by the legacy of four years of recession and under-investment, and Brazil's continuing debt burden. Local suppliers proved unable to keep up with the demand for meat and consumer goods.

By as early as June 1986, Funaro's aides were aware of the build-up of dangerous pressures that, unless they were rapidly defused, would threaten the success of the whole plan. The price freeze had also caught many manufacturers at a bad moment. Though some industrialists held back stocks deliberately in anticipation of the Plan's failure, others were genuinely producing goods at a loss, and were thus unwilling to increase output to satisfy the booming demand. Shortages of essential goods were creating strong inflationary pressures that the price freeze was artificially repressing, but with increasing difficulty.

Similarly, the freeze on rents had discouraged construction companies from carrying on with housing projects. Yet the population of the big cities was still expanding, swollen by the population growth and the continued drift to the cities of poor peasant families. As the government, hard-pressed for resources, had failed to carry out the big popular housing programme that it had promised, the pressure on housing was growing steadily, though once again it was hidden by the freeze.

Buoyed by the initial popularity of the price freeze, the PMDB won a landslide victory in November's elections. Before all the votes had been counted, Funaro was pushing through important new policies, aimed at eliminating some of the Cruzado's weaknesses. But, as some of the team had feared, the changes came too late. Inflationary pressures had become uncontrollable and, once the sluice gates were opened, the head of water swept the plan away. As inflation soared to unprecedented levels, Sarney's prestige crumbled. By February 1987, Sarney had won the doubtful honour of being the president who had achieved both the highest and lowest ratings in the opinion polls.

By then, Brazil was facing a serious balance of payments crisis. Manufacturers had been unable to satisfy local and foreign demand. On the whole, they had put the domestic market first, leading to a sizeable drop in exports. At the same time, booming domestic demand had led to local shortages and forced the government to permit increased imports, even of such basic goods as beef and rice, which Brazil should have been able to produce itself.

The net result was a dramatic fall in the trade surplus, from about US$1 billion a month in early 1986 to about US$100 million in early 1987. Brazil's foreign reserves were rapidly depleted, and, in late February, with the country on the verge of insolvency, the government had little option but declare a moratorium. Sarney tried, belatedly, to claim that his government was finally standing up to its creditors, but the country, angry at Sarney's earlier manipulations, did not respond. From a political point of view, the moratorium was a resounding flop. Ironically, the only solid source of support came from the armed forces, where economic nationalism still holds sway.

Cruzado and Debt

Foreign creditors watched from the wings as the play unfolded. During the first few months after he took over, Funaro had attempted to negotiate an austerity programme with the IMF. But, partly because of his determination to maintain economic growth, he had failed to reach agreement. Finally, in early 1986, before he announced the Cruzado Plan, Funaro stated unequivocally that he would be halting negotiations. Brazil would go it alone and 'never again would an IMF official step foot in the country to negotiate an austerity plan'. Brazil would try to negotiate its own rescheduling agreement with foreign creditors, outside the influence of the IMF.

Along with the other radical changes Funaro's close aides wanted the government to rethink its old, conciliatory policy on the debt. They argued that it would be far better for Brazil to seize the initiative and to declare a temporary moratorium on its foreign debt payments while it was still in a strong position, with a strong domestic economy and high foreign reserves. The economic rationale was clear. For the moment, Brazil was managing to pull off what most economists had considered impossible: high domestic growth (8 per cent in 1985 and 1986) and full debt-servicing (thanks to the large trade surplus, of US$12.4 billion, in 1985). But the existing burden of debt made this a difficult juggling act.

For a short time, manufacturers would have little difficulty in increasing production rapidly, to satisfy domestic and external demand, for they had been bringing back into use capacity that had been made idle during the recession of 1981-83. But this leeway would soon be exhausted. Soon manufacturers would have to opt between satisfying either the local market or their foreign customers, eating into Brazil's trade surplus as they did so. If manufacturers were able to invest in new capacity, the problem would eventually be resolved. However, the lack of investment over four years, combined with the difficulties of financing it where imported machinery was involved, made a temporary bottleneck inevitable.

Competition among consumers for scarce goods was thus bound to increase inflationary pressures, already generated by the strain of maintaining an unnaturally high trade surplus over a long period. When manufacturers sent goods abroad, they were paid in dollars (or any other foreign currency), which they deposited with the Central Bank which then paid for them in local currency. The Central Bank used these dollars for debt-servicing. So far, so good. But if imports ran at a lower level than exports (just half, in Brazil's case in 1985), then exporters were paid local currency for which there was no equivalent supply of goods on the local market. There was too much money chasing too few goods — a classic inflationary pressure.

Funaro's aides argued that for these reasons Brazil's success on the external front was very precarious. Even if the Cruzado Plan managed to eliminate inflation for a few months, new inflationary pressures would emerge, unless the pressure of excessively high debt payments was removed. With a buoyant domestic economy, Brazil was unlikely to preserve indefinitely trade surpluses, running at over US$1 billion a month.

With hindsight, it is obvious that this analysis was all too accurate. In February 1986, it convinced Funaro, but not Sarney or the ruling PMDB, both of whom rejected such a dramatic and obviously risky break with the old economic order (from which most of them

152

benefited), and whose destruction could hardly be encompassed without a social upheaval which might damage their election chances and their relationship with the military. Sarney himself is a highly conservative politician, who favours Brazil's close integration into the international capitalist system. Funaro's aides were pressing the President, first, to declare a moratorium on its debt (while the country still had abundant foreign reserves) and then to demand radical changes in the rules of the game, so that the country's debt burden would be permanently alleviated. They argued that, in the end, once the creditors realised that their bluff had finally been called, they would agree to a new rescheduling deal, in which far more favourable conditions would be provided for Brazil. But it was evident that such action would cause an unprecedented furore on the world's financial markets, with Brazil being accused of subversion, betrayal of western values and communism — all anathema to Sarney and to the military commanders whose shadowy presence still troubled Brazil's civilian regime.

The only way of facing such high-powered attacks would be through political mobilisation at home, with a nationwide campaign to make people aware of the issues and to win support for the new tough stance. But such a strategy was abhorrent to Sarney. And, indeed, it would have entailed risks for him. Once public opinion was mobilised in favour of a radical new policy on the foreign debt, it could turn its attention to inequalities at home, and dare to demand a far-reaching programme of agrarian reform and redistribution of wealth.

So Sarney backed away from the challenge. Because he identified so closely with highly conservative factions in Brazilian society, he was incapable of carrying out a truly radical foreign debt strategy. Perhaps a nationalist, bourgeois leader, such as a Brazilian version of the Peruvian President, Alan García, might have grasped the opportunity, but Sarney did not represent anything new in the Brazilian political scene. Brazil paid the price of its cautious — and incomplete — transition from military rule to democracy. Its experience demonstrates, graphically, the fundamental importance of politics in any foreign debt strategy. The Latin American debt crisis is the result, not only of the extraordinary greed of the ruling elites in the industrial countries, but also of the dramatic failure of progressive sectors within Latin America to gain the political ascendancy.

So the Cruzado Plan did not receive the back-up it needed with a new radical stance on the debt front. Instead of gaining bargaining power from a temporary moratorium, declared from a position of strength, Sarney carried on with the old-style negotiations. Though the foreign creditors were clearly unhappy with developments in Brazil, they wisely decided to avoid any aggressive action that could provoke Sarney into following the advice of his aides and toughening his stance. While refusing to provide Brazil with a multi-year rescheduling deal, as Sarney wanted, they agreed to roll over the debt for one year. Brazil became the first big debtor nation to sign a rescheduling deal without the back-up of an IMF austerity programme. Sarney proclaimed it to be a victory, but, in fact, it was little more than the creditors skilfully playing for time.

Funaro, who reportedly had favoured a moratorium for over a year, tried hard to make the best of a bad job. He visited the world's financial capitals, speaking forcefully of the need for far-reaching reform that would lift the debt burden from the developing world. He was much disliked by bankers, who laughed at his earnestness ('Just because he has survived cancer, he thinks that it is his mission to save the developing world' was one scornful response) and who complained that his very terms of reference were different from theirs. The moratorium was nonetheless not a complete failure, since it secured Mexico the best rescheduling yet, forced bankers to make their first ever loan loss provisions to cover the costs of possible default by a major debtor, and indirectly inspired them to move from a rhetorical compliance with the Baker Plan towards new strategies for coping with the debt crisis.(see chapter six) One can only speculate what a carefully-planned moratorium called in 1986, with full public backing, could have achieved.

The Failure of the Cruzado Model

Given its internal weakness and external burden of debt, the Cruzado Plan ended in yet another spurt of hyperinflation, reaching 186 per cent in the first six months of 1987, and an astounding 365 per cent by the year's end. Wage-earners gained relatively little from it (see table 7.4) and even by mid-1987, their wages over the year were less than they had been at the outset of civilian rule in 1985. For some the situation was even worse: many state employees lost their right to an automatic adjustment for inflation in early 1987, as state governors pleaded bankruptcy and unilaterally abolished the trigger laid down in the Plan.

Union organisation suffered from an acute demoralisation, as workers who had hoped for the elimination of inflation, and carefully organised to retrieve some of the losses they had made during the 1981-83 recession, saw these gains wiped out over a matter of weeks by inflation running at over 20 per cent a month. Disillusion with the benefits of democracy spread. Unemployment began to loom as a serious threat again, as the local market for consumer goods once again contracted.

For employers and the self-employed, life was still comparatively comfortable. However, some were caught between the Cruzado price freeze and interest rates which at one point reached 2,000 per cent a year. Throughout 1987, employers took the public position that no price freeze could avoid the multifold imperfections which dogged the original Cruzado Plan. Volkswagen and Ford, the joint owners of Autolatina, Latin America's largest car firm, took the government to court in late 1987 to avoid a freeze on their prices, and successfully increased the cost of a car to local consumers by 780 per cent during the year, twice the average rate of inflation. By the end of 1987 employers were mounting an increasingly vociferous attack on the state itself, as Sarney's commitment to such pharaonic projects as the North-South railroad and the failure of successive Finance Ministers to reduce state expenditure even by a drastic freeze on civil service wages, increased the general discredit in which Sarney's government was held.

Meanwhile, employers scrambled over one another to preserve price advantages, feeding the very inflation they complained about so much. They also fought hard to preserve their own share of government subsidies, and even pressured central government to offer extraordinary loans to save firms caught by the renewed outbreak of hyperinflation from bankruptcy, and their bankers from a string of bad debts (see box p.156) — thus piling yet futher pressures on the government's growing deficit. By the end of 1987, the government owed an additional US$70 billion to Brazilian creditors, over and above its commitments on the foreign debt.

With politicians distributing political largesse to the private sector as a way of preserving their careers, and employers cooperating with them in a frantic effort to protect the real value of their patrimony, no economic team had much chance of imposing order on inflation. Any attempt to do so was bound to weigh more heavily on wage-earners in compensation for a lightening of the burden on the property-owner classes.

In May, Funaro was replaced by Luiz Carlos Bresser Pereira, a well-known São Paulo economist, who like Funaro, had close ties with local employers, but also with heterodox economists and even with the relatively progressive local church. In June 1987, he introduced a new economic package, Cruzado Three. Heterodox economics were now formally abandoned: the cause of the original Cruzado Plan's failure was reckoned to be not the ability of employers to raise prices regardless of price controls, but an excess of demand.

Prices were frozen for 90 days, with negotiable increases thereafter,

155

What's a Government for? Bailing out the Banks...

Before the Plano Cruzado, a proportion of [Brazilian] bank profits had come from the manipulation of inflation itself, from the *industria de float* — the management of that portion of their funding which was 'free', unremunerated, unindexed current account deposits. After the Plan, banks went through a harsh period of adjustment and scaling down. Most were in the red for three months. Payrolls were whittled down by as much as 20 per cent, reducing the national bank force by some 150,000. Five hundred branches were closed.

But by the end of 1986, they were on even keel again, and most turned in their best profits for years. What happened next was not predictable. After eight months of low inflation — rates of under 2 per cent a month — inflation embarked on its fastest and most violent upturn in history: 3.3 per cent in November, 7.3 per cent in December, 16.8 per cent in January, ... 20.9 per cent in May.

'With inflation rising at that rate, the banks acted very fast — and our bankers are probably the fastest in the world — borrowing at yesterday's rate, lending at today's,' said Wadico Waldir Bucchi, director of banking affairs at the Banco Central. Money market rates lept up by as much as 100 per cent annually in a day.

But the corollary was that by April, borrowers had started to fall behind with payments. By mid-May, an average 30 per cent of banks' loan portfolios was overdue by more than 30 days.

'Between January and March, banks made the highest profits in their history,' said Bucchi. 'Between 1.5 per cent of Brazil's GNP changed hands through the financial system during that period, and a good portion of that stayed in the financial system. Banks were making 30-40 per cent more profits than they should have been.'

Banks were forced to roll over working capital loans en masse. For a few tense weeks, the economy hovered on the brink of real danger, the threatened domino effect of the so-called 'industry of liquidations' — an anomaly in Brazilian law that allows companies in trouble to apply for *concordata*, a two-year rescheduling in which debts are frozen at nominal rates. In the first quarter, *concordatas* had been restricted to small firms, but by the middle of May, the *concordatas* of a handful of sizeable companies sent the market into near-panic.

At the end of April, finance minister Dilson Funaro was replaced by Luiz Carlos Bresser Pereira. One of the new economic team's first moves was to provide an emergency US$1.2 billion credit line for small and medium companies — those firms that had expanded with the Plano Cruzado boom and now faced foreclosure.

Source: *Euromoney*, September 1987.

but there was now no talk of zero inflation. Wages were frozen over the same period, and then granted monthly adjustments in a complex formula which offered workers nothing in compensation for the ground lost during June. Meanwhile, fuel prices were increased once again, although the removal of wheat subsidies was delayed through fears of its inflationary impact.

The package succeeded in halting inflation for a time, but it was insufficient to put a final stop to the headlong career of prices. Bresser Pereira attempted to repeat it in late November, designing a new package in which restraints on demand were equated with an end to soft government loans and other forms of government subsidy to the private sector. He also proposed a wealth tax on all transfers of assets worth more than US$80,000, citing World Bank support for the introduction of progressive taxes, and World Bank figures which showed that Brazil had not only one of the highest, but also one of the most regressive tax systems in the Third World. The plan was vetoed by Sarney, following rigorous protests from businessmen.

Cruzado Three thus did little or nothing for the local economy, like the more orthodox IMF plans on which it was largely based. It did succeed in restoring Brazil's trade surplus, which by the second half of 1987 was once again running at US$1 billion a month. Bresser Pereira had promised a more conciliatory attitude to both the IMF and Brazil's foreign creditors, but in practice he preserved the moratorium and attempted some tough negotiations with the banks, in the hope of forcing them to accept the losses on Brazilian loans which they had prepared against in March, and of persuading them to accept a lower rate of interest. This effort, known as the Plan Pereira in banking circles, met with immediate repudiation from the US Treasury Secretary.(see chapter six)

The end of Brazil's moratorium in December 1987 was seen locally as a capitulation, not so much because of what Brazil paid — the agreement left the country's 70 major creditors to put up the money for most of the unpaid arrears of interest — but because it committed Brazil to resuming full interest payments in January, without guarantees of refinancing. Meanwhile, the country faced the most serious economic crisis in its history — and its fourth Finance Minister, and fifth President of the Central Bank, in the three years of Sarney's tenure.

Conclusion

Brazil is a deeply conservative country, whose ruling elite has never had much time for the country's poor, and whose governments have traditionally put the preservation of private sector profits — for local businessmen and foreigners — at the top of their list of priorities. Its conservatism in this sense goes a long way towards explaining the

157

enthusiasm of bankers for the military governments of the 1970s, when the original debt was contracted. The advent of democracy did not change the nature of the regime, leaving military men and landowners still in key positions of power. The fond hopes placed in the end of dictatorship by Brazil's poor, and some of its middle classes — such as the young academics in Funaro's team — were thus bound to be disappointed. The story of Brazil's first civilian regime in twenty years is still the story of a government trying desperately to preserve private profits at the expense of wages and social expenditure — in spite of the PMDB's rhetorical commitment to eliminating the so-called social debt.

But there is another side to the story, clearly manifest in the problems of hyperinflation which neither the Cruzado Plan nor its successor could resolve. In the 1980s, as the banks presented their astonishing bill for services, even a deeply conservative civilian government was finding it difficult to meet the country's international commitments and simultaneously preserve profits for its own private sector. The scramble of businessmen, Brazilian and foreign, to avoid the staggering losses implicit for them in a transfer of more than a third of export earnings abroad, does much to explain the persistent problems of hyperinflation, just as it also explains the failure of the Brazilian state itself to control the public sector deficit.

8. Peru

Since 1985 Peru has gained notoriety in the world's financial press as the country which stood up and said 'no' to the IMF and to the international banks. Soon after its electoral victory in April 1985, the centre-left government of Alan García declared that it would pay no more than 10 per cent of the value of its annual exports on servicing the foreign debt. It also made it clear that it would not implement IMF-dictated economic policies.

This forthright stand was no accident. Not only was it patently impossible for the country to continue servicing its debts normally, but it had become clear that a series of IMF adjustment policies adopted since 1977 were simply worsening the country's problems. By 1985 painful experience had taught the majority of Peruvians to reject the claim that belt-tightening was a necessary short-term prelude to sustained and more soundly-based growth. They had seen their standard of living fall for ten years, while the IMF said over and over again that Peru's main problem was one of excess demand. So, in adopting a hard line towards the country's creditors, the new government was responding to political demands it could not ignore. But the strident rhetoric was to mask caution and pragmatism. Despite achieving some economic recovery, it was to prove much harder to sustain this expansion and to keep promises for a radical redistribution of income and wealth in favour of Peru's poor.

The Genesis of the Crisis

Peru is no stranger to debt crises. From the Independence period onwards, governments have tended to amass substantial debts — typically for unproductive military spending or for expensive infrastructure — while the country's export base has remained vulnerable to both the exhaustion of raw materials and to the collapse

159

Table 8.1
Peru's External Debt, 1973-86

US$m	1973	1976	1979	1981	1983	1985	1986 (p)
Long-term	2,709	5,250	7,941	8,173	11,007	12,677	13,013
Public	1,491	3,554	5,764	6,210	8,339	10,510	11,018
Central Bank	17	385	869	455	1,088	825	781
Private	1,201	1,311	1,308	1,508	1,580	1,342	1,304
Short-term (Public and Private)	1,432	3,134	1,393	1,516	1,513	1,117	1,295
Total	**4,132**	**7,384**	**9,334**	**9,689**	**12,520**	**13,794**	**14,398**

Source: Central Bank.
(p) Preliminary figures.

Debt Coefficients

	Total Debt as % of GDP	Long-term public debt* as % of GDP	Long-term public debt service† as % of exports of goods and services
1977	67.3	33.4	29.6
1978	86.0	47.4	29.2
1979	66.8	41.3	19.7
1980	55.7	35.1	28.6
1981	47.6	30.4	45.8
1982	56.5	33.6	36.7
1983	77.2	51.6	20.1
1984	78.8	57.0	17.4
1985 (p)	94.6	72.1	16.3
1986 (p)	68.2	52.1	15.0

Source: Central Bank Memoria 1986.
*Excludes private sector debt and short term debt.
†Includes payment in kind.
(p) Preliminary figures.

of world market prices. In 1826, 1876 and 1930, debt problems and export collapse led to balance of payments crises, which in turn led to default.

However, the country has never faced such a prolonged period of crisis as the one which first emerged in 1975 and which it is still living with today. Nor have the social effects ever been so devastating. Like many other countries of Latin America, Peru borrowed heavily during the early 1970s. The public sector foreign debt nearly quadrupled to US$4 billion between 1970 and 1975. The vast majority of new

Table 8.2 Who Is It Owed To? 1970-85*				
%	1970	1975	1980	1985
Governments	29.4	35.0	38.3	30.5
Multilateral agencies	19.9	7.9	11.3	18.6
World Bank	16.7	5.4	7.4	n.a.
Private commercial banks	14.5	41.1	36.9	35.9
Suppliers	36.1	16.0	14.4	15.0

*Public medium and long-term debt, including undisbursed.
Source: World Bank.

borrowing was on the Eurodollar market from commercial banks, their confidence in Peru bolstered by the country's potential as an oil producer. While borrowing from commercial banks amounted to only 14.5 per cent of the total in 1970, by 1975 it accounted for over 40 per cent.(see table 8.2) In their enthusiasm to lend to Peru the banks undertook little proper analysis of the projects or other purposes for which they were lending. And in their enthusiasm to borrow when money was cheap, the Peruvian military governments (1968-80) took little heed of the economic risks they were taking. Nor did they do much to ensure that the money was spent on programmes which would generate an economic return. Some projects like the giant Majes irrigation project near Arequipa absorbed huge quantities of foreign exchange, but were never intended to increase Peru's export potential.

The Peruvian debt crisis arose well before the 1982 Mexican default caused bankers to stop lending to Latin America. Having first tried to do a deal directly with the banks in 1976 without going to the IMF, the government of General Morales Bermúdez was forced into approaching the IMF in 1977, agreeing in return to implement a stabilisation programme. The social effects of the government's economic policies, including massive sackings in the public sector, helped prompt a series of general strikes, the first and most successful taking place in October 1977.

By 1979, however, things were looking better: the balance of payments difficulties had receded, and the recessionary impact of the IMF programme had given way to growth.(see table 8.3) People at the time even talked of the Peruvian miracle. In world financial circles Peru was briefly held up as a model of the good effects IMF stabilisation policies could have. In fact, the reason for the recovery was that exports had doubled as two major investments projects — the northern oil pipeline from the jungle fields to the sea and the giant

Table 8.3
Annual Growth Rates, 1975-86

Year	GDP Growth	GDP per capita Growth	In 1970 *Intis*
1975	+ 2.4	− 0.4	20.52
1976	+ 3.3	+ 0.6	20.52
1977	− 0.3	− 2.9	20.05
1978	− 1.8	− 4.3	19.19
1979	+ 4.3	+ 1.6	19.50
1980	+ 2.9	+ 0.2	19.54
1981	+ 3.1	+ 0.4	19.62
1982	+ 0.9	− 1.7	19.28
1983	−12.0	−15.3	16.53
1984	+ 4.7	+ 2.1	16.88
1985	+ 1.9	− 0.7	16.77
1986	+ 8.5	+ 5.8	17.74

Source: Central Bank Memoria 1986.

Cuajone copper mine in the south — both came on stream, just as copper prices improved.

Belaúnde and Structural Adjustment

The debt strategy of the elected centre-right Belaúnde administration, which took office in July 1980, was premised on the idea that Peru had everything to gain, nothing to lose, by following liberal economic policies and doing its utmost to pay the debt on the nail. Many of the government's top officials had worked with international commercial banks, or with the World Bank or the IMF. Some were even ridiculed for appearing to speak better English than Spanish. In 1981 the government even went so far as to pay back debts ahead of schedule. In 1982 it also entered voluntarily into a new agreement with the IMF, this time a three-year Extended Fund Facility, taking upon itself to push ahead with adjustment. This meant devaluing the currency, tightening monetary control and cutting public spending to bring down the fiscal deficit. The Belaúnde government also sought to relax controls on foreign investment (particularly in the oil business), increase competitiveness among Peruvian banks, reduce legal protection for workers and liberalise foreign trade by reducing tariffs.

The Peruvian miracle proved to be a very transient phenomenon. Faced with a surge in imports (helped along by the reduction of tariffs and despite devaluation of the *sol*), a disastrous fall in the market prices for most major export items, the greatly increased cost of debt

Table 8.4
Central Government Spending, 1972-84 (as % of total expenditure)

	1972	1974	1976	1978	1980	1982	1984
Health	5.1	4.5	5.4	4.5	4.8	4.4	4.3
Education	18.5	18.2	16.8	11.6	13.2	13.7	11.6
Defence	14.5	15.8	21.9	21.5	17.8	21.6	11.9
Debt	26.3	24.1	16.6	35.6	31.0	31.4	44.5

Source: Central Bank.

servicing (with the post 1981 rise in real interest rates), and the cut-off in new commercial bank credit in the wake of the Mexican crisis, Peru ran swiftly into a new balance of payments crisis. The current account, which had actually been in surplus in 1979 and 1980, turned sharply negative again in 1981 and 1982. The Central Bank found itself rapidly using up the reserves it had managed to accumulate in the two previous years.

As Peru's economic performance deteriorated, meeting the conditions imposed by the IMF in 1982 became increasingly difficult. Though the government did what it could to comply with the targets, it failed repeatedly. The IMF finally rescinded the Extended Fund Facility in October 1983, when formally it still had nearly two years to run. Though a new standby loan was negotiated in March 1984 by the Finance Ministry (headed at the time by a former Vice-President of Wells Fargo, a prominent US creditor bank), the terms were broken by Peru almost before the ink on the final agreement was dry.

As elsewhere, the main thrust of the IMF stabilisation strategy centred on reducing the pressure of demand in the economy. The favoured method was to cut progressively public sector spending. Reducing the fiscal deficit became the most important and revered target. But it proved hard to achieve. On the income side a high percentage of government revenue comes from taxes on trade (export taxes and import duties) and other indirect taxes. The drop in export earnings combined with tariff reductions on imports to produce a serious erosion of tax income. To compensate, the government resorted to increasing domestic fuel prices, which in turn fed inflation. Little, however, was done to get wealthy Peruvians to pay direct taxes: tax evasion in Peru was, and remains, widespread.

On the spending side, the Belaúnde government faced limited options: the main items of expenditure were debt servicing (sacrosanct, at least until 1983/84), the military budget (another

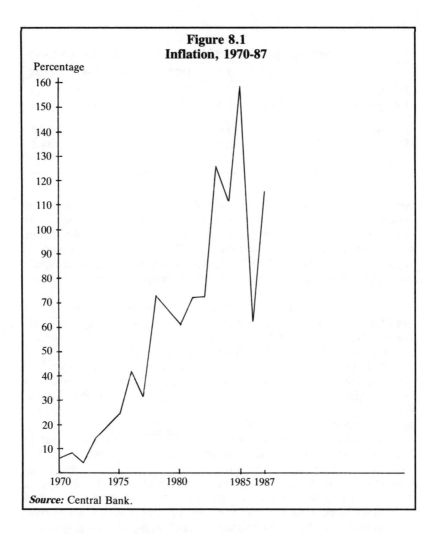

Figure 8.1
Inflation, 1970-87

Percentage

Source: Central Bank.

untouchable for political reasons), and the public sector wage bill (difficult to cut substantially without provoking serious labour unrest). (see table 8.4) The axe therefore fell on food subsidies — always regarded with hostility by the IMF — which inevitably hit the poor hardest. It also fell on public sector investment projects, which meant mortgaging future sources of government income and exports, and postponing the expansion of basic services like electricity and water supply.

164

Table 8.5
Unemployment and Underemployment, 1970-84

	Unemployment	Underemployment	Total
1970	4.7	45.9	50.6
1972	4.2	44.2	48.4
1974	4.0	41.8	45.8
1976	5.2	44.3	49.5
1978	6.5	52.0	58.5
1980	7.0	51.2	58.2
1981	6.0	47.9	53.9
1982	7.0	49.9	56.9
1983	9.2	53.3	62.5
1984	10.9	54.2	65.1

Source: Labour Ministry (quoted from L. Figueroa, *Economic Adjustment and Development in Peru: Towards an Alternative Policy*, UNICEF).

The Economic and Social Cost

Mainly as a result of these stabilisation policies Peru became a victim of stagflation, a combination of economic stagnation and inflation. Historically, inflation had never been a serious problem in Peru. Between 1950 and 1975, annual inflation rates never exceeded 20 per cent. But from 1976 onwards inflation accelerated relentlessly, finally hitting 158 per cent in 1985.(see figure 8.1) In an economy where industry depends to a high degree on imported raw materials and other inputs, and where food imports are high, a policy of continual devaluation was bound to speed up inflation. Other policies compounded the inflationary pressures: the maintenance of high real domestic interest rates which companies simply passed on to the consumer, ever increasing prices of fuel on the domestic market, the removal of subsidies on basic consumer goods like food, and various attempts to increase the prices of the goods and services provided by the state.

Far from embarking on the reactivation it promised in 1980, the Belaúnde administration oversaw the worst economic depression since the 1930s. A slight recovery from the slump post-1975 had taken place during the years of the Peruvian Miracle, but in 1982 the economy stagnated, and in 1983 Peru felt the full force of recession. The 12 per cent negative growth rate in 1983 was the worst in its recorded history. This was a year of freak climatic conditions, drought in the south and floods in the north, and low export prices, but the recession was deepened by the insistence of the IMF that Peru should pursue recessionary economic policies.

There is no doubt that the stabilisation policies successfully reduced aggregate demand as they were supposed to. Inflation and recession brought with them an unprecedented fall in living standards. Per capita income fell from the equivalent of US$1,232 in 1980 to US$1,055 in 1985. Far from creating the million jobs he promised the electorate in 1980, unemployment and underemployment increased substantially under Belaúnde's government.(see table 8.5) The number of people fully employed dropped from just under 42 per cent of the workforce to under 35 per cent in five years. For those fortunate enough to have a job the purchasing power of wages also fell sharply during 1981-85.

Undoubtedly, those least able to defend themselves tended to be those who suffered the most. In contrast, Peru's wealthy elite found many ways to keep abreast of inflation. The owners of industry could pass on increased costs to their customers, while keeping their money in dollars or putting it into bank accounts abroad. They also found it easier to dodge their tax obligations. Despite the severity of the recession, relatively few companies went broke. But wage-earners, particularly those on or near to the minimum wage which lagged far behind inflation, suffered badly. And, with cuts in social spending on health, education, and housing, it was the poor who were the main victims of government austerity. (see box p.167)

But as economic realities for the majority of Peruvians worsened, new forms of social organisation arose, which began to express themselves politically. Trade unions were not alone in attacking government economic policy (through periodic one-day or two-day general strikes). In the slums of Lima and other cities a myriad of neighbourhood groups, often linked to the progressive church, played a leading role in organising communities and mobilising them in response to communal needs. Community-based eating facilities, for instance, were set up: milk supply networks created; and neighbourhood building and improvement schemes launched. In rural areas too, peasant communities fought for solutions to their economic problems through local and national peasant union federations.

The political consequence of falling living standards, therefore, was the growth of mass-based opposition to the government. As the popularity of the Belaúnde government nosedived, the two main opposition groupings, APRA and the United Left, sought to organise and give political direction to the groundswell of discontent. The degree of hostility to the Belaúnde government was revealed in the massive swing to the Left in the November 1983 municipal elections when Lima elected its first-ever socialist city council. It became even more evident by the time of the 1985 presidential elections. Elected

166

Debt and the Nation's Health

Falling living standards and prioritising debt repayments since the mid-70s have contributed to a sharp reversal in earlier trends towards better health in Peru. By 1987 more people than ever were dying of diseases attributable to poverty, malnutrition and inadequate public hygiene. At the same time cuts in health spending had led to a notable deterioration in medical services.

Between 1976 and 1984 the number of reported infectious diseases more than tripled, and the rate of disease per head of the population doubled. The incidence of tuberculosis, for instance, rose by a third between 1979 and 1983. Over the same period cases of gastro-enteritis and dysentery, the most common causes of infant mortality, multiplied more than threefold. Bronchitis and other severe respiratory diseases (particularly common in Lima) were nearly twice as common in 1984 than 1981. In 1983 these three types of disease accounted for 77 per cent of the total registered number of infectious diseases.

In Peru half of all deaths are of children under five. It is more common to die in infancy than in old age. According to USAID estimates, around half of Peru's eight million children suffer from some sort of malnutrition. More than 70,000 children are thought to suffer from third degree malnutrition at any one time. In 1985 the average calorie intake in Peru was only 85 per cent of requirements, compared with 97 per cent in 1979, according to the World Bank; per capita protein intake was 50 grammes, compared with 59 grammes in 1979.

Hospital and general medical facilities provided by the state have deteriorated in recent years, largely as a result of lower spending. In 1970 the government spent nearly 6 per cent of its budget on health, but by 1984 this was down to 4.3 per cent. Although health provision has expanded, it has failed to keep up with growing demands on existing facilities. Assuming that 1972 represents a base of 100, the number of hospital beds per head of the population fell to 97 in 1974, 88 in 1979 and 80 in 1984. Low pay in state hospitals and clinics led more and more doctors to move into the better-paid private sector, while students coming out of higher education tended to opt for other professions. In 1972 there were 1.7 doctors per 1,000 head of population, but in 1984 this had dropped to 1.1; in 1972 there were 2.9 nurses per 1,000, but in 1984 only 1.4.

with 46 per cent of valid votes in 1980, Belaúnde's party, Acción Popular, was all but wiped out in 1985, when it received barely 6 per cent of the vote. Though Belaúnde's handling of the messianic Maoist Sendero Luminoso insurgency undermined his personal standing, and though his patriarchal political style did nothing to inspire popular enthusiasm, it was his government's economic record which contributed most to this crushing defeat. Alan García's revamped APRA party (see box p.168) was the best placed to take advantage of

The APRA Party: Transforming the Image

When Alan García became General Secretary of APRA (literally the American Popular Revolutionary Alliance) in 1982, few predicted that within three years he would lead the party to a landslide election victory. Demoralised by its poor election performance in 1980, and beset by a serious internal rift, the party seemed plagued by its past reputation for political opportunism, narrow sectarianism, and virulent anti-communism. If anything, the Marxist Left seemed best placed to oppose the right-wing Belaúnde administration. García's task — accomplished with extraordinary success — was to cast aside wrangles within APRA, to project a new image for the party, to widen its appeal to the voters, and to give it the leadership it had lacked since the death in 1979 of its founder and guiding star, Victor Raúl Haya de la Torre.

Inspired by the success of the Mexican Revolution, APRA took root in Peru during the 1920s and early 1930s. Its popularity quickly overtook that of the fledgling Communist Party. Its radical and nationalist appeal, transmitted largely through Haya's charisma, found a strong echo in a country dominated politically by a small elite and economically by foreign companies. Unlike the Communist Party, however, APRA appealed to a fairly wide social spectrum. Its initial radicalism was quickly toned down, however, as repression forced it to negotiate the terms on which it was allowed to participate politically. The 1950s found the APRA in alliance with extreme conservatives, as in the climate of the Cold War the party became strongly pro-US, its anti-communist streak coming to the fore.

Right until his death Haya exercised absolute personal control through the party's hierarchical and highly vertical structure. No dissidence in its ranks was tolerated, and there was little or no internal democracy. *Aprista* leaders at the local level, especially among the unions, became well known for their bully-boy tactics against their opponents, particularly those on the left. APRA's conservatism, however, led to the erosion of its former strong union presence. By the 1970s the *Aprista* CTP (Peruvian Workers' Confederation) had largely lost out to the Communist-led CGTP (Peruvian Workers' General Confederation) and individual federations further to the left. The CTP was also widely believed to have had close ties with the CIA.

García's priority in 1982 therefore was to bury this tarnished image. He sought to resurrect APRA's earlier radicalism while giving it a modern gloss, almost as if he was trying to blend the style and image of Haya with that of Spain's Felipe Gonzalez. Under García APRA's hostility towards the Marxist Left was muted in the pursuit of maintaining dialogue. But many aspects of the old APRA still lived on: as in the past, the driving force of APRA's appeal was its nationalism — Peru's creditor banks replaced the formerly foreign-owned mining and oil companies as a target for attack; APRA still stood for a class alliance, which extended to the business elite; and García ran the party in a highly personalist, perhaps even authoritarian, fashion.

168

the desire of most Peruvians for a government which put Peruvian interest first and those of foreign banks last.

García's Debt Stand

Addressing a packed Congress on 28 July 1985, the day his constitutional mandate began, Alan García announced his decision to limit Peru's foreign debt service payment to the equivalent of 10 per cent of annual exports. He also used the occasion to underline his earlier commitment to avoid using the IMF as an intermediary in the renegotiations of its debt with foreign creditors.

Both these new policies caused a profound impact in Peru itself, even though most of the other presidential candidates had advocated putting limits on debt servicing. By opting for 10 per cent, García took as radical a line as APRA's main parliamentary adversaries, the United Left. In the build-up to the elections the United Left had called for a moratorium on some debt payments — notably to commercial banks — but had not specified what percentage of exports would be paid. APRA's own election manifesto had mentioned 20 per cent.

But it was among international bankers that the move caused the biggest stir. For the first time a country unilaterally chose to limit debt payment to its perceived capacity to pay. More importantly, it was the first time that a Latin American debtor country elevated non-payment to a key aspect of economic policy. Earlier non-payers, like Bolivia and Nicaragua, had tended to go about it quietly. Peru, in contrast, was shouting it from the roof-tops. The small size of Peru's debt in relation to the biggest Latin American debtors meant that non-payment would cause little more than a blip on the balance sheet for its major creditors. But it was the exportability of the model that gave bankers sleepless nights. What if Brazil, Argentina or Mexico were to 'do a Peru'?

Careful Wording

García and his government, however, were careful to choose words which would not offend the international financial community unduly. He was emphatic that Peruvian debt policy did not represent a rejection of all liability to pay which Cuba's Fidel Castro was advocating at much the same time. In his speech to Congress García said that his stand did 'not mean that we will ignore our responsibilities to our foreign creditors'. 'Peru,' he went on, 'would resume its payments in full when external circumstances permitted. We want to pay because we are honest, and though we are mindful of the injustices

169

of that debt, we assume our responsibility as a people that stands by recognising its own mistakes.'

A total moratorium was also deliberately ruled out, not least because Peru hoped to continue borrowing from some of its creditors. Only later did it become clear that some creditors (commercial banks in particular) would get virtually nothing. Moreover, initially at least, the 10 per cent limit was not to be open-ended but to last only 12 months. Strategically this was important since creditors could reasonably be expected to wait for the duration of these 12 months without taking reprisals in the hope that a more satisfactory settlement could be worked out in the meantime.

García was also careful to stress his willingness to continue negotiations with creditors, thus forestalling the accusation that Peru was blocking all dialogue. The problem from the banks' point of view was that the government was not prepared to negotiate the 10 per cent nor the question of the veto on the IMF, but only long-term debt restructuring on terms the banks considered impossible.

While Peru thus used language designed to allay fears that it was reneging on its debt obligations, the 10 per cent formula also allowed García considerable scope in defining what debt service and exports were to consist of. Only in the course of time did it emerge that the definitions used permitted the maximum possible repayment while technically staying within the 10 per cent limit.

First, it transpired that the debt limit referred only to the public or publicly guaranteed debt, and did not include the private debt. (In Peru, though, the overall size of the private debt is relatively small in comparison to the debts of the government and the public sector.(see table 8.1)) Then, in due course, it became evident that the 10 per cent referred to the public medium- and long-term debt. It did not cover payments on short-term borrowing, undertaken mainly to finance trade. It also emerged that the 10 per cent was not to include payments in goods, mainly minerals, to creditor countries. Since 1983 this had become an important way of paying off governments in the eastern bloc, mainly the Soviet Union, which had lent large sums to Peru in the early 1970s for arms purchases. Nor did it include payments to Latin American multilateral agencies (like the Andean Development Corporation), Latin American governments or suppliers. Lastly, but not least, the 10 per cent definition did not refer only to goods exported (the usual definition of a debt-service ratio) but to goods *and* services. Services include official transfers, payments for shipping and (an important item in Peru) tourism.

Partly because of the confusion over definitions, economic analysts in Peru found it very difficult to pin the government down on the

170

Table 8.6
Who Got What? Public and Central Bank Foreign Debt Service Payments*, 1985-86

US$m	1985	1986
1. Officially *included* in the '10 per cent'		
a. Public Sector	418	350
— to governments	14	37
— to banks	133	21
— to multilateral organisations	154	234
— to suppliers	99	58
b. Central Bank (to IMF)	79	74
Total	**497**	**424**
2. Officially *excluded* from the '10 per cent'		
a. Public sector	212	173
— to governments	19	36
— LA multilaterals	17	15
— payment in kind	160	108
— LA suppliers	16	14
b. Central Bank	79	72
Total	**291**	**245**

*Excludes private sector and short-term payments.
Source: Central Bank and Drago Kisic, *De la Correspondibilidad a la Moratoria: El caso de la Deuda Externa Peruana 1970-1986*, CEPEI/Fundación Friedrich Ebert, Lima 1987.

question of compliance with the 10 per cent target. Using more conventional definitions of the debt service ratio, in 1986 — the first full year of debt service limits — the García administration paid out considerably more than the equivalent of 10 per cent of exports to foreign creditors.(see tables 8.6 and 8.7) Total debt service payments as a percentage of exports came to nearly 35 per cent.

In a press conference two days after his inaugural speech to Congress, García sketched out his government's policy towards deciding who it would pay and who it would not. The rule of thumb, at least, was to give priority to creditors with whom net lending (new loans less debt service) was in Peru's favour. In practice, however, the government at times made payments in response to pressures on a very ad hoc basis. Apart from suppliers and government export guarantee departments which extended trade lines (excluded from the 10 per cent), those non-Latin American creditors which did best at first were undoubtedly the World Bank and other multilateral banks like the Inter-American Development Bank (IDB). Both these institutions

Table 8.7
What 10%? Debt Service Ratios (Exports of Goods and Services),
1985-86

	1985	1986
1. Service included in the official 10 per cent definition (see table 8.6)	13.6	13.0
2. Total service of public sector debt, medium and long term, excluding Central Bank payments	17.2	16.0
3. Total service of public sector and Central Bank debt, medium and long term (see table 8.6)	21.6	20.4
4. Total public, Central Bank and private debt, medium and long term, including 'retained' interest on short term	31.7	26.6
5. Total public, Central Bank and private debt medium and long term, including 'retained' interest on short term as % of exports (FOB)	38.9	34.7

Source: Central Bank and Kisic, *op.cit.*

had extensive programmes in Peru, considerably enlarged under the Belaúnde government, with large sums which had been agreed upon in the past but which had not been fully paid out or disbursed. Extending the payment ban to these banks would have had an immediate and negative impact. Second in order of priority came government-to-government loan repayments. There was little interruption on payments to eastern bloc countries since payment in kind had been excluded from the 10 per cent equation. Payments to other countries were also made — intermittently — often because of the threat that non-payment would lead to an interruption in aid flows. At the bottom of the list came the international commercial banks and the IMF. During the course of the first 12 months up to July 1986 the banks received only US$63 million and the IMF US$35 million.

Attacking the Fund

The restriction of debt repayment was accompanied by an aggressive posture towards the IMF. García's rhetorical offensive against the Fund was aimed both at domestic public opinion and at bolstering his radical credentials among the leaders of other Third World countries. Initially, at least, Peru used every opportunity in international forums to criticise the Fund's role and approach to the debt crisis. Addressing the UN General Assembly in September 1985, García even threatened to withdraw Peru from IMF membership, though he later admitted that this would be 'a last resort measure'. Luis Alva Castro, Finance Minister during the first two years of the APRA government, took much the same message to the annual IMF and World Bank meetings in Seoul in October 1985. In Seoul, however, Alva was reminded that were Peru to decide to leave the IMF it would also have to leave the World Bank, and this in turn could oblige the country to repay all past loans from the Bank in one go. Less rhetorical was the government's refusal to repay the IMF for past loans. Despite symbolic payments in April and August 1986, the build-up of arrears led to Peru's being declared 'ineligible' for further IMF loans on 15 August 1986.

Bankers' hopes that the end of García's first twelve months in office would bring a change of policy and the abandoning of the 10 per cent stance, were dashed by García's Independence Day message on 28 July 1986. Not only was the 10 per cent limit to be extended for another twelve-month period, but the repayment of private debt was to be affected as well. This was a recognition that private sector debt payment had been extraordinarily high during the government's first year in office (US$305 million between the beginning of July 1985 and the end of June 1986). Government officials took this to be a symptom of capital flight, with private businesses using exaggerated debt repayments as a way to get their money out of the country. At the same time the government announced the introduction of new controls on profit remittances, royalty payments, and the payment of dividends abroad. Faced with no likely improvements on the export front, the virtual certainty that paying more debt service would not bring any new loans and the inevitable criticism from the left-wing opposition at home, it made little sense to soften the debt policy at this stage.

The Bankers' Response

When García told the world he was unilaterally restricting Peru's servicing of its debt, attention immediately turned to how the country's creditors would react. In the recent past the response to debt payment delays in Bolivia had been measured. Though some banks had threatened to seize assets abroad and to suffocate foreign trade by withdrawing trade credits, in practice they preferred not to provoke confrontation. It was obvious that Bolivia was not in a position to service its debts normally — even if it wished to do so. But Peru was rather different. Although in 1984 the Belaúnde government had fallen seriously into arrears on payment of both capital and interest to the banks, it had done so without making a major issue out of it. The banks had been prepared to wait and negotiate with Belaúnde's successor. But with García, creditors were keen to rap the country over the knuckles for deliberately setting an example that others might be tempted to follow.

The first major salvo against Peru came in October 1985 when US government agencies declared the loans of US banks to Peru value impaired. This forced US banks to set aside bigger provision to cover their loans to Peru. This classification meant not only that commercial banks would be less likely to lend new money (hardly a likelihood anyway), but that Peru's ability to borrow in other markets would be undermined as its international credit rating dropped. In theory, the decision by the US regulators to declare a country value impaired follows technical criteria related to the length of time arrears have accumulated. In practice, however, there is considerable room for discretion. The Belaúnde administration avoided having its debt similarly dubbed largely because the US administration felt it unwise to further politicise the debt issue in the build-up to the 1985 presidential elections.

The commercial banks' concern about Peru, however, tended to dissipate as other major debtors in Latin America and elsewhere made it abundantly clear that they would not 'do a Peru'. In the twelve months after García's announcement only two countries — Nigeria and Zaire — stated they would limit debt service to a percentage of exports. In both cases this was more a bargaining ploy than a real statement of principle. As with Bolivia the banks adopted a 'wait and see' approach, letting Peru — in the words of one banker — 'stew in its own juice'. The main threat, voiced repeatedly by Citibank (the bank which chaired the steering committee representing 287 commercial banks) was that the steering committee would be dissolved. Such a move would leave it up to individual banks to use their own judgement on how to get their money back, opening up a greater possibility of Peruvian assets abroad being seized and embargoed in retribution.

In anticipation of possible reprisals Peru announced in February 1986 that it had shipped back to Lima around half its gold and silver holdings abroad (an important part of its international reserves) valued at US$700 million. Then in an attempt to get renegotiation talks going, Peru paid the steering committee US$17.7 million at the end of April. This floundered on the banks' insistence that Peru pay off a meaningful amount of the arrears, which by then totalled US$450 million. By September when the bankers met a Peruvian delegation in New York, the figure had risen to US$630 million. At the same time Peru let it be known that it wanted a rescheduling on terms far more favourable than those granted anywhere else in the world — hardly a gesture designed to please.

Some banks, however, took more seriously Peru's offer to start repaying debt in goods rather than cash. With Peruvian debt trading on the secondary market at a fraction of its face value, this prospect had its attractions. Also the banks found it galling to see the Soviet Union and other eastern bloc countries being exempted from the 10 per cent equation. By the middle of 1987 discussions on such a scheme were well advanced with First Interstate Bank of California and the Midland Bank. Even so it appeared most unlikely that any large amount of Peruvian debt would be paid off in this way.

One area where pressure from the commercial banks (and government export credit guarantee departments) was felt more directly was through the drop in trade lines available to Peru. Before the onset of the Latin American debt crisis in 1982, Peru enjoyed short-term credit lines worth around US$850 million. By early 1987 these had fallen as low as US$250 million making it more difficult for even reputable importers in Lima to buy the goods they sought abroad. As the year progressed, the Central Bank announced an improvement of up to around US$350 million, but this appears to have only been possible thanks to the Central Bank's providing creditors with 100 per cent collateral guarantees. Repayment on short-term trade lines was not affected by the 10 per cent limit.

The IMF and the World Bank

Faced with Peru's growing repayment arrears, the IMF also came to adopt a tough line. The Fund's decision in August 1986 to declare Peru ineligible for further lending was a further blow to the country's credit rating. Peru joined a select club of other countries declared ineligible — including Sudan, Liberia and Cambodia — at the bottom of the world credit rating lists. The IMF's decision did not itself make much difference to Peru, since the APRA government had no intention of asking for more money from the Fund. However, it did lead to a further deterioration in relations with the World Bank and the IDB. The Fund's initial policy towards Peru since 1985 appears to have been to avoid giving García any pretext for accusing it of vindictiveness. Like the bankers, Fund officials were initially worried that other countries would follow Peru. The decision to declare Peru ineligible followed a lengthy period of bargaining. In April 1986 the Fund agreed to hold fire, as Peru made its payment of US$35 million on arrears of US$140 million, and promised to pay off the rest over four months. Subsequently García ruled out making any further payment. Arguably it was US$35 million wasted.

Deterioration of relations with the World Bank paralleled the row with the IMF. Though the Peruvian government told the World Bank that it would get preferential treatment under the 10 per cent policy, it became clear — well in advance of the IMF's decision on ineligibility — that the Bank was scaling down its operations in Peru. One sign was the non-replacement of the Bank's representative in Lima when he ended his stint in 1985. The IMF's decision, though, hardened the Bank's resolve. It became evident that there would be no new Bank lending, and that the drawdown of already agreed loans would be slowed down. In addition, when the Bank's criticisms were publicised on the President's pet project to build an urban railway in Lima, it once again crossed swords with the Peruvian government. The project was a key element in APRA's successful campaign to win the 1986 municipal elections in the capital. At the beginning of 1987 Peru decided to stop repaying the World Bank because it was paying back to the Bank more than it received in loans. As a consequence in May the Bank suspended all lending, including funds for new projects, and put Peru on a non-accrual basis. The Bank argued that the reason the flow to Peru had become negative was due largely to the APRA government's failure to come up with new projects for World Bank finance. There was considerable truth in this. The Belaúnde government had run down the administrative capacity of the state, which García was unable to rectify.

Official Government Lending
Government-to-government links were also affected. The García administration's stand on debt inevitably contributed to the deterioration in relations between Washington and Lima. Soon after his inauguration García met with Secretary of State George Shultz in Washington, who reportedly commented on his government's distaste for García's anti-imperialist rhetoric. With masterly understatement Paul Volker, Chairman of the Federal Reserve, told pressmen shortly after García's 10 per cent speech that 'that kind of approach seems to contain some arbitrary elements that in my judgement aren't conducive to the best progress on the problem'. US constitutional amendments, however, guide with considerable precision the ways in which non-payment of debt affects the disbursement of funds on either military or economic aid programmes. Repeatedly the Peruvian government waited until the last moment before paying: on several occasions amendments were invoked as the time limit passed. Each time, though, Peru paid up what was owing so that aid flows were not seriously disrupted. With other government lenders, especially in Europe, the García government sought to make use of its own political

176

contacts (through the Socialist International, for instance), to get new lending from friendly governments for specific projects. Any renegotiation of official government-to-government debt through the Paris Club was subject to Peru's reversing its policy on debt and seeking a new agreement with the IMF.

Implicit in García's debt policy was the (perhaps a little naive) hope that other debtor countries would follow suit. Their failure to do so effectively isolated Peru. Most countries believed it in their best interests to play the game, even though they may have benefited indirectly from Peru's more radical stand. One by one their leaders and debt negotiators, while paying tribute to Peru's courage, opted to respect the case-by-case approach.(see chapter three) Two years after the Peruvian debt strategy was announced, the reprisals against the country had been less stringent than many observers had originally expected. A major reason for this was precisely that the danger of the Peruvian example spreading had been successfully contained by the international financial community — at least in the short run. The creditors opted for a waiting game, in the belief that, sooner or later, under the pressure of circumstances, García would be forced to eat humble pie.

The Heterodox Policy Mix: Disinflation and Growth

Peru's debt policy grew out of the basic conviction that economic growth could not take place so long as the country continued to devote a large proportion of its resources to servicing the external debt. It also stemmed from the belief that unless there was economic growth, and an improvement in the living standards of the poorest in Peru, then it would become increasingly difficult to contain and undercut growing popular sympathy for the violent methods of change exemplified by Sendero Luminoso. But while it was relatively easy to fix a limit to debt repayment, it was less obvious how to go about reversing the recession and reactivating the economy. This difficulty was compounded by the inexperience of García's economic team in managing economic policy.

Indeed, when they took up their jobs in July 1985, García's top officials and ministers had little grasp of what had to be done. But clearly something had to be done and quickly, so as to keep the political initiative. APRA's policy blueprint, supposedly completed before the elections took place, was never deemed worthy of publication. In fact it seems that the new government, aware that a break was needed with past policy, found more inspiration in the United Left's *Plan de Gobierno*. This had been the result of months of work by a number of Peru's leading left-wing economists, and

177

represented a comprehensive attempt to come up with coherent alternatives to IMF orthodoxy. Another source of inspiration was Argentina's Austral Plan, which had been unveiled on 15 June 1985, six weeks before García came to office. Alfonsín's subsequent visit to Peru in July appears to have played a crucially important role in helping García decide what to do.

The shape of the policy package, announced the week after García's inauguration, bore some striking resemblances to aspects of the Austral Plan as a short-term counter-inflationary strategy. It included a freeze on both wages and prices, a one-off devaluation followed by the freezing of the exchange rate, a progressive scaling down of domestic interest rates, and the introduction of a new currency — the *inti* — which knocked three noughts off the old, much devalued *sol*. Unlike the Austral Plan, though, the Peruvian programme did not form part of an IMF-approved debt rescheduling strategy. While the Austral Plan led to a fall in demand in Argentina, the Peruvian plan included a wage rise to boost demand. In this García's approach was more akin to Brazil's later Cruzado Plan, which also used wage rises to stimulate economic growth.(see chapter seven) In Peru the government ordered an 18 per cent average across-the-board wage rise before imposing the wage freeze.

In many respects the García government's heterodox approach involved doing exactly the opposite of what had been done for so long in Peru — with such conspicuous lack of success. The fundamental challenge to the IMF articles of faith was the proposition that inflation was not generated by excess demand in the economy, but by those

178

cost-push factors which orthodox policies encouraged such as devaluation, higher interest rates, fuel price increases, and the reduction in subsidies. Indeed, it was strongly argued that demand would be increased without inflationary effects since industry was working at only a fraction of its installed capacity. Only when this idle capacity was used up would continuing high demand encounter a supply ceiling causing inflation to pick up again. With its catastrophic fall in living standards over the previous ten years and its accelerating inflation rate, Peru had become a text-book example of the fallacies inherent in the orthodox approach. The IMF's preoccupation with public sector over-spending as the main cause of excess demand also seemed misplaced in a situation where government tax revenues had fallen to such an extent with the decline in the level of economic activity. Hardly surprisingly the Peruvian model came in for sharp criticism from the IMF and the World Bank. (see box p.178)

Initial Successes

Despite the initial lack of forward economic planning, the anti-inflation policy was surprisingly successful in 1985 and 1986, confounding the sceptics who had argued that price controls would never work in a country like Peru. Though Peru never got its inflation down to zero, as Brazil did for a time in the wake of the Cruzado Plan, the fall in the monthly consumer price index was notable.(see figure 8.2).

As inflation came down, and as the government awarded pay increases over and above the prevalent inflation rate, domestic demand began to pick up. This was slow during 1985 and the first part of 1986, but by the middle of 1986 the country's growth rate began to show unmistakeable signs of recovery.(see table 8.3) Despite the existence of price controls (which were never rigidly adhered to) and higher wages, most Peruvian companies saw their sales increase rapidly and their overall profitability grow. The problem for the government was to find ways of encouraging firms to invest their profits in expanding their factories or building new ones.

A major ingredient in the initial success of Peru's heterodox approach was the government's ability to keep the exchange rate under control. An obvious danger to the programme was that the market rate for the dollar would prove difficult to stabilise, with the official exchange rate against the dollar being driven upwards, and inflationary pressures being rekindled because of the increased cost of imports. In fact the exchange rate was to prove remarkably stable during the first 18 months. From July 1985 until early 1987 the free

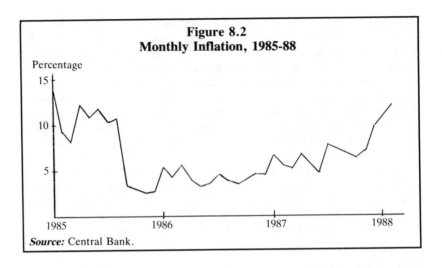

Figure 8.2
Monthly Inflation, 1985-88

Percentage

Source: Central Bank.

market rate — the rate at which dollars were bought and sold on the street — stabilised at around 20 *intis* to the US dollar. The official rate of exchange and the so-called financial rate (each of which governed the prices at which different types of goods were imported) stabilised at 14 and 16 *intis* to the dollar respectively. If the street rate had not held, then a growing black market in dollars would have evolved which, sooner or later, would have obliged the government to devalue the official and financial rates.

One of the reasons why the government managed to stabilise the market rate was because reduced debt payments meant there were more dollars available with which the Central Bank could intervene on the market. Mainly as a result of the leeway created by restricting debt servicing, the Central Bank's reserves grew from just under US$1 billion when García took office to over US$1.5 billion by March 1986. A second, less quantifiable source of dollars which may also have helped in currency stabilisation was the country's rapidly growing cocaine industry, worth perhaps as much as US$800 million a year. Though the vast majority of dollars earned from cocaine exports probably never entered the financial system, those that did may have helped stave off balance of payments pressures.

Reduced debt payment also helped the government to maintain or increase expenditure without further pushing up the fiscal deficit. The huge burden of debt repayment on public finances is revealed by the fact that in 1984 and 1985 debt service (on both debts owed to Peruvians as well as foreign debt) accounted for around 45 per cent of

The View from the Ground

An Interview with Esther Moreno, Mayoress of Independencia, a shanty town in the north of Lima.

'We continue to see living standards fall in Independencia. You can see it clearly with health. Tuberculosis has increased — we have some 2,000 cases of TB registered. The health centres in which it is treated operate under appalling conditions. We had high hopes that under Alan García health provision here would be expanded and improved. But we have seen no improvement at all since 1985.

To give you an idea, we had planned to build eight medical posts as long ago as 1983. Provision for them was included in the 1985 national budget. Then it was all postponed by the government to 1986. 1986 came and went, though we did have a visit from the Minister of Health. But still nothing happened, so here we are in 1987 no further forward.

So far as medicines are concerned, there was a government decree which said that all TB sufferers would get free medicine. But medicines have now all but disappeared. We've only been able to get medicines by organised pressure from the TB sufferers themselves. They've had to collect money on the streets to buy the drugs they need. They even went to the extent of holding a demonstration outside the Ministry of Health, but the Minister didn't even have the decency to listen to what they had to say. There's now even talk that the government's TB programme will be scrapped.

In theory, the government's Health Law is fine; the problem is that it is not implemented. The health centres do not have even basic supplies, like syringes and gauze.

During the Belaúnde government things got far worse on the economic front, but we managed to help each other pull through by means of the organisations we set up. Some of these were very small, like the communal eating facilities which helped people to survive by making it cheaper to feed themselves, or the communal workshops. What happens now is that far from valuing the hundreds of small organisations that have sprung up in Independencia and places like it, what they [the APRA government] do is to try and take them over and neutralise them. We did not think that those who claim to be left-wing and progressive, would proceed to destroy the people's autonomy, co-opt it, or include them in their own programmes which are mostly interested in nothing else than political indoctrination.

Price increases have been less frequent under García than Belaúnde, but that does not mean that people feel better off. The people here are still poor. Women and children still have to look for work or beg on the streets for the family to survive. What happens is either that price controls do not work, like with chicken, or the goods disappear altogether. We've denounced this continually, but to no avail.

In 1986 the government invested 100 million *soles* [1 million *intis* or about £3,000] in education in Independencia. With help from the municipality of Lima [controlled by the United Left] we invested at least ▶

181

> ten times that figure. The officials at the Education Ministry agree with us: what can you do with 100 million *soles*? At the beginning of the school year the Ministry failed to supply children with writing books. Parents and children had to march to the Ministry before they paid up. We have only one secondary school in Independencia. With some 28,000 young men of school age we can only offer vocational training to 80. Is it surprising we have a lot of juvenile delinquency?
>
> Where we live we're only about 15 minutes from the centre of Lima. They can't claim they don't know. They say they're paying only 10 per cent of export income on the debt. They can't say there's no money, because there must be a saving on debt payment. And they say that education and health are priorities for spending. But in Independencia health and education have not improved at all.'

the government's total spending.(see table 8.4) In 1986 the ratio fell to 33 per cent, giving the government more leeway in meeting other demands for spending. Even so, there was considerable doubt as to how much more money was spent on health and education, and how much filtered through to the poor. (see box p.181) Not all the money went on social spending, investment, or on paying better wages to state employees. In 1986 spending on national security — the armed forces and the police — absorbed more than 40 per cent of current spending, 12 per cent more than in 1985. (see box p.183)

At the end of 1986 the government could justifiably claim credit for the success of its economic policies. The economy grew in 1986 by 8.9 per cent, the fastest rate in Latin America and the best annual performance in Peru since 1960. At the same time the lid was kept on inflation. The annual rate was 63 per cent compared to 158 per cent in 1985 and 111 per cent in 1984. Few economic pundits, either in Lima or elsewhere in the world, had predicted that reactivation at such a rate was possible — although growth was from a very low base. Even top government officials admitted — off the record — that they had been surprised by the year's results, which showed particular dynamism in manufacturing industry and construction, the two sectors worst hit by the recession of the Belaúnde years. But as the surprise wore off, discussion turned to whether growth had in any way altered the distribution of wealth, and indeed to whether the model itself was sustainable.

Who Benefited?

Alan García's political honeymoon lasted longer than any analyst would have dared predict at the time of his inauguration. After two

Defence Spending

Since the time of the military governments (1968-80) Peru has been one of the Latin American countries to devote most resources to its armed forces. This did not change substantially when the military handed over to a civilian government in 1980. According to the International Institute for Strategic Studies (IISS), in 1984 Peru had the highest percentage of government spending on defence of any country in the region — even more than the Pinochet dictatorship in Chile.

Border disputes with Chile to the south, and with Ecuador to the north, provide the justification for massive military outlays. The threat of war with Chile in the 1970s and a skirmish on the Ecuadorean border in 1981 also gave new impetus to military spending. But, as the armed forces appreciated when they ousted Belaúnde in 1968, the main threat to national security was not external but internal. This point has been rammed home since 1980, when Sendero Luminoso launched its popular war in Ayacucho against the Peruvian state.

In its attempts to keep to IMF prescribed spending targets, the second Belaúnde administration made cuts in social spending, but military budgets continued as one of the main items of public expenditure. Amounts were agreed upon with minimal consultation with Congress and largely free of interference from the Ministry of Economy and Finance. Himself thrown out of the presidential palace in his pyjamas in 1968, Belaúnde was not one to question the importance of military spending. The lack of civilian control came clearly into focus in 1983 (the worst year for the Peruvian economy since records began) when the military announced its intention to purchase 26 new Mirage 2000 interceptors and to build a large new naval dockyard at the port of Chimbote.

The military's inability to eradicate Sendero Luminoso revealed deficiencies in equipment, weaponry and manpower. This became the new justification for increased spending. Excluding police contingents, by 1987 10,000 troops were deployed on counterinsurgency operations in the Peruvian highlands.

Despite the threat from Sendero, Alan García started off promising to reduce military spending. Shortly after coming to office the Mirage deal was renegotiated, and the order reduced to 13 jets. The Chimbote scheme was put on the back-burner, and steps were taken in conjunction with Chile to reduce the number of troops deployed on the southern frontier.

Although accurate figures for military spending in Peru are usually impossible to find, Central Bank figures show that military spending has as a percentage of total central government spending steadily increased under the APRA government: it amounted to 26 per cent of expenditure in 1984, 29 per cent in 1985 and 30 per cent in 1986.

Table 8.8
Wages, 1984-87 (1979 = 100)

	White collar	Blue collar
1984		
February	97.5	77.1
May	89.9	73.6
August	93.9	74.8
November	91.6	72.6
1985		
February	87.9	65.4
May	81.5	59.9
August	82.7	59.3
November	89.5	68.9
1986		
February	98.4	71.3
April	101.9	76.6
June	101.1	80.4
August	105.0	86.7
October	110.0	91.3
December	108.9	89.2
1987		
February	108.7	84.3
April	111.0	85.9

Source: Central Bank.
Note: These figures come from a regular sample survey conducted by the Labour Ministry of factories and offices with more than ten workers in Lima. Information prior to 1986 has been adjusted due to changes in the methodology used.

years in government, his standing, though marred by specific incidents like the massacre of 300 Sendero prisoners in Lima's jails in June 1986 and charges of fraud in the November 1986 municipal elections, was still remarkably high by Peruvian or Latin American standards. His popularity was due in part to his youth, apparent dynamism, and his political flair in projecting his image. But fundamentally this support was due to the success of the reactivation strategy in 1986, in which the Peruvian economy grew and the fall in most people's living standards was checked. In fact many Peruvians were considerably better off at the beginning of 1987 than they had been twelve months before. It was partly as a result of this that APRA did well in the November 1986 municipal elections.

Charting out who benefited the most from García's reactivation programme is hampered by the lack of reliable information (the last census took place in 1981, and the next one is due in 1991). But the information that is available confirms the recovery in income levels. Indeed, it was on the basis of the extra demand that this created that the economy grew by nearly 9 per cent in 1986. Not surprisingly, the government was quick to claim credit not only for an increase in average incomes but also for an improvement in income distribution.

Wages

Wage earners saw an increase in their spending power (see table 8.8), though real wages by April 1987 were still nowhere near what they were in 1982, let alone 1973 — the year the long-term decline set in. Labour Ministry figures suggest that workers who belonged to a union fared better than other wage earners. Their real purchasing power increased by 46 per cent in the two years between April 1985 and April 1987, though it was still 15 per cent lower than its 1982 level. The wages of government employees, for instance, were still nearly 40 per cent lower than their 1982 level. But among some groups of workers there was little or no improvement: in the depressed mining industry, miners in the large companies saw their wages fall 5 per cent between the end of 1984 and the end of 1986. Even among unionised workers the increase did not mean that people enjoyed anywhere near a reasonable standard of living. To cover basic items such as food, housing, furniture, transport, clothing, education, and health, it cost the average Peruvian family (two adults and four children) the equivalent of £200 a month, whereas the average wage of a unionised worker amounted to only £117 a month.

The situation appears to have been less favourable for non-unionised workers who were getting about 14 per cent more in April 1987 than in July 1985. Although the minimum wage was increased to the equivalent of £31 a month in April 1987, up 36 per cent on July 1985, in real terms this was still lower than its 1980 level.

Employment

The economic recovery, especially in labour-intensive and relatively unskilled activities like construction, increased employment. Although Labour Ministry statistics are based on a relatively small sample of larger firms, they suggest that the increase was particularly strong among manufacturing companies where numbers in employment went up 12 per cent in the first eighteen months of the APRA government. Employment also rose by 11 per cent in commercial firms and by 3 per cent in service industries.

The increase in demand also increased employment in smaller firms and in the informal sector, where wages were lowest. The

185

government's job creation programme known as PAIT — which employed mainly women in the shanty-towns to undertake tasks like street cleaning, planting trees and painting public buildings — also helped to boost family incomes and employment levels. The PAIT programme offered jobs to between 27,000 and 35,000 people between October 1985 and July 1986. Because of its political value, the PAIT programme was expanded to over 150,000 workers in the build-up to the municipal elections, though it was reduced afterwards. PAIT was an important element in APRA's social programme, proving to be a relatively cheap way to boost employment and to strengthen party organisation in left-wing dominated districts.

Profits
At the other end of the social scale, the dramatic increase in sales of goods and services meant that, despite price controls and wage rises, company owners and shareholders benefited from higher profits. In 1986 the private sector had its best year for a long time. The economic model adopted by the García administration presupposed privileged treatment for local firms. Since it was clear from the outset that Peru would get little by way of new capital inflows either through loans or through investment from abroad, the government had to rely on domestic sources of capital if it was going to push ahead with economic expansion. Initially, the huge under-utilisation of fixed capacity meant that output could be increased without major new investments. From the end of 1985 onwards the García government made a concerted appeal to the private sector to invest. Companies were offered numerous special tax incentives and other sweeteners like changes in job security restrictions which made it easier for employers to sack workers. Though García secured promises of support from the heads of Peru's biggest industrial combines, known as the twelve apostles, by mid-1987 there was still little evidence that the private sector was making major new investments. This was one of the pretexts for García's decision to nationalise private financial institutions, discussed below.

Rural Peru
The effect of the 1986 reactivation on rural Peru is even more difficult to measure than its impact in the cities. However, it is clear that higher earnings in the cities produced a higher level of demand for food. Given the low level of average family income in the cities, it was logical to expect that the majority would spend the largest portion of any extra income on buying more food. As demand for food outpaced supply, prices for agricultural products in both wholesale and retail markets

increased — irrespective of the government's system of price controls. Despite official attempts to boost agriculture through increased credit, the volume of output rose by only 4 per cent in 1986. If chicken farming — basically an industrial pursuit — is excluded, growth was only 2.8 per cent.

Though the terms of trade between rural producers and urban consumers improved for the first time in many years, those who did best were not the poorest, nor the majority, but relatively prosperous cash crop producers with access to the urban market. Among the Lima suppliers for instance, the producers in the coastal valleys and in the Mantaro valley in the central highlands appear to have been the main beneficiaries. Agro-industrial interests also did well as demand in the cities increased sharply for processed foods like vegetable oil, flour and wheat. Also, a substantial proportion of food consumed in the urban market is traditionally imported. Afraid of the political effects of food shortages in 1986, the government resorted to importing even more than usual, contrary to their original priority of boosting agricultural production, and especially the traditional sector: Peru even ended up importing potatoes. Food imports were up by 75 per cent on 1985, though the low world price of agricultural commodities meant that in monetary terms the increase was less.

Peru's reactivation in 1986 certainly improved incomes among some sectors of the population. Unionised wage earners and richer rural producers were substantially better off than they had been in July 1985. But the benefits of growth do not seem to have been shared to the same extent by non-unionised workers, the unemployed and the vast majority of the Andean peasantry who remained the poorest of the poor. Despite Alan García's commitment to a new deal for the poorest, Peru's huge inequalities in income distribution remained.

The Model Runs into Trouble

As the García government entered the second half of its five-year term of office in January 1988, there were no obvious signs that it was contemplating any major shift in its position on the debt. The freedom from conditionality from creditors had permitted it to pursue an economic programme to reactivate the economy, while achieving lower rates of inflation. This achievement was in stark contrast to the preceding Belaúnde administraton. At the same time, Peru had escaped relatively unscathed from the bankers' vengeance. As for Alan García himself, his stand on the debt had won him kudos both at home and abroad.

For their part, Peru's foreign creditors were unwilling to take any steps which might be construed by other debtors as letting Peru off the hook. They ruled out any further negotiations until the García government offered hard and fast evidence of mending its ways. Although some banks pushed ahead with specific deals, notably the Midland Bank which arranged to receive some payment in the form of goods, no comprehensive agreement for rescheduling and refinancing appeared to be on the cards. The government continued to rule out IMF policy conditions as the price for an arrangement.

So there was deadlock. The big question for the banks was whether (or how soon) Peru's experiment with heterodoxy would flounder; and whether or not this would force García — like it or not — back to the IMF and orthodoxy. Even by early 1987 clear difficulties had begun to emerge which cast doubt on the longer-term viability of the economic model. As the year passed, these doubts did not diminish.

The first problem was how to reactivate the economy without bringing on new balance of payments difficulties. The growth of the economy led to a dramatic increase in imports during 1986 and 1987. As well as importing food and other consumer goods, the country's industries are highly dependent on a variety of foreign-produced inputs and raw materials. At the same time, low oil and mineral prices led to a notable drop in exports. The value of Peru's exports in 1986, for instance, was the lowest since 1979. With the local boom in demand, some exporters of finished goods, like textiles, found it much easier to offload on to the domestic market than to sell their goods abroad. By the middle of 1986 Peru's trade surplus disappeared for the first time since 1982, and stayed that way until 1987.

As a result, there was a further deterioration in the balance of payments. Despite the limit on debt repayment Peru continued to pay back more than the country received in new loans. This negative cash flow plus the trade deficit led to the sustained erosion of foreign reserves. Net reserves peaked at US$1.5 billion in March 1986; by the end of 1987 they had reached dangerously low levels.

The second key problem which faced the García strategy was how to compensate for the lack of foreign savings entering the economy either in the form of new lending or direct foreign investment. One way was to step up the rate of domestic capital accumulation. Strapped for cash, especially with the slowdown in disbursements from agencies like the World Bank and the IDB, the García government was forced into reliance on the Peruvian private sector to sustain the model.

In the past, Peru's private sector had never distinguished itself for its contribution to developing the national economy. The lion's share of investment has historically been carried out either by foreign companies, and, especially in the last 15 years, by the Peruvian state.

188

The García government, however, tried to court private firms. It used generous sweeteners and incentives to encourage them to reinvest the profits made by the 1986 consumer boom, especialy in potentially profitable sectors of the economy like agroindustry. With industry on average still running at substantially below its installed capacity this was not an immediate problem. But if the economy was to continue to grow on the lines that official predictions claimed it would, then lack of new investment posed a major threat to the model.

García's carefully nurtured relationship with key figures in the private sector was upset by his sudden decision in July 1987 to nationalise privately-owned banks. The economic rationale behind the nationalisations was to make up for the lack of investment and to stem capital flight, but politically the move was bound to anger Peru's business elite, as most of them have interests in the financial sector. García's timing appeared mainly to respond to his desire to wrest the political initiative from the Left at a moment when his popularity was falling fast. In stark contrast to the 10 per cent limit, however, the move failed to capture the imagination of the popular sectors. In fact, the main effect of the move was to grant the initiative to his opponents on the Right. The novelist Mario Vargas Llosa emerged as the leader of a well-orchestrated campaign to stop the nationalisation from going ahead, supported by many of those who García had hoped would commit their money to back the reactivation strategy.

The failure of the nationalisation plan was compounded by the deteriorating economy, which gave the Right even more ammunition to attack García's record. By the end of 1987, the pace of growth was faltering. Though the average rate compared to the average for 1986 was around 7 per cent, the quarterly growth rate had fallen as the year proceeded. At the same time, inflationary pressures were building up. The annual inflation rate was 115 per cent, double the 1986 figure. There were clear signs of rapid acceleration during the last three months of the year.

Faced with the need to correct the trade deficit and to generate foreign currency, the government reverted to a time-honoured method: devaluation. Though there had been pre-announced devaluations early in 1987, the official rate was formally frozen in July 1987. But in the last quarter there was an average 25 per cent devaluation in October, followed by a further large 50 per cent devaluation in December. Following discussions with the World Bank, the government also announced that it intended not only to continue devaluing in 1988 but to revert to the policy used by the Belaúnde government to reduce the fiscal deficit: regular increases in the price of gasoline. A turning-point in the thrust of economic policy had apparently been reached. As *La Republica*, a generally pro-government newspaper, wrote in one of its editorials, 'this is where growth through demand reactivation stops, and where demand restriction to cure external imbalances begins'.

The third and perhaps most fundamental difficulty facing García's economic strategy was that it required certain structural changes to take place to make it work, to avoid many of the pitfalls of the past. As Rosemary Thorp, a British economist whose writing is considered to have influenced Peruvian government policy, has stated, 'If heterodoxy is to come to mean no more than reactivation with unorthodox inflation management, without accompanying structural change, there could be little prospect of survival beyond the short term'.

To avoid new balance of payments difficulties, Peru had to develop the ability to produce for itself what historically it had always tended to import, especially food; it needed to build up an industrial base less dependent on imported raw materials and other inputs; it needed to develop new lines of export goods, thereby reducing its dependency on oil and a handful of price-volatile minerals, and to diversify the markets in which it sells goods abroad; and perhaps most of all, it needed to tackle with new urgency the age-old problem of huge inequality in income, wealth and power. A small rich elite still coexists with some of Latin America's poorest people. While this remains the case, the motor for long-term, sustainable and domestically-generated growth and development will be missing.

Alan García has said he wants to achieve such structural change, and his government's policies during the first half of his term stand in contrast to those of his predecessor. But the deeper transformation has yet to take place.

9. Costa Rica

In mid-1987 Costa Rica's foreign debt stood at US$4 billion — a paltry sum compared to the hundreds of billions owed by Brazil or Mexico, but a huge amount for a small country with a vulnerable and export-orientated economy. Each Costa Rican owed US$1,500, one of the highest per capita debts in Latin America and more than double the Central American average. Moreover, the country had become one of the Latin American countries least able to maintain its debt repayments, according to the two key criteria used by economists to judge a country's capacity to pay, namely the ratio of debt to exports and debt to GDP.(see table 9.1)

As the debt crisis began to bite, Costa Rica became so tightly constrained by debt repayments that it was in danger of losing its reputation as the 'Switzerland of Central America'. As every student of Central American politics knows, since the 1940s Costa Rica has essentially been a modern capitalist democracy, with a tradition of political pluralism, non-violence and less social polarisation than its neighbours. Successive governments have been committed to a substantial public sector role in the economy, and a developed health, education and welfare system which together underpinned four decades of political stability. But with the onset of the debt crisis, such 'privileges' began to be eroded.

Although Costa Rica's welfare state helped to mitigate the worst effects of the social cost of the adjustment policies imposed to pay off the debt, nevertheless social services were cut back, wages were constantly held below the rate of inflation, and malnutrition and illiteracy rates began to rise. At the same time, the heavy debt burden forced the country into the hands of the IMF and other international financial institutions (IFIs). This not only meant a surrender of Costa Rican control over key economic policies, but also caused social protests and tensions to flare up, which were increasingly met with

191

Table 9.1
Debt and Debt Indicators, 1970-86

	1970	1975	1980	1981	1982	1983	1984	1985	1986
Total Publicly-guaranteed Debt (US$m)	134†	421†	3183	3360	3497	3848	3955	4804**	4000
% at variable interest†	7.5	29	47	52	52	57	57	57	n.a.
Debt per capita (US$)	n.a.	n.a.	1396	1453	1451	1557	1563	1618	1585
Debt as % of GDP	n.a.	n.a.	143	154	173	186	181	n.a.	n.a.
Debt as % of exports	48†	70†	265	286	313	336	326	440	373
Total Debt Service (US$m)	28†	64†	295†	197†	138†	745*	375*	574*	568*
Debt service as % of GDP	n.a.	n.a.	13	9	6	36	17	16*	15*
Total Debt Service as % of Exports	10†	11†	18	28	36	33	31	28	23

Sources: CEPAL, except figures marked with † (World Bank Debt tables), and * (Republic of Costa Rica Information Memorandum, September 1986).

Debt by Creditor, Year-end 1985

Type of creditor	US$m	%
Commercial Banks	1459	39
Bilateral Agencies	905	24
Multilateral Agencies	1036	28
Bonds & FRNs	74	2
Suppliers	50	1
Certificates of Deposit	185	5
Total	3709**	100

**Discrepancy is due to different sources.
Source: Republic of Costa Rica, Information Memorandum, September 1986.

government repression — previously a rare event in the country. The Costa Rican example also illustrates the potential political cost of the debt crisis: in this case, the US giant to the north took advantage of the vulnerability of the Costa Rican economy to severely restrict the country's professed neutrality in the regional conflagration.

'The Switzerland of Central America'

Costa Rica's reputation as a haven of peace and democracy in the midst of a strife-torn region is of fairly recent construction. In the colonial era any Spanish settlers who found their way to what was then an isolated backwater worked the land alongside family farmers, which contributed to the common perception among Costa Ricans that they are 'a nation of equals'. However, any egalitarianism there may have been did not survive the brief civil war of 1823 which led to independence from Spain and the introduction of coffee and bananas as export crops.

Nineteenth century politics were largely a family affair amongst the coffee barons and were characterised by frequent electoral fraud, armed revolts, interventions by the army and a bewildering array of new constitutions. By the time of the Second World War, the coffee oligarchy was weakened economically by the Great Depression and threatened politically both by the communists, who enjoyed a strong trade union base in the foreign owned banana plantations and the capital, and by the urban middle classes who were increasingly influenced by the philosophies of Social Christianity and New Deal Liberalism.

The weakening of the oligarchy helped to create the political conditions for the institutional framework of modern Costa Rica to be laid down during the presidency of Rafael Angel Calderón (1940-44) and his successor, Teodoro Picado (1944-48). Calderón's professed Catholicism — a rarity among Costa Rican public figures — led to church support for the Social Guarantees, fifteen constitutional amendments which opened the way for comprehensive state intervention in a wide range of social and economic fields. They included the establishment of the National University; a labour code which guaranteed the right to strike, collective bargaining, job security and a minimum wage; social security measures including health insurance; and provisions for squatters to acquire titles to lands they cultivated.

When his party split over the issue of the Guarantees, Calderón turned for support to the communist Popular Vanguard Party (PVP), and the ensuing coalition under the candidature of Picado won an easy victory in the 1944 election. Picado's presidency was marked by increasing violence as the oligarchy, already deeply hostile to Calderón's reforms and implacably opposed to communist participation in government, was roused to fever pitch by Picado's attempt to introduce direct taxes on income. When Picado tried to use constitutional manoeuvres to ensure the succession of Calderón for a further term following the blatantly fraudulent 1948 election, the country was faced with the prospect of a further round of dictatorship or chaos.

This was prevented by the decisive action of José Figueres Ferrer, widely known as Don Pepe, whose political vision and enormous ambition had not found expression in the established parties. When Figueres launched an armed revolt, he was swiftly backed by the oligarchy and the US government, who were both attracted by his anti-communist rhetoric. The ensuing civil war (the so-called War of National Liberation) was short; in order to avoid bloodshed and widespread destruction, the communist militia defending the capital agreed to surrender in return for an assurance that the Social Guarantees would not be repealed.

Figueres assumed the presidency at the head of the Founding Junta of the Second Republic, which during its 18-month term prepared a new constitution and enacted decrees which went beyond anything conceived by Calderón: the banking system was nationalised, a network of autonomous public sector agencies was established to administer public utilities, education, housing, finance and welfare, the vote was extended to women and a 10 per cent surtax on large bank deposits was introduced. In addition, following an abortive Calderonista invasion launched from Nicaragua, and to prevent further meddling with the democratic process, the army was abolished and constitutionally proscribed.

Ever since 1949, the presidency has since alternated between the social-democratic National Liberation Party (PLN), founded by Figueres in 1951, and coalitions of conservative groupings defined more by their opposition to the PLN than by any internal ideological coherence. Until the 1980s this political rhythm was reflected in the domestic economic policy, whereby the PLN expanded state involvement in the economy, along with public sector employment and welfare provision, which they funded by borrowing during the periodic decline of coffee and banana prices. The expansionary process was then halted, but not reversed, by the succeeding conservative president. At the same time, attempts were made to diversify the export base of the economy, with the establishment of sugar, cacao and beef farming, while industrial output grew rapidly following Costa

Rican membership of the Central American Common Market (CACM) in 1962.

Impressive growth rates in the 1960s and 1970s and the emphasis on social welfare programmes helped to ensure that most Costa Ricans enjoyed a higher standard of living and a greater degree of political stability than their neighbours in the other Central American countries. Per capita income doubled over the two decades, while social improvements were also impressive: between 1948 and 1978, infant mortality fell from 117 per thousand to 17 per thousand; life expectancy increased from 60 to 74 years; illiteracy almost disappeared; and a welfare system encompassed 80 per cent of basic needs.

The Genesis of the Crisis

The fiesta could not last forever. By the mid 1970s, growth had begun to slow down. The expansion of agricultural output halted as accessible virgin lands became exhausted, while economic recession and increasing political turmoil in the rest of Central America combined to reduce industrial exports. At the same time, the expansionary state intervention policies of the Oduber administration (1974-78) increased the central government deficit while private institutions also ran heavy losses. Both the public and private sectors were able to take advantage of the flood of petrodollars recycled through the international banks in order to fund their deficits. Under Oduber the public sector debt tripled, while the proportion owed to private banks (rather than international agencies or governments) rose from 22 per cent in 1970 to 53 per cent in 1979.

The second OPEC price rise in 1978, together with the collapse of world coffee prices, had a disastrous effect on the economy. International rates of interest almost doubled as a consequence of the oil shock, increasing proportionately the burden of the private debt Costa Rica had contracted at market rates. (see table 9.1) The writing was on the wall. In the final days of his administration, the IMF offered Oduber financial assistance in return for significant changes in domestic policy: restrictive credit and demand policies, tight control of the money supply, and increased indirect taxation. Oduber rejected the package. 'The IMF', he declared, 'restricts and damages countries' sovereignty by imposing limits on their economic and social development and translating the reality of control of the national economy to Washington.' Subsequent presidents have shared his sentiments, but their capacity to resist the blandishments of the Big Brother of the international financial system was steadily reduced.

Under Oduber's successor, the conservative Rodrigo Carazo (1978-

Table 9.2
Main Economic Indicators, 1980-86

	1980	1981	1982	1983	1984	1985	1986
GDP (%)	0.8	−2.3	−7.3	2.9	7.5	1.6	3.0
GDP per capita (%)	−2.1	−4.8	−9.8	−0.2	−4.8	−0.9	0.4
US$ Exchange Rate	8.6†	22†	40	43	48	54	59
Inflation (%)	18	65	82	11	17	11	14
Trade Balance (US$m)	−459	−127	73	−14	0	−75	50
Open Unemployment (%)	5.3	8.3	8.5	7.9	6.4	6.2	6.0
Underemployment (%)	13.5	17.5	21.8	18.1	15.1	14.0	14.0
Central Government Deficit (as % of GDP)	9.1	4.3	3.4	5.1	4.8	4.1	5.7

Sources: CEPAL except figures marked with † (IMF International Statistics).

82), the crisis deepened. The public sector consumed an ever greater quantity of domestic credit, while the private sector continued to draw funds from international banks. By 1982 the external debt had tripled again, to some US$3.5 billion. As exports stagnated, the trade balance moved into severe deficit. Carazo was unable to force through devaluation against opposition from the PLN and powerful interest groups within his own coalition, particularly the industrial sector, who were producing more and more for the domestic, instead of the regional, market and were heavily reliant on imported capital goods. Inflation rose to over 60 per cent, open unemployment to 8.3 per cent.(see table 9.2) Foreign reserves drained away, while government gold holdings fell by three quarters between 1980 and 1981.

In 1979 the IMF offered a stabilisation deal, but Carazo was unable to deliver the austerity measures required, and the IMF suspended payments. A harsher package the following year was equally unfulfilled. In July 1981 Costa Rica became the first nation in Latin America to suspend unilaterally all payments on foreign debt. The IMF closed its office, and Costa Rica was isolated from further international loans. Carazo bequeathed an economy in chaos to his PLN successor, Luis Alberto Monge.

The Monge Administration (1982-86)
— Stability at a Price

Monge's most immediate problem on taking office was the renegotiation of the debt to the international, and mainly US, commercial banks. But any deal with the banks was impossible without first satisfying the IMF, which implied adopting the standard package of 'reforms' — reduction of public sector spending, deflation, and deregulation of both the financial system and production and distribution. But the problem did not end there; the burden of debt servicing was so great — well over half of annual export revenue — that a fresh inflow of funds was essential to maintain even the necessary minimum of imports, on which the industrial sector as well as consumers depended.

At the same time, Monge initiated a programme of economic adjustments which aimed to provide a long-term solution to the country's economic problems. The import substitution model of development, which for two decades had required protection for Costa Rica's national industries, was according to Monge, 'exhausted', and had to replaced by one that was 'more profitable'. Instead, he favoured exposing the external economy completely to market forces in a move towards non-traditional industrial and agro-industrial products which could be exported to the US. This fitted neatly into the IMF and US Treasury scheme of thinking as it required the creation of an economic climate supposedly favourable to attracting foreign, especially US, private investment. But no amount of redistribution of resources from domestic consumption to the export sector — dominated by large enterprises and foreign capital — within the debt strangled domestic economy was going to supply the capital required for such a transformation.

In fact, Monge applied many IMF-type measures before IMF conditionality was imposed. A drastic credit squeeze, increases on taxes and on the prices of government supplied goods and services, a freeze on government expenditure, cuts in the budgets of the autonomous agencies, and a devaluation of the exchange rate achieved a certain measure of stability by December 1982 when the IMF offered a US$100 million standby credit.

On the positive side, the rate of inflation was slowing down, and the free market exchange rate was beginning to improve. But on the negative side, during 1982 GDP in real terms fell by a record 7.3 per cent, per capita GDP by 9.8 per cent and industrial production by 7.7 per cent. Exports, hit by low coffee, meat and sugar prices, fell by 14.1 per cent. While wages rose by 16 per cent, the rate of inflation of consumer prices was over 80 per cent; real wages had fallen by almost a half in the three years from 1979. (see box p.211) Visible unemployment was approaching 10 per cent. The number of families classified as poor had risen from 79,000 (25 per cent) in 1973 to 177,000 (51 per cent) in 1982. Official figures showed that the proportion of low income families had risen from 42 per cent in 1980 to 71 per cent in July 1982, and a staggering 83 per cent in rural areas. Malnutrition was once more being observed at health clinics. The housing shortage of 100,000 units was officially declared a national crisis.

The government fiscal deficit was still over 5,000 million *colones* (₡5,000 million) equivalent to 9.5 per cent of GDP, despite hefty increases in telephone charges and electricity tariffs over the year. If all that were not enough, the external debt of US$3,497 million — US$1,451 for every Costa Rican — represented the total production of the economy for 13 months. Repayments of US$745 million due for 1983 were worth 85 per cent of exports, the interest payments alone 65 per cent of exports and 18 per cent of GDP. Repayment on that scale, according to Economy Minister Federico Vargas, implied 'a reduction in the standard of living of Costa Ricans to the level of the 1920s'.

The price exacted by the IMF for readmitting Costa Rica to the circles of international financial respectability was higher than the terms offered to either the Oduber or Carazo governments. Prices for public sector goods and services were to continue to increase, and subsidies to fall. The fiscal deficit was to be held to 4.5 per cent of GDP, implying drastic cutbacks in the welfare state, while wage increases were to be held to a minimum. In addition, interest rates were to rise, a measure strongly opposed by the retailing and manufacturing sectors, whose need for credit had risen with the surge in import costs. The burden on the lowest paid of these measures was to be partly offset by a ₡3,000 million programme of income, employment and housing support.

Nevertheless, the December IMF deal swiftly enabled the urgent debt problem to be tackled, in the short term at least. In January 1983 the government creditors of the Paris Club agreed to reschedule 85 per cent of debt arrears over seven years, with repayments to begin in 1986. In September the commercial banks rescheduled US$655 million — 83 per cent of the total debt — with a period of grace until 1987. These agreements put off the repayments crisis until the term of office of the next president, and gave Monge three years in which to reactivate the economy along the lines of his longer-term adjustments.

'By the Scruff of our Neck'

'The IMF has got us by the scruff of our neck.'
President Monge, 19 December 1983.

As 1983 wore on, resistance and protests by farmers, consumers and unions, as well as more progressive elements of the PLN, ate into the proposed cutbacks. (see box p.200). Opposition groups were able to achieve partial success in resisting the reductions in welfare spending. For example, restoration of a cut in the budget of the Family Aid programme was paid for by a 10 per cent increase in business taxes. It soon became apparent that the spending targets given in the letter of intent to the IMF would not be reached. In November the last US$20 million was withheld, together with US$60 million from USAID. In addition to demanding a further reduction in the fiscal deficit for 1984 to 2 per cent of GDP, the IMF required abolition of the 1 per cent tax on exports, while USAID appended a demand for the abolition of controls on foreign exchange. The 1984 budget, overseen by the IMF, proposed further price tariff and tax increases, decreased controls and subsidies, continuing tight control of wages, as well as further encouragement for exporters. A new letter of intent was signed in April 1984.

During the second half of Monge's presidency he continued to pursue his balancing act between the demands of the international agencies and the protests by those on whom they fell. Movement in the direction programmed by the agencies was inexorable, however much Monge attempted to stall and hedge.

The watershed was reached in mid-1984. While the IMF was satisfied with emergency measures passed in January, both the World Bank and USAID continued to press their own demands. The former demanded further restrictions on public spending and insisted upon the privatisation of CODESA, the state institution which had been responsible for coordinating much of Costa Rica's industrialisation, but which ran an average loss of ₡114 million per month between September 1982 and June 1984. It also began to exert pressure for a new Central American Common Market (CACM) tariff regime at lower rates. USAID chose this moment to withhold its funds until the currency reforms which it had requested since 1982 were implemented. Henceforth, dollar loans were to be paid directly to private institutions in *colones*, bypassing the Central Bank, while payments overseas were to be made in dollars instead of by reference to the official exchange rate of ₡20 to the dollar (compared with an interbank rate of over ₡45). This had the effect of transferring to the Central Bank the financial cost of the successive mini-devaluations.

Despite a desperate search for funding from Mexico and Europe, the hold up by the World Bank and USAID made the April agreement with the IMF impossible to fulfil. The IMF responded with a call for a further cut in the government deficit, and a new letter of intent was agreed allowing the deficit to reach 1.5 per cent of GDP. At the same time, however, the letter also promised a new accord with the World

The Popular Response

A central element of Monge's internal policy and an essential prerequisite for debt renegotiation and an IMF agreement was the maintenance of social p_ace — in other words, the containment of political opposition to the austerity programme especially from local communities, farmers and unions.

Local Communities: Protests by community organisations against the decline in rural bus services and the rising price of water supplies were a regular occurence. But the most serious and sustained mass opposition to Monge's economic strategy came during the 1983 campaign against electricity price increases.

In 1982 the state electricity agency was the most indebted in the public sector, with its external borrowings of US$619 million representing 20 per cent of Costa Rica's total external debt. In mid-1982 the government raised tariffs by 70 per cent, followed by a further 90 per cent increase after the IMF agreement. There was little public opposition until April 1983 when the increase over 16 months reached 227 per cent. Demonstrations began in San José in May, organised by a committee in the suburb of Hatillo in which the Popular Vanguard Party played a leading role. On 6 May negotiations with a PLN-dominated committee led to agreement for a tariff freeze at the February rate. But when cut offs began on 6 June, the response was swift. Street barricades were erected in Puriscal, and spread rapidly to over 30 towns and communities. A list of demands formulated by a coordinating committee, which included representatives of the most militant communities, was signed by 140 local organisations and 52 trade unions. The government had little option but to give in. From May, tariffs returned to the December 1982 level, cancelling all but 20 per cent of the IMF inspired increases, along with other concessions.

In general though, the community organisations and their left-wing leadership proved incapable of extending the gains they had made into other areas. This was partly because the development of autonomous community organisations had always been intimately linked with the local branches of the PLN, which gave the administration an important means of restraining popular discontent at a neighbourhood and village level.

Small Farmers: By mid-1983, the all-important agricultural sector was in severe difficulties because of the decline in the value and volume of Costa Rica's main agroexports. Farmers at all levels demanded easier access to credit: large coffee producers were strongly opposed to the higher interest rates demanded by the IMF, while small farmers campaigned for a reduction in duties on fertilisers and greater state support. UPANACIONAL, an organisation of small and medium-sized coffee and vegetable growers predominantly of the Central Plateau founded in May 1981, quickly became one of the most effective pressure groups in winning concessions from the government, which had been elected on a 'Back to ▶

▶ the Land' ticket. In February 1983 UPANACIONAL began a strike to press its demands, and started blocking roads the following month. In a significant U-turn, the government acceded to its demands for lower input costs and credit and tax breaks.

The problem of the landless was less tractable. In July 1,000 families invaded unoccupied lands, followed by a further 250 in August. Less organised invasions of squatters were reported weekly, to which the government responded by expelling the new occupants by force.

Unions: The focus of union opposition to Monge's economic programme was the wage control mechanism introduced from January 1983, which the unions were generally unable to reverse. Unions also attempted to combat government attempts to exert steadily tighter control over public sector employment and pay, including the non-payment of arrears due to employees, in order to bring its IMF-imposed spending targets under control. From January 1984 the Monge government also restricted the right to strike in the public sector and froze further appointments. As protests over back-pay continued, the government increasingly resorted to the previously rare practice of jailing union leaders.

Bank. The conservative opposition in the assembly made its agreement conditional on measures providing for the autonomous agencies and state banks to guarantee government expenditure, which amounted to a further cut in welfare spending. USAID, meanwhile, pressed through the privatisation of CODESA'S 18 companies.

Monge's austerity programme, however successful in satisfying international creditors, offered in no sense any solution to the structural problems of the economy. The reduction of inflation and the budget deficit to around a quarter of what they were when he took office brought a fragile stability to the domestic economy, but the external pressures were in no way relieved.

Foreign debt rose by around 15 per cent between 1982 and 1984 to US\$3,955 million. Little comfort was to be drawn from the fact that this enormous sum now represented 1.6 per cent, rather than 21.6 per cent, more than the country's entire national output for the year. Debt repayments in 1983, following the defaults in previous years, represented around a third of GDP and a third of exports. 1984 was better, but the balance of payments on the current account deteriorated by 15 per cent to a US\$315 million deficit. Moreover, both debt repayments and the foreign trade deficit were on a rising trend, while the improvements in industrial production and the slight recovery in income levels since 1983 both fuelled the trade deficit by stimulating demand for imports. The economy was so strangled by debt repayments that Monge was highly vulnerable to economic and political pressure from the US.

The Reagan administration, through USAID, provided Monge with just sufficient funding to keep the economy afloat. In addition to demanding economic changes which favoured US multinationals, the US used the debt crisis as a bludgeon to secure a shift in Costa Rica's traditional stance of neutrality in the region. Many interpreted it as a straight swap: Monge would get aid in exchange for his turning a blind eye to Costa Rica being used as a base for contra operations against Nicaragua.

US Aid and the Nicaragua Dimension

Monge was of course constrained by the Sandinista victory in Nicaragua in 1979. The two countries had long been traditional enemies: Nicaragua provided a ready haven for Costa Rican rebels in the nineteenth century, while the Somoza family dictatorship was particularly abhorred in Costa Rica for its aid to the two Calderonista invasions in 1948 and 1955. There was therefore, a generalised sympathy amongst Costa Ricans for the Sandinista cause which was reflected in the provision of refuge and supplies during the insurrection.

However, with the overthrow of Somoza, the historical enmity combined with the profound anti-communism common to both conservatives and the PLN to transform the sentiments of support to those of paranoia. Monge took office at a time of considerable social unrest, including sporadic outbreaks of urban guerrilla activity. Nicaragua provided a convenient peg on which accusations of foreign agitation could be hung, as it was far easier to lay responsibility for the growing civil disorder at the door of the Sandinistas than to acknowledge the domestic roots of the crisis. Few were prepared to take on board an analysis which called into question the reality of the national myth of egalitarianism and the economic basis of Figueres' second republic.

Throughout 1982 relations were strained. The Sandinistas consistently denounced Costa Rica for providing a base for both the political leadership of the contras and the armed forces belonging to ARDE (Revolutionary Democratic Alliance) under Eden Pastora ('Commandante Cero') — accusations which were repeatedly, and increasingly hollowly, denied by the Monge government. At the same time Costa Rica pursued a staunchly pro-US line as a member of the Forum for Peace and Democracy and refused any suggestion of bilateral discussions on matters such as navigation rights on the Rio San Juan frontier.

Predictably, US economic aid to Costa Rica leapt up. In 1981, the US contributed a modest US$15.3 million, two thirds of which came in loans. In 1982, this amount jumped to US$52 million, all but US$9 million in loans. Monge also accepted US$2 million for equipment and training for the Civil Guard. In 1983 aid suddenly soared to over US$200 million, almost a quarter of it as a grant. The following year, although the total fell back to US$179 million, almost two thirds came in grants, with an additional US$9 million for security assistance.(see table 9.3) Costa Rica became the largest recipient of US aid on the continent after El Salvador, and the largest per capita recipient of aid after Israel. By 1984 the US contribution represented a staggering 5 per cent of GDP, 20 per cent of the cost of total imports (or half the cost of imports from the US), 25 per cent of government expenditure and twice the central government deficit — and these figures represented a substantial reduction from the levels of 1983.

In 1983 there was a slight change of tack. Monge initially supported enthusiastically the Contadora peace initiative, launched in January by Mexico, Colombia, Venezuela and Panama in an attempt to find a political solution to the Central American crisis. Relations with Nicaragua improved. Costa Rica also refused to cooperate with plans for regional manoeuvres and to support the US invasion of Grenada in October. Furthermore, in November, Monge launched a new policy of active neutrality, and introduced a proclamation of neutrality, for which he was unable to obtain the two-thirds majority in the legislative assembly required to give the measure the force of a constitutional amendment. The same month, the IMF announced that it was holding back the last payment in its 1983 programme pending further revision of government spending targets.

However, throughout 1984 Costa Rica joined the key US allies, El Salvador and Honduras, in stalling the Contadora process, in particular by raising US-sponsored objections to the arms control and verification provisions. In January 1985, it failed to attend a Contadora meeting and in February refused another invitation using the issue of political asylum for a Nicaraguan draft evader as the pretext. On 8 April, the ambassador to Managua was withdrawn and three days later Monge expressed his 'enthusiastic support' for a new Reagan peace plan, adding his appreciation for the 'contribution your illustrious government has made towards strengthening peace and Costa Rican democracy'. In May, the government set up a military camp at El Murciélago, 16 kilometres from the Nicaraguan border, where US advisers could train the Costa Rican Civil and Rural Guard in 'anti-

Table 9.3
US Aid to Costa Rica, 1962-88 (US$m)

	1962-79	1980	1981	1982	1983	1984	1985	1986	1987	1988*
Total Economic Assistance	198.9	16.0	15.3	51.7	214.1	178.9	198.2	154.5	118.7	118.1
Loans	119.6	12.0	10.0	42.7	166.2	74.6	26.6	n.a.	n.a.	n.a.
Grants	79.3	4.0	5.3	9.0	47.9	104.3	171.6	n.a.	n.a.	n.a.
Security Assistance	6.9	—	0.03	2.05	2.6	9.15	9.2	2.6	1.7	2.5
Loans	5.0	—	—	—	—	—	—	—	—	—
Grants	1.9	—	0.03	2.05	2.6	9.15	9.2	—	—	2.5

*Requested.

Sources: M. Edelman, *NACLA Report on the Americas*, Nov/Dec 1985, p.41 (1962-85); Centro de Investigación Social, Estados Unidos, *Centro America Boletín de Análisis e Información*, No. 14-15, Feb-Apr 1987, p.19 (1986); and *Coalition* #55, 5 March, 1987 (1987-8).

terrorist measures'. Diplomatic relations with Nicaragua were broken off in the same month after an exchange of gunfire on the border in which two Civil Guards were killed, by Nicaraguan troops according to Costa Rica, and by contras according to Nicaragua.

Diplomatic developments apart, acceptance of government denials of contra activity on its soil flew increasingly in the face of observable facts. The government explained that the small number of security forces (some 5,000 men) could not adequately police the borders. But there were frequent allegations that officers of the Rural Guard knew about contra movements but ignored them.

As the run-up to the February 1986 presidential election began, the contest at first appeared to be akin to that between Tweedledum and Tweedledee. The most significant difference appeared to be the degree of enthusiasm shown by the main candidates for an economic policy, determined by the IMF, and a foreign policy, increasingly influenced by the Reagan administration. The PLN strategists decided to campaign on a peace platform, and accordingly Monge reintroduced the proclamation of neutrality on 19 November. After a public opinion poll revealed 70 per cent support for a non-belligerent stance towards Nicaragua, the PLN campaign moved into high gear. The PLN's adoption of the peace ticket was widely considered to be a major factor in Oscar Arias' subsequent victory — only the second in which the ruling party had retained power since 1948.

Following the victory, Monge spent the last months of his presidency mending fences with Nicaragua, but plans to establish an international team of observers to police the border came to nothing. At the same time some measures were taken which appeared to suggest that contra activity was at long last being brought under control. Monge altered the location of a high profile road building exercise by US military engineers from close to the Nicaraguan border to close to the Panamanian.

But according to evidence which later emerged during press investigations of the Irangate scandal, Monge agreed to requests by US Ambassador Tambs (who told him that a Nicaraguan invasion was imminent) for the construction of an airstrip some ten kilometres from the El Murciélago base. The Monge government claimed that the airstrip was part of a tourist project, but according to the Tower Commission report, the airstrip was in fact used for the direct resupply of the contras from July 1985 to February 1986, and thereafter as the primary abort base for damaged aircraft. (see box p.206).

Project Democracy

The construction of a secret airstrip in northern Costa Rica in summer 1985 was apparently one of the operations undertaken by Project Democracy, [a term used by LtCol North to describe a network of secret bank accounts and individuals involved in contra resupply and other activities]. In a September 30, 1986, memorandum to VADM Poindexter, LtCol North described Project Democracy's role:

'The airfield at Santa Elena has been a vital element in supporting the resistance. Built by a Project Democracy proprietary, (Udall Corporation S.A. — a Panamanian company), the field was initially used for direct resupply efforts [to the contras] (July 1985-February 1986)... the field has served as the primary abort base for aircraft damaged by Sandinista anti-aircraft fire.'

[....] [A] CIA field officer told the Board that construction of the Santa Elena airfield was a pet project of US Ambassador Louis Tambs. According to the CIA field officer:

'When Ambassador Tambs arrived in Costa Rica [July 1985], he called together the Deputy Chief of Mission, the Defense Attache and myself, and said that he had really only one mission in Costa Rica, and that was to form a Nicaraguan resistance southern front.
[The Santa Elena airstrip] was a matter which I had been monitoring, kind of as an aside, but it was essentially the Ambassador's initiative.'

[...] In August 1986, Costa Rican authorities took measures to stop further use of the airstrip. US authorities sought to avoid public disclosure of past activities there. [...] On September 9, LtCol North informed VADM Poindexter that he had completed a conference call with US Ambassador to Costa Rica Louis Tambs, Mr. Abrams and the Director of the CIA CATF who all agreed that LtCol North would call Costa Rican President Arias to insist the press conference [to announce the presence of the airfield] be stopped. LtCol North said that they agreed he would take a tough line with President Arias, threatening to withhold US assistance [worth US$80 million from USAID].
[...] Reporting after the fact, LtCol North asked VADM Poindexter to understand the grounds for taking steps that LtCol North admitted may have been extraordinary:

'I recognize that I was well beyond my charter in dealing with a head of state this way and in making threats/offers that may be impossible to deliver, but under the circumstances — and with Elliott's concurrence — it seemed like the only thing we could do.'

Later that day, VADM Poindexter replied: 'You did the right thing, but let's try to keep it quiet.'
Source: *Tower Commission Report*, pp. 470-473.

The Arias Administration (1986-): Déjà vu?

The arrival of Oscar Arias heralded a significant break with Monge's policies towards the contras and repaying the debt, but not in the overall direction of the Costa Rican economy. Arias' first move was to exercise firmer control over the activities of the contras. Shortly after he took office in May, he learnt of the airstrip near El Murciélago and informed Ambassador Tambs that it was not to be used. Despite threats from Lt.Col Oliver North that he would cut off aid to Costa Rica, Arias publicly announced the 'discovery' of the airstrip and had it closed by the Costa Rican security forces. Although Tambs reportedly twice urged him to reopen it, Arias remained firm.

Arias also gained some breathing space from the withdrawal of Eden Pastora from the armed conflict, leaving the remains of his ARDE forces under the control of the main contra leadership but isolated from its supply lines in Honduras. Although contra activity from within Costa Rica declined, a sizeable force did remain and reportedly received US$10 million of the US$100 million package approved by Congress towards the end of 1986.

But as in 1983, the movement away from strict adherence to the US foreign policy line was accompanied by a hold up in payments by the international agencies. In October 1985 the World Bank delayed US$40 million, citing the exceeding of public expenditure targets, while the IMF retained US$20 million and USAID US$30 million, citing technical reasons due to the fall in oil prices and the gains in coffee.

Just as on his foreign policy Arias was carrying out a balancing act between the Costa Rican general desire for regional peace (as evidenced by the elections) and the US demand for support for the contras, so on his economic policy he was caught between the demands of the international lending agencies and the protests of the people on whom they fell. The top priority was once again the acceptance of a letter of intent by the IMF and further public spending cutbacks as a preliminary to the urgent necessity of rescheduling the repayments postponed by Monge. Arias had campaigned on a platform of greater stability and growth, increased employment and action to tackle the housing shortage, but the IMF, World Bank and USAID between them demanded a further reduction of the government deficit to 1 per cent of the GDP, the abolition of a 12 per cent import duty, further increases in the cost of government services and sales taxes, the ending of subsidies to grain farmers, a cut of 5,000 in public sector employment and the ending of all control over the credit policies of the private banks. In short, more of the same.

Arias began to confront the same problems as Monge. Control of government expenditure again proved impossible. In particular, the financial deficit of the Central Bank was soaring out of control as a result of the USAID enforced exchange control liberalisation in 1984. To help reduce the deficit, the Arias government continued the trend started by Monge of shifting the burden of taxation from business groups to middle income consumers by extending the range of taxable goods almost to its limit. In January 1987, the government introduced a range of new consumption taxes, including ones on luxury housing and car ownership, in an effort to raise revenue and fund a substantial decrease in company taxes demanded by the Chambers of Commerce.

Promised social programmes once again were difficult to implement. Arias' campaign pledge to complete 80,000 new houses by 1990 was soon revised to include rehabilitation and extension of dwellings. Invasions of empty lands by squatters continued to be widespread, and demonstrations against declining water, transport and electrical services increased.

However, it was the effect of cutting subsidies to producers of corn, rice and beans that promoted the first successful resistance to the externally-imposed policies. Once again it came from small farmers. Cutbacks in rice subsidies had led to a situation by the end of 1985 where the cost of milling rice exceeded its retail price, or so the processors claimed in initiating a suspension of payments to growers. The growers, denied cash and therefore credit for new plantings, mounted a campaign of demonstrations and roadblocks. The processors received concessions. When the further subsidy cutbacks demanded by the IMF were applied in July 1986, grain producers again blocked roads, which the government cleared with the help of the Civil Guard. On 17 September a demonstration in San José was organised by small farmers, corn growers and members of the Atlantic Small Producers Union, who protested against the elimination of the subsidies and imports of US-subsidised corn into Costa Rica as a result of the IMF measures. More than 20 people were arrested and 40 injured by the US-trained anti-riot police amidst the worst scenes of violence seen since 1948.

In the wake of public outrage, and resignation threats by the protectionist Minister of Agriculture, Alberto Esquivel, the subsidies were reintroduced in October, along with other concessions. The World Bank, accordingly, suspended payment of US$26 million. But this was the pro-subsidies faction's last victory. Following the completion of the draft agreement with the IMF in March 1987, the hard-line Central Bank President Eduardo Lizano, who had been increasingly at odds with the Agriculture Ministry, resigned. With

208

rescheduling talks pending, the attacks launched on him by his former opponents after his departure caused such embarrassment that he was recalled the following month, while Esquivel was sacked in favour of a more IMF-minded replacement favouring the ending of subsidies. Lizano's victory confirmed the definite shift in the Costa Rican economy away from an import-substitution model towards a much greater reliance on exports, a process which Monge had initiated and Arias continued.

The tax reform package and reduction in subsidies were essential measures to comply with the demands set by the IMF, whose agreement was in turn essential for Costa Rica's foreign creditors to agree to a rescheduling of the debt. Since mid-1986 Costa Rica had, in a 'friendly and non-confrontational moratorium' in the words of Lizano, made no repayments of principal on its foreign debt, and limited interest payments to 4 per cent of export earnings, equivalent to about US$5 million a month. In addition, in October 1986 the government submitted a proposal to the Steering Committee of the foreign banks which called for repayment of principal over 25 years with a period of grace of seven years, lower interest rates and payments to be pegged to GDP growth. The banks rejected the proposal and insisted on a prior agreement with the IMF.

In July the following year, the Steering Committee again rejected a similar plan, despite similarities with proposals which had recently been submitted by Argentina and Mexico and accepted by the banks. While some saw the decision as evidence of the banks' displeasure at Costa Rica's unilateral reduction in interest payments, others speculated that the dark hand of Washington was behind it. In general, Arias' more principled opposition to both the contras' presence and Reagan's Central American policy led to less favourable treatment at the hands of the Reagan administration and the IFIs.

In 1986 when Arias arrived, Costa Rica received 29.6 per cent of the US aid to four Central American countries (El Salvador, Honduras, Guatemala and Costa Rica), but in 1987 this figure dropped to 19.1 per cent. In 1987 as Arias began to take a high international profile with his Peace Plan for Central America, USAID held up a crucial US$120 million of aid until September, while the IMF held back a US$55 million stand-by loan and insisted on further reductions in the budget and fiscal deficit. Government officials complained that in sharp contrast to the Monge period, Washington support during negotiations with the IFIs was virtually absent. As the Guatemala-based weekly, *This Week*, of 27 July 1987 expressed it, 'During the cosy Monge era, when rollover talks with the commercial banks seemed stymied, Costa Rican officials used to call for help to AID chief Daniel

Chaij. Not infrequently cabinet-level officials travelled to Washington to talk directly to White House officials or top level IMF personalities. But political favours can no longer be sought from Washington.'

Conclusion: Who Paid?

Between 1982 and 1987 the burden of the debt crisis became a burden of austerity. Wealth was redistributed from consumers towards national large-scale exporters and multinational investors. By 1985 standards of living and real wages of the average Costa Rican had still not regained their 1979 levels. (see box p.211) Falling incomes were mainly suffered by wage earners, especially state employees, who had a margin of consumption which they could be called upon to sacrifice in the national interest. At the same time, prices of the basic services provided by the state and the essential goods subsidised by it multiplied, sometimes, as in the case of electricity prices, beyond the level which the population could tolerate.

With the reduction in food subsidies, between May 1982 and August 1986 the retail price of such staples as white maize increased by 130 per cent, rice by 100 per cent and beans by 164 per cent. The sharp increases were also due to the fact that the National Production Council, which regulated basic grain prices, had to close down some of its watchdog functions and turn them over to private business, as a result of pressure from the IFIs. Smaller producers could no longer rely on the government to pay them a set price and had to compete with larger producers who could underprice them with their greater access to capital and technology. In general, small and medium-sized basic grain producers suffered badly from government measures to promote non-traditional agricultural exports in order to generate more foreign exchange to pay off the debt. While favourable terms were offered to producers of the non-traditionals, limits were imposed on the amount of land used for basic grains.

But it would be illusory to conclude that the burden of austerity was borne only by those who were required to pay for it in monetary terms through increased taxes and prices, or reduced subsidies. The social wage, extended over 30 years of development of the welfare state, used to account for some 80 per cent of basic necessities and it was this sector on which the government axe fell. Education, health, social security and housing, which between them accounted for 54.3 per cent of government spending in 1979, represented only 41.5 per cent in 1984, the share of education falling by a fifth and health by a third.(see table 9.4) There were visible signs of the effects of the cuts; by 1987,

Squeezing the Working Class Average Wages, 1979-85*			
Year	Average Wage	Price Index	Index of Real Wages
1979	1737	100	100
1980	1983	119	96
1981	2301	163	81
1982	3255	325	58
1983	5309	409	75
1984	6703	458	84
1985	8176	525	89

*Colones/month, July of each year, except 1984 (average of March & November). **Source:** Director General of Statistics and Censuses, quoted in CEPAS, *Balance de la Situación*, No.18 (Oct-Dec 1986) p.17.

As the table shows, workers received a massive cut in their real wages as the austerity measures came into full effect in 1982. A main plank of the austerity programme was the wage control mechanism first introduced by Monge in January 1983. Pay increases were determined twice yearly by reference to increases in the price of a 'basic wage basket' of 18 necessities. This index consistently lagged behind both the general index of consumer prices and that of an already established basket of nutritional necessities comprising 39 items, only eleven of which were represented in the wages index. Its application at six-monthly intervals ensured a time lag before wages caught up with the last round of price rises.

Arias introduced a new wage adjustment mechanism. The small wages index was replaced by an index of 158 goods as the unions had long demanded, but increases were only granted when this index rose above 7 per cent. The capacity of unions to protect living standards was also restricted by the Arias government's announcement that no new collective bargaining agreements would be concluded in the public sector, and that those already in force would be subordinated to overall budgetary control.

the education system lacked 42,000 places, and many buildings were in extreme disrepair, while the rate of matriculation to university was falling sharply as expenditure cutbacks led to staff reductions. At the end of 1986, the rector of the University of Costa Rica criticised the government tendency to privatise higher education, thereby making it a privilege of the elite. Also, due to budget cuts the same university was forced to reduce its staff by 400 while raising tuition costs.

Epidemic and malnutrition-related diseases were reappearing, while figures for hepatitis in 1986 were the worst for 23 years. At the same time, partly because of cash shortages, by 1987 the housing deficit was approaching 300,000 dwellings. There was also no solution

Table 9.4

Proportion of Government Expenditure on Social Services, 1978-84

	1978	1979	1980	1981	1982	1983	1984
Total (%)	52.0	54.3	52.5	45.2	41.0	40.3	41.5
Education	16.0	15.5	15.3	15.4	13.8	12.3	12.6
Health	24.8	26.5	25.7	21.1	18.3	17.4	17.6
Social Security	8.9	9.7	8.0	6.7	7.2	6.9	8.7
Housing	2.3	2.6	3.5	2.0	1.7	2.7	2.6

Source: Cameron Duncan, *IMF Conditionality, Fiscal Policy and the Distribution of Income in Costa Rica*, unpublished thesis, Dept. of Economics, American University, Washington DC, quoted in CEPAS, *Balance de la Situación*, No.16 (Jun-Jul 1986), p.12.

in sight for the large number of landless peasants, which amounted to 10,400 families in 1978 — even before the economic crisis of the 1980s brought with it rapidly rising rural unemployment. In 1983 the Office of Technical Services to the legislative assembly had concluded that since 67 per cent of the cultivable land was in the hands of a few landowners (dating back from the concentration of land in the nineteenth century in the hands of the coffee and banana growers), the only solution was land redistribution. However, landowners were unwilling to surrender available land and no funds were available to open up inaccessible virgin land on the northern and southern borders. While national levels of unemployment had declined from a peak of 8.5 per cent in 1983 to 6 per cent in 1986, many rural workers were still being forced to join the ranks of the self-employed in personal services like domestic and odd job work.

The slow erosion of the welfare state brought with it disturbing political implications, since it was on the basis of benign paternalism that both Costa Rican democracy and the PLN had flourished since 1948. As its progressive critics frequently pointed out, the economic policies of the PLN since 1982 were not only largely contradictory to its historical practice, but also largely borrowed from the conservative opposition. This in part reflected the political ascendency within the PLN of a younger generation, headed by President Arias and much influenced by the philosophies of the US business schools where they studied, over the old-guard, more reformist wing of the party.

The traditional political foundation of the republic as a pluralist and non-violent society also came into question as the government increasingly relied on the use of its security forces as a means of repressing popular discontent by evicting squatters, and dispersing protest marches and demonstrations. At the same time the Civil and Rural Guard, originally kept strictly separate to limit their political influence, were brought under unified control as part of a US-inspired 'professionalisation' plan which also involved increased training and a larger provision of arms. The unions had their traditional freedom of action increasingly circumscribed by wage control legislation (see box p.211) and government use of the courts to control strikes. Increasingly they began to turn to hunger strikes as a last resort. All these developments are common enough in the rest of the region, but Costa Rica had long prided itself upon their absence.

A complete break with the political legacy of 1948 was only a threat, but in the economic sphere it was already a reality. The traditional commodity exports were affected by falling prices and output; the regional market for industrial goods was in recession, and although Costa Rica ran a trade surplus, its partners, with debt problems of their own, frequently defaulted. The PLN governments' preferred solution was a shift in emphasis towards non-traditional exports which favoured multinationals setting up assembly operations (the fastest industrial growth area) but did little to aid established, import substitution, industries which were threatened by the reduction in external tariffs and whose market was reduced by the demand restriction measures intended to reduce labour costs. Although new agricultural exports such as vegetables and flowers were growing at a fast rate, they still contributed under five per cent of total exports and did not offer the prospect of generating living standards comparable to those of the recent past.

Within the chamber of industry, wholehearted support for the government/IMF policies was only forthcoming from large enterprises, five-sixths of which exported a fair proportion of their output. This was true of only a quarter of small firms, who lacked the capital to adjust to, let alone take advantage of, the new emphasis on exports. The shift within the chamber of industry mirrored a redistribution of resources towards larger, export-oriented enterprises. A similar change of emphasis also occurred in farmers' organisations such as UPANACIONAL, whose acknowledgement of the future needs of small farmers was in doubt.

State spending, the traditional engine of growth, came under continual IMF pressure, and was hard pressed to maintain a level of welfare provision at anything like the level the population had come to expect. At the same time Costa Rica had clearly compromised its capacity to form its own economic policies by allowing the World Bank, the IMF and USAID to dictate economic priorities. Budgetary control was now by the IMF, while the regulation traditionally

213

Table 9.5			
Net Capital Transfers, 1983-85 (US$m)			
	Inflows	**Outflows**	**Net Position**
1983	624.5	744.7	−120.2
1984	350.2	374.6	−24.4
1985	334.2	573.9	−239.7

Source: Republic of Costa Rica, Information memorandum, September 1986.

exercised by the state over a wide range of areas from credit and foreign exchange to tariffs and industrialisation policy was in the process of being removed, to be replaced by the operation of market forces which would further benefit the multinationals. Most notable — but least publicised — of the changes demanded by the IFIs in the financial sector was the substantial reduction in the role of the Central Bank in the economy in favour of private banks. By 1987 the Central Bank had less control over credit policy and setting interest rates, and was no longer the only channel for, or recipient of, foreign exchange or aid, thus breaking a tradition of 30 years since the banks were first nationalised in 1948. Dollar inflows were paid directly to private institutions in *colones*, bypassing the Central Bank. The Bank was then forced to purchase foreign exchange at a later date to meet debt repayments, the losses running in proportion to the devaluation of the *colon*, and worsening the fiscal deficit.

While the resources to finance further development and maintain spending on the welfare state dwindled, until May 1986 Costa Rica maintained its debt repayments. Despite massive inflows of dollars, between 1983 and 1985 the country became a net capital exporter (see table 9.5), while between 1979 and 1984 private dollar deposits in the US by Costa Ricans grew from US$203 million to US$528 million.

Already a hostage to the demands of USAID, the future held out the prospect of increasing dependence on the US for markets for new products and on US companies for the investment to make them. Costa Rica was also still highly dependent on the good will of Washington for bailing out the economy with large hand-outs of aid.

However great Costa Rica's debt problems may have appeared to Costa Ricans, in international terms they were insignificant. Although it was one of the most indebted nations — in per capita terms — in Latin America, its debt represented only 1.5 per cent of the total Latin American debt. By itself, therefore, it had little hope of winning exceptional terms from the international banks. Any hope based on the establishment of a new international economic order was equally founded on circumstances over which it had no control.

The best possibility for Costa Rica to establish a measure of control rested on a solution to the regional conflict, which could ease the political and economic constraints imposed by the Reagan administration. In this light, the new peace plan launched by President Arias in March 1987, and endorsed by the Central American Presidents in August 1987, represented not only a sincere desire to achieve peace in the region but also a desperate attempt to prevent a prosperous, peaceful and democratic Costa Rica becoming nothing more than a memory.

10. Sentenced to Debt

'There are no such things as technical formulas [...] When a family has an income of US$50 a month, spends US$100, needs US$200, and owes US$1,000, I'd like to know what technical formula can solve that problem. Well, in fact there is a technical formula — very technical — and that is to cancel the US$1,000 debt and give the family the US$200 they need.'
Fidel Castro to the Fourth Congress of the Latin American Federation of Journalists, 6 July 1986.

Since the debt crisis first emerged into Western consciousness in 1982, economists, journalists, politicians and lawyers across the world have all bent their minds to working out an answer. Within two years, one banker claimed to be carrying 200 solutions in his briefcase. Felix Rohatyn, the financier who saved New York from bankruptcy, had his proposals ready in 1983, based on the creation of an international agency to buy up bank debt and convert it into long-term bonds. Anthony Solomon of the New York Federal Reserve Board proposed an interest rate cap in 1984 (see chapter six), only to see it rejected by the banks. Britain's Lord Lever, a former Labour party adviser, chairing a group of Commonwealth experts, came up with others.(see box p.217)

The emergence of debt-equity swaps as a strategy favoured by the banks inspired a host of less self-serving imitations. Environmentalists have argued for debt-environment swaps, preserving Latin America's threatened jungles. (see box p.219) UNICEF has argued for a debt-child survival swap. The IDB has suggested debt-development swaps. The problem with this proliferation of solutions has never been a lack of technical ingenuity. The problem has been a lack of political will within the OECD to find a long-term solution — a solution made all the more urgent by events on Black Monday.

216

Debt Remedies

Transferring Real Resources?

Through IMF soft loans:

- The IMF Compensatory Financing Facility could be expanded to cover the entire cost of falling export revenues caused by external shocks, providing loans over and above the level of the debtor's own quota, the present limit [Brandt, Lever, Fabian Society].
- IMF conditionality should generally be loosened, not tightened [Fabian Society].
- Unconditional loans to developing countries could be increased through an increase in Special Drawing Rights [Fabian Society].
- New IMF loans might be financed through additional levies on members, or by floating loans on financial markets — the latter solution limiting the concessions which could be made in lower interest rates on soft loans.

Through increased World Bank loans:

- The Baker solution, perhaps expanded, perhaps with less rigid conditionality. A key issue here is whether funds would be provided by OECD countries or whether they would be raised by the World Bank itself on international capital markets, and thus tied to market interest rates even when set at a lower level [Lever].

Through co-financing between World Bank and commercial banks, or commercial banks loaning out World Bank-guaranteed loans: [The David Rockefeller solution.]

Debt 'Forgiveness'?

Just the interest payments?

- For low income countries only? The Lawson solution for Africa in which existing loans are converted into grants, in other words written off, rejected by US and West German governments in 1987.
- For official loans only?
  Similar to the Lawson proposals.
- Through an interest rate cap:
  This would set a ceiling on the level of interest paid by Third World debtors:
  — perhaps an absolute ceiling [Fabian Society]
  — perhaps a fixed rate financed by the creation by Western governments of an interest compensatory fund [as proposed by Mr Herrhausen, a leading German banker]
  — perhaps a fixed percentage of relief over a certain period [3 per cent for a year, in the Bradley Plan]

> — perhaps a ceiling on current payments, with the bulk of unpaid interest capitalised, i.e. added to the existing principal (though this is hardly real forgiveness) [New York Federal Reserve Board, 1984].

- By limiting interest payments to a certain percentage of exports: the Alan García solution, also supported by the Socialist International.
- By replacing debt at current market interest rates with long-term low interest bonds: The New York model solution, first proposed by Felix Rohatyn, or the Pereira solution proposed by Brazilian Finance Minister Bresser Pereira in September 1987 (see chapter six).
- Interest-development swaps: proposed by Sr Ortiz Mena, President of the IDB. Part of the interest on foreign debt would be deposited in local currency by the debtor, in an escrow account, administered by the IDB. The funds would be used for productive expenditure within the country, monitored by the IDB.

The principal?

- Debt-equity swaps: (see chapter six) [Chairman of Citicorp John Reed; Nigel Lawson].
- Debt-environment swaps: (see box p.219)
- Debt-child survival swaps: [UNICEF].
- Existing bank debt revalued at secondary market levels: i.e. Brazil's as 55 per cent of US$110 billion, Bolivia's as 22 per cent of US$3.8 billion [Milton Friedman, Bresser Pereira].

Sources: GATT-Fly, *Debt Bondage or Self Reliance?*, 1985; Fabian Society, *The Debt Crisis: the Third World and British Banks*, London, 1987; S. Griffith-Jones, 'Bargaining in the Debt Crisis', *mimeo*, 1987.

Black Monday

'Today's news is that the New York Stock Exchange has tumbled [...] this Monday has shown just how fragile is a system founded on injustice and inequality, and the obligations on nationalists around the world to act with foresight. We must not now repeat the error of 1930, when every Latin American country thought it could obtain a better individual agreement through bilateral negotiations with an unstable international system. We must understand what today is obvious: there will be no economic recovery, except under a more just international economic and monetary system.'

Alan García, preface to *El Futuro Diferente*, Second Edition, Andina, Lima 1987.

The castles in the air on which, for sixteen years, the world busily constructed its increasingly integrated world economy, began to disintegrate on 19 October 1987. On that Black Monday the world's stock markets suddenly woke up to the fact that nothing was holding them in place.

218

A Ransom for the Amazon — Swapping Debt for Trees

In twenty years the forests of the tropics will be stripped largely bare unless Third World countries slow their ravenous logging and mining. Many species of plants and animals will die in 'the greatest extinction since the end of the age of the dinosaurs,' says Harvard biologist E.O. Wilson. But biology lectures carry little clout with countries desperate for cash to pay huge foreign debts. Now US environmental groups are making an imaginative offer to Third World governments: we'll pay your debts if you'll spare your trees.

It's not a cure for the world's debt or deforestation problems, but the notion makes economic sense. Conservation International, a Washington organisation, struck the first big deal last month. It will buy US$650,000 of Bolivia's US$4 billion external debt at a discounted price of US$100,000 from banks eager to dump the largely uncollectable loans. In exchange, Bolivia will set aside 3.7 million acres of Amazon river country adjacent to the existing Beni Biosphere Reserve, home to endangered species of plants and animals. The Bolivians will retain ownership and management of the land. Costa Rica is financing its Guanacaste National park with a similar deal, and Ecuador announced it too seeks foreign benefactors. A new resolution introduced in the US Congress encourages lending institutions such as the World Bank to let poor countries suspend loan payments if they protect tropical forests. 'We've just begun to scratch the surface,' says Thomas Lovejoy of the World Wildlife Fund.

As the debt crisis intensifies, bankers are more willing to trade their bad debts for investments in developing nations — but hotels and factories are more what they have in mind. Swapping for national parks 'will only work where the banks have written the debt down to next to nothing and can claim some real benefits from a tax or political perspective,' says Gary Caesar of the BankAmerica Corp. Otherwise, the bank's shareholders might object. Caesar thinks Bolivia was the perfect charity case. Its debts have been discounted to 10 to 15 cents on the dollar since its economy collapsed in the early '80s from low tin prices and high inflation. By contrast, Brazil's debt goes for 60 cents on the dollar, raising the cost of a tree's ransom.

Environmentalists face a tough sell convincing the countries with ambitious development plans that could be hampered by restrictions on land use. Lovejoy argues that nations ought to 'protect their biological capital' since the tremendous diversity of life in these virgin tracts may be invaluable in the future to genetic engineers searching for new drugs and crops. Brazil, which holds Third World records for both debt and deforestation, is committed to a vast scheme for dams and highways in Amazonia.

Newsweek, 10 August 1987.

Table 10.1
The Underlying Imbalances in the World Economy,
Deficits and Surpluses on Current Accounts, 1985-88 (US$ billion)

	1985	1986	1987*	1988*
United States	−117.7	−140.6	−155.0	−135.0
Japan	+49.2	+86.0	+82.0	+70.0
West Germany	+15.1	+37.1	+35.0	+25.0

*Forecast.
Source: 'The International Economy', *Barclays Bank Review*, November 1987.

The essential cause was the collapse of another band-aid. By the beginning of 1987, Japanese investors began to show increasing reluctance to fund the US trade and budget deficits, leading to a collapse in the bond market. The OECD powers stepped into the breach, sending their Central Banks to buy dollars on the open market — in theory, to keep the price of the dollar level, but in practice, to help fund the US financial gap by some US$90 billion, as they had throughout the late 1960s when the crisis of US hegemony began. This new band-aid was formalised in the Louvre agreement, signed on 22 February 1987.[1]

In October, Secretary James Baker announced that it was not enough: West Germany and Japan would have to take rapid steps to expand their own consumer markets, to suck in more US exports and so cure the underlying imbalances in the world economy.(see table 10.1) Otherwise, the dollar would be allowed to slide, which would hurt their exports, and those of other countries, triggering depression outside the US. The stock markets recognised a point of no return, and within days had wiped 22.5 per cent, or nearly US$1 trillion, off US share prices — equivalent to the entire value of all Third World debts. British shareholders lost £150 billion, more than the individual debts of Mexico or Brazil.[2] By December, the fall in share prices had reached 30 per cent.

Latin American debt only contributed indirectly to this new debacle, but the uncertainty surrounding future Latin American payments to the banks nonetheless figured in stock market calculations. To attract the funds needed by the US economy, the Federal Reserve Board announced a new rise in US interest rates in September, quickly followed by similar announcements on the part of US major banks, whose prime rate reached 9.25 per cent.[3] That increase, combined with others earlier in the year, would have added US$2 billion to the interest payments due from Third World debtors: a jolt which the stock market took badly, rightly looking at the difficulties bankers were having with Brazil.

The Vampire Solution

Black Monday thus brought the West's debt crisis to the end of a chapter. The band-aid solution put in place back in 1982 had assumed that the world economy was safe as long as Latin America kept paying interest on the banks' paper mountain of non-existent assets created by the combined effect of the dance of the millions and the Reagan hike in interest rates. Given this essential plank, the rest of the world economy was in good enough shape to ensure growth in OECD country imports from Latin America to allow it to keep repaying the debt.

These assumptions masked a sophisticated juggling exercise, of the kind which OECD governments and World Bank economists were quick to condemn when used by Latin American governments in 1982. In fact, the US economy was no longer able to export enough to pay for its own consumption, or to earn enough on its overseas investment to plug its growing trade deficits. Essentially, it was now dependent on a continuous flow of funds into the US economy, some of them from Latin American interest payments, much more from loans and direct investment in the US economy on the part of the British, West Germans and Japanese.

The foundations of the post-war world economy had shifted. In the days of Bretton Woods, the US was a net exporter of capital with investments strung across the globe. The days of the band-aid solution turned it into a net importer, with increasing debt obligations of its own, giving rise to a growing preoccupation with the US economy's ability to sustain its own interest rate burden. These worries intensified as the weight of US investment abroad (generating profits on behalf of the US economy) was increasingly outstripped by the weight of foreign investment in the US (generating profits for other countries).(see table 10.2) Yet the US remained the world's Central Bank, coiner of the' world's trading currency, and the most important market for OECD exports. The dangers in this situation were clearly apparent to British bankers in 1979 — well before Black Monday, and before the debt crisis broke in 1982.[4]

Within the overall juggling exercise which sustained the unsustainable situation during the 1980s, the band-aid solution played a small but important part, shoring up Western banks whose collapse could have triggered a general crisis of confidence. The band-aid forced Latin Americans to keep up interest payments on debts whose

221

Table 10.2
The Growing Burden of US Obligations on Foreign Investments,*
1982-86 (US$ billion)

1982	+136.2
1983	+88.5
1984	+4.4
1985	−107.4
1986	−232.0

*US assets abroad less foreign assets in US at year-end.
Source: R. Dornbusch, 'External Balance Correction: Depreciation or Protection?', *Brookings Papers on Economic Activity*, 1:1987.

absolute size jumped by 50 per cent after the introduction of higher interest rates in 1981 — interest rates geared higher precisely to protect the flow of funds into the US economy. They achieved their purpose, nearly doubling foreign assets in the US within four years, from US$500 billion in 1980 to US$926 billion in 1984.[5]

US banks were thus presented with a premium of undeserved and unanticipated income from Third World debtors. This extra income was, in fact, one of the crucial props in the elaborate edifice of 'confidence' in the world economy which OECD governments were nailing in place, with the help of an artificial boom in the US, and artificial depression elsewhere. This extraordinary levy on the poor of other countries also helped the US banks to survive a rash of bad debts in the US energy and agricultural sectors, which might otherwise have generated an uncontainable banking crisis, and brought both the US boom and the continued prosperity of the global economy to a premature close.

The rich of Latin America accepted this arrangement, both because they were genuinely afraid of the consequences of a financial collapse, and because they were the least affected in the region. Many of them acquired a stake in the US economy, through bank deposits earning interest in New York, or other investments in property, or increased holdings of US Treasury bonds. By 1985, the total assets owned by Latin American and Caribbean private citizens in the US amounted to US$200.3 billion — compared with the equivalent liabilities on their part to the US banks of US$208.4 billion.[6]

Black Monday showed the sacrifice of the poor for what it was: economically irrelevant, because the solution did nothing to restrain the madness of an integrated world economy tying its future growth to the unearned consumption of a single country, and unneccessary, because the total debt in whose name the poor had been sacrificed amounted to the gains made by speculators on the world's stock market in a single year.

Solutions in a Crumbling World?

'If recession is to be avoided, and the world's surplus savings to be used wisely, lending to developing countries needs to be restored. If the indebted countries and the banks are left to solve the problem on their own, a satisfactory solution looks impossible.'
Editorial in the *Financial Times*, 1 December 1987

Morally speaking, Black Monday left the real victims and heroes of the debt crisis clearly defined. Practically speaking, it was a watershed, but one whose impact was difficult to predict. Latin America's immediate prospects of survival worsened, thanks to the almost inevitable contraction of their best export market, the US. US protectionism, already troubling Brazil (see box p.224), was now bound to be used with increasing vigour against all those countries whose exports the US could not hold at bay by devaluing the dollar. Interest rates were also likely to rise. The US still desperately needed foreign finance, and foreign investors would need higher interest rates in compensation for the dollars which the Reagan administration was pushing ever further downwards, in its desperate attempts to avoid a slump before the November 1988 presidential elections.

In the long run, the real question now became whether the OECD countries were capable of organising a global solution, or whether their internal power battles would bring the world's economy crumbling down first. OECD governments themselves faced the threat of a new Great Depression, making the ten-year-old logic of recycling attractive once again. They were caught in a structural dead-end. The weight of the US consumer market in the integrated world economy on which industrial development in the 1970s and 1980s was based, made it difficult to replace, even if Japan and West Germany set about expanding their own economies. The US economy accounts for 40 per cent of the combined GDP of the 24 OECD nations, and Japan for a relatively insignificant 14 per cent. Furthermore, the Japanese and West German economies were historically geared to export in a fashion which made it relatively difficult for them to organise an international consumer boom.[7]

After Black Monday, financial analysts in the Western press could be heard to mutter that if the debt crisis could only be resolved, there was much to be said for a transfer of resources to the Third World, which could then provide a timely market for OECD exports,

---

US Protectionism Hits Brazil

Following the recent reemergence of the trade dispute between Brazil and the US over the computer industry, Brazilians have been totting up the accumulated effect of protectionism in the US since the debt crisis broke in 1982.

That year, US companies initiated 18 separate proceedings for government relief against imports from Brazil. The affected products included steel, leather goods, orange juice and aircraft.

By mid-1984, Brazil had lost US$44 million worth of sales in textiles, US$22 million in footwear, and US$30 million in steel.

Between 1984 and end-1986, as a result of further restrictions, voluntary and involuntary, Brazil's overall exports to the US fell by US$932.8 million.

Though in all cases it has been US companies which claimed to be harmed by the evolution of bilateral trade, it is interesting to note that in the same period, US exports to Brazil increased by US$1,226 million.

Latin American Weekly Report, 29 October 1987.

---

particularly those of the US, thus saving the world from a slump. 'Debt relief for the less developed countries,' commented one such expert wistfully, 'would do wonders for American exporters in the markets they are best able to supply.'[8] By the end of 1987 however, this solution was still a shadow on the horizon. Two essential preconditions would have to be met before it was put in place: some domestic Western solution, to persuade the banks to write off their mountain of uncollectable debt, perhaps through tax concessions; and some general agreement to transfer money to the Third World. Both faced a stumbling block in the US government.

Towards the end of the year, the European financial press was clearly talking itself into a position where the revaluation of Latin American debt in line with the secondary market was acceptable, in combination with hefty government tax relief on Third World debts for the banks.[9] The British government had accepted their arguments, allowing the UK banks to claim tax relief on 80-90 per cent of their 1987 loan loss provision, at a cost to the British taxpayer of an estimated US$850 million in the first half of 1987 alone.[10] Baker's abrupt rejection of the Pereira solution proposed by Brazil in September showed that the US government was still reluctant to take any such step.

Still more depressing from the Latin American point of view, was the persistence with which governments and bankers looked to satisfy the Third World's desperate need for new financial resources by raising funds on the world's capital markets, even when they chose a multilateral institution like the IMF or World Bank as the appropriate agent of transfer. The implication was that this new money would have to be paid for at interest rates close to the market rate, at worst piling debt on debt, at best leaving open the possibility of another edition of the recycling fable.

The recalcitrance of the Reagan administration had its roots in a combination of peculiarly US problems. Banks have been politically unpopular in the US since the massive foreclosures on farm land in the 1930s. US governments are traditionally loath to take any public measures amounting to bailing them out, the more so under an administration ideologically opposed to any public intervention at all. The original band-aid solution was in part an attractive political fudge: Third World countries were pressured into bailing out the banks to save the US government's face. Following Black Monday, the Reagan administration was faced with implementing drastic cuts in government spending to satisfy the world's stock exchanges. The political cost of tax concessions to the banks accordingly rose sharply.

Furthermore — a constant headache throughout the debt crisis — the US itself was now in no position to finance a second Marshall Plan. In principle, Japan and West Germany, the two surplus countries, had sufficient funds available to transform the position of the Third World. In practice, the US has consistently set its face against restructuring the finances of any multilateral agency in any way which would challenge US control. Control of the IMF and other multilateral agencies depends on the relative weight of US financial contributions compared to those of other countries. Latin American proposals to seek increased funds for the IDB from the Europeans and East Asians came to grief on the US rock in 1982.[11] This conundrum dogged attempts to solve the world's trading problems by raising contributions to the IMF from the time of the 1979 OPEC crisis, and the Reagan administration agreed to a general rise in subscriptions only in the wake of the Mexican crisis of 1982, when it had no alternative.

The existence of this constraint helps to explain the durable popularity of compromise solutions to the debt crisis which involve the IMF and the World Bank raising additional funds on the world's commercial financial markets. While ruling out any solution to Third World needs through the obvious mechanism of cheap government loans and grants, which would minimise the repayment burden, they avoid the delicate question of who contributes what to the IFIs, and what power each country could expect in return.

By December 1987, the real financial squeeze on the US's role in IFIs was evident, with the US behind not only in its payments to the

UN (always unpopular in Congress), but even to the organisation of the OECD itself.[12]

Old and New Baker Plans

Faced with a trade deficit with Latin America running at US$37 billion a year in place of its traditional trade surplus (see table 10.3), the US might be thought to have good reasons for seeking an end to debt-linked adjustment, particularly since US$37 billion represented no less than 30 per cent of the US trade deficit in 1985. Over the Third World as a whole, with the trade deficit in excess of US$50 billion, the arguments were even more compelling. By 1986, the US Overseas Development Council estimated that the country had already lost 1.6 million jobs due to debt-linked recession in the Third World.[13]

In practice, the Reagan administration's own preferred solution has not been as self-destructive as it seems at first sight. It is based upon a fairly explicit trade-off between short-term trade imbalances with Latin America, and the long-term benefits of using increased economic leverage in the region to force the removal of existing barriers against greater economic dependence on the US. Latin American countries which have financed debt payments by expanding their exports to US consumers, face increasing pressure from the IMF to open up their own economies to US exports and US financial services. This hidden programme was built into the process of rescheduling under the band-aid programme from an early stage (it has a long history in IMF policy, as suggested in chapter three). The Baker Plan changed nothing. It simply transferred responsibility for opening up Latin America from the IMF to the World Bank, as an explicit part of restructuring, with the carrot of additional finance to keep up interest payments and the stick of much longer-term supervision over the results.

Beyond its long-term interest in opening up further opportunities for US exporters and banks in the region, the Reagan administration remained committed throughout 1987 to organising US responses to the debt crisis in line with the perceived needs of US banks. The failure of the Baker Plan to generate any further growth-oriented reschedulings following the 1986 Mexican agreement, caused very little serious concern. Openly critical of Citicorp's intransigence in the Mexican negotiations, US Treasury Secretary James Baker nonetheless gave wholehearted support to Citicorp's adoption of a menu of options, and particularly to debt-equity swaps: as well he might, since debt-equity swaps are an obvious extension of the principles of restructuring and can only strengthen US interests in

Table 10.3
US Trade Balance with Latin America, 1975-85
(US$ billion in current dollars)

	1975	1980	1983	1984	1985
US exports to LA	15.7	36.0	22.6	26.3	27.9
US imports from LA	11.8	30.0	35.7	42.3	43.4
Merchandise Trade Balance	+0.6	−4.6	−29.9	−38.1	−37.6

Source: Statistical Abstract of the United States, 1987, US Department of Commerce, Washington DC, 1986.

Latin America. Both were adopted as part of an updated version of the Baker Plan.

Given the banks' reluctance to provide new money, and their explicit demands for greater government finance to developing countries to take up the slack, towards the end of 1987 the US government began to consider further funding for both the World Bank and the IMF. Government budgets did not need to be tapped: the proposed additional US$80 billion could be raised by floating long-term bonds on the world's financial markets. The IMF was allowed to return to its old OPEC-era practice of providing soft conditionality loans to the poorest countries faced with external shocks, such as declining commodity prices or new peaks in interest rates (which the US policy of devaluing the dollar would certainly bring in its train). But the US government itself made no contribution to the US$8.4 billion fund set up for this purpose, citing budgetary constraints, even though the IMF, too, was to be lent its new funds at commercial interest rates. All these measures left the Reagan administration's restructuring programme firmly in place, with the World Bank playing an ever-more-important role in any new crisis. They also fell far short of a new Marshall Plan.

Before the New Year, US banks offered Mexico a new twist to their menu of options, with significant benefits both for themselves and for the US government deficit. Mexico would exchange current debt for 20-year bonds, at the ratio of US$1 in bonds to US$1.30 in old debt. The principal on these bonds, though not the interest, would be guaranteed by the US government, with the Mexicans spending US$1.86 billion of their reserves to buy US Treasury bonds, paying no interest now but redeemable in 20 years for US$10 billion. The banks would accept a loss on part of their Mexican debt, roughly equivalent to the 30 per cent loan loss reserves which they had already credited themselves earlier in the year.

In the context of a rapidly worsening world economic scene, the deal simultaneously gave the banks some insurance against default on their existing assets, and found the US government relatively cheap finance for its government deficit. As the *Financial Times* commented, 'It will replace bank debts, which will probably never be repaid, with bonds which will... [The US Treasury] has contrived a solid capital guarantee which will not cost US taxpayers a cent.'[14]

Mexico was an attractive target for these new proposals because of its build-up of substantial foreign exchange reserves over the previous year, out of which they could be financed. The deal has to be seen in part as an attempt by the banks to recapture some of the reserves for which they had provided the finance under the 1987 rescheduling agreement, for national use. Less plausibly, the new package was also offered to Brazil.[15]

What was it worth to the Mexicans? Bankers calculated about US$137 million a year, assuming that the banks were willing to sell Mexico US$13 billion worth of existing debt for US$10 billion in bonds. The figure compared poorly with the US$8.8 billion Mexico paid in interest charges in 1986. But while it made little difference to Mexico's debt problems, the deal did sweeten Mexican-US relations and their continuing negotiations to liberalise trade between the two countries.

The Democrats' Alternative

Congressional opponents of the Reagan administration, particularly the Democrats, have been a source of hope for Latin American debtors since 1985, when Congressman Charles Schumer suggested that between 70-80 per cent of existing bank loans was illegitimate, representing money loaned out since 1979 simply to pay banks back the interest on old loans. Schumer proposed to make this procedure illegal in the case of new loans. Meanwhile, at least in the case of Mexico, one third of the debt should be simply be wiped off the books. The cost should be paid by the banks.[16]

A better indication of the principles which might guide an incoming Democratic president in 1988 is the Bradley Plan, announced by Senator Bill Bradley in Zurich in June 1986. Well aware that IMF austerity policies were not only damaging to Latin America, but also hurting US exporters, Bradley focused on the need to eliminate short-term trade imbalances and radicalise the restructuring process. Bradley proposed a writing down of the value of Third World loans by 3 per cent to the cost of the banks and creditor governments. Interest rates should be cut by three percentage points, though only for a single

228

year. The Baker Plan should be continued, together with all its efforts to fit Latin American countries into a 'restructured' mould. Latin American countries who agreed to introduce economic policies in line with the free market philosophy of the US should be offered a further incentive in terms of a 9 per cent write-off on their debts.[17]

Bradley's proposals are far from generous to Latin America. In the long run, they fit perfectly well with the strategy of using debt as a lever to restore US hegemony in the region. The difference between Bradley and Baker lies essentially in the fact that Bradley is in a hurry — and apparently more willing to accept the imposition of some costs on US banks. In 1986, the Bradley proposals were denounced by Paul Volker, then President of the US Federal Reserve Board, for being entirely unrealistic, because they involved a loss of 6-7 per cent on banks' Latin American assets, or US$12 billion spread over the 24 US majors.[18]

Richard Feinberg of the US Overseas Development Council has suggested a more generous version, involving a 30 per cent write-down of the value of Latin American debts over ten years. He has estimated that this would add a total of US$52 billion to US exports over the decade, and boost US employment by 177,000. But as he warns, 'No improvement in the debt-trade equation that serves to destabilise the US banking system will be in the national interest.'[19] Calculating the room for manoeuvre enjoyed by an incoming president in 1989 is a delicate business. Faced with continuing bank vulnerability, an incumbent president might well feel he could not go much beyond a selective use of the 30 per cent discount implicit in the banks' 1987 loan loss provisions.

Japanese Solutions

Japanese banks had an important stake in the Latin American debt crisis, but nothing like the involvement of the US major banks. The end of the 1970s had seen them mobilising enormous funds for overseas investment, and by 1985, they were beginning to dominate the world's financial markets.(see chapter two above) But although Latin America owed US$22 billion to Japanese banks in 1982, compared to US$53 billion to the US money centre banks and US$17 billion to Britain's 'big four', these loans represented a much lower proportion of the Japanese banks' world loan programme, and only a third of their overall loans to the Third World. Only one Japanese bank made total loans to the region in excess of its total equity — even though the equity level of all Japanese banks, compared to their outstanding loans, was notoriously low.

For Japan, then, the debt crisis was always manageable. US and European regulatory agencies made an attempt, nonetheless, to use Japanese exposure to Third World debt as an excuse to justify forcing them to raise equity levels, in an attempt to limit Japanese competition in other OECD financial markets. In February 1987, Japanese banks took evasive action with the support of the Ministry of Finance, setting up a wholly-owned subsidiary in the Cayman Islands tax haven to act as a government-supported secondary market, buying Japanese bank loans to Mexico at a heavy discount, in order to resell them to Japanese or other investors. The banks' intention was to extend this operation from Mexican debts to Brazilian, and ultimately any troublesome Latin American loans.[20] The unfortunate debtors were expected to receive very little benefit from the discounts, the intention being that they should offer any investor the full face value of the debt in local currency.

With Japanese banks' own Latin American problems thus firmly under control, the Japanese were free to consider making concessions to the US on global funding of the Third World debt burden. Japan's willingness to provide general funds for the Third World was a direct reflection of the extreme pressure being put upon it in 1986 and 1987, to reduce its own trade surpluses and thus relieve the pressure on other OECD countries. Threats were made of deliberate restrictions on markets for Japanese goods in Britain and the US. The long term impact of the decline in the dollar was also worrying Japanese officials, as it promised to make Japanese exports to the US much more expensive in local terms, and US exports around the world much more competitive.

In the course of a visit to Washington in May 1987, Prime Minister Nakasone therefore made an offer to recycle US$20 billion of its trade surplus over three years to developing countries, in addition to US$10 billion already offered to multilateral institutions at the beginning of 1987, and a US$1 billion Japanese contribution to the Mexican agreement of 1986. In terms of the size of Japanese surpluses (see table 10.1), the Nakasone offer was not obviously generous: a total of US$30 billion over three years, US$10 billion a year. Much of it was to come from loans floated on Japanese capital markets. Some funds were to be committed outside Latin America, in Africa and Asia. The Nakasone Plan was clearly *not* a possible solution to the Latin American debt crisis, given that Brazil alone needed around US$8 billion a year in new money just to lift its February 1987 moratorium on interest payments.

Nonetheless, the gesture briefly raised Latin American hopes of additional funds. By mid-1987 these had been dashed. Most of the new money, it seemed, would go to Japan's hinterland in South-East Asia.

230

Japan intended to help the South-East Asian countries prepare an infrastructure which would ease the process of future Japanese investment there, in economies tied to the dollar, from which its multinationals could export to the US when dollar devaluation and trade restrictions made it impossible to continue doing so from Japan itself.[21]

Other Japanese solutions have been mooted, including a Japanese version of the Marshall Plan first proposed by ex-Foreign Minister Saburo Okita in April 1986, of US$125 billion over five years or US$25 billion a year. In detail, however, even the Okita plan would hardly provide a solution to the debt crisis. Of its US$25 billion, US$5 billion would be loans from the Japanese capital market to the IMF, for on-lending to low-income countries with balance of payments problems, thus excluding Latin America entirely. US$10 billion would take the form of government-guaranteed loans from Japanese commercial banks to a Japanese Trust Fund lending to country-specific projects in liaison with the World Bank: their origins in the Japanese capital market would, in practice, tie these closely to current Japanese interest rates, and the choice of recipients would be determined by Japan in line with its own interests. A further US$10 billion would be available in untied credits from Japan's own Export-Import Bank. Even this programme met with criticism from the Japanese government for assuming too great a role for government funding, since the Japanese trade surplus was essentially in private sector hands.[22]

In practice, then, efforts to tap Japan's trade surpluses and so promote a general recycling process to the benefit of Latin American debtors have been severely limited by Japan's own vision of its global interests. Japan's close ties with Third World countries are confined to East Asia. In the 1980s, the Japanese had no ambition to replace the US as the dominant world power, still less to displace US capital in a region which US politicians clearly regarded as their own backyard. Japan's primary concern was the protection of its trading profits in the face of coming attacks.

European Solutions

A global response to the debt crisis should include... new public control over the private international banking system, in exchange for support to private banks as a result of debt relief measures taken by governments. *Global Challenge*

European Social Democrats have gained a reputation for attempting to resolve North-South tensions, especially since the publication of the

Brandt Report of 1979, *Common Crisis* in 1983, and *Global Challenge* in 1985. These have been Opposition documents. Outside Southern Europe, France and the Scandinavian countries, Europe has been dominated by Conservatives throughout the era of the debt crisis.

Until early 1987, these governments gave US management of the debt crisis loyal support. British backing for the band-aid solution has been consistent and often voluble, with the first break in a depressingly consistent pattern visible only in 1987, when, faced with disaster in sub-Saharan Africa, Chancellor Lawson began to urge OECD governments to cut the interest rates they themselves were charging on African debts (directly challenging the US view that even government loans must be directly tied to the rates prevailing in commercial markets). The silence of the West German government under Chancellor Kohl has been even more impressive, given the fact that Germany is one of the world's trade surplus countries.(see table 10.1) Lacking Britain's historical involvement in colonial Africa, and with a relatively minor stake in Latin American debt, the disasters which both these areas have suffered have not inspired the Germans to come up with solutions of their own.

Like Senator Bradley, the Brandt reports strongly emphasised the mutuality of interests between developed and developing countries' seeing aid to the South as a means of curing high unemployment in the West and North. Unlike Bradley, the ex-German Chancellor Willy Brandt and Swedish Prime Minister Olaf Palme set their seal on a much more radical approach to North-South problems, stressing the need to confront growing problems of hunger with growth through redistribution, and showing much greater faith in the justice of Southern complaints about the behaviour of Northern markets and Northern firms. They also offered an explicit alternative to the market-dominated philosophy of Western conservatives, calling for the creation of powerful government institutions at a global level to cope with the crumbling of the post-Bretton Woods world.

The presence of this alternative model for the construction of a world economy has had some influence on European politicians. Elements of it have appeared in statements on the debt crisis by former Austrian Chancellor Bruno Kreisky in 1984, and by President Mitterand in another call for a Marshall Plan for the Third World in 1986, to be effected by raising OECD aid commitments from their present levels of less than 0.35 per cent of GNP per year to 0.5 per cent, and eventually 1 per cent, thus transferring resources of US$35-70 billion a year. Arguably it has had some influence even on West German bankers, not themselves particularly at risk from Latin American default. In November 1986, the Speaker for Deutsche

Bank's Management Board, Herr Herrhausen, proposed an interest fund on Third World loans paralleling Brandt proposals for a commodity fund. Interest rates on existing loans would be fixed at a given level, the difference between this and market rates to be subsidised initially out of the loan-loss provisions already established by the private banks. If and when market interest rates fell below this level, the difference between the fixed rate still paid by Third World debtors and the rates actually prevailing on world markets, would be paid into the compensatory fund.[23]

The end of the 1980s thus suggested that Europe was the one region of the industrialised world which might just be prepared to turn its back on the OECD countries twenty-year love affair with international financial markets which created the original debt crisis, and contemplate a government-organised transfer of resources to revive Third World economies, and thus its own. But any Latin American hopes deposited here would still rest on very slender foundations: the possibilities of a Social Democrat victory, the possibilities of a reconciliaton of Europe's own divisions (West Germany opposed Lawson over the issue of concessions to Africa), and perhaps most slender of all, the possibilities of a divided and weakened regional economy surviving yet another US attempt to use the structure of the post-Bretton Woods system to preserve its own economic interests at the expense of the rest of the world.

After Black Monday: the Latin American View

'The declaration of Acapulco is good news. It would be even better news if Latin Americans declared a unilateral moratorium, for which the financial community is already prepared.'

Rudiger Dornbusch, MIT economist and *eminence grise* of economic policy-making in Argentina, Brazil and Peru, interviewed by the Lima *El Comercio*, 1 December 1987.

Five years after the outset of the debt crisis, Latin America was US$121 billion poorer — most of it taken from investment in the new industries and infrastructure necessary to give their countries a future. Every Latin American economy was in bad shape. Morale was low, and the region was not well prepared to defend itself against the prospect of an increasingly aggressive US drive to control its economies.

The heterodox plans of Brazil and Peru, which during 1985-86 had provided a brief glow of hope as a way of avoiding IMF austerity measures, restoring economic growth and controlling inflation, by the end of 1987 had begun to run into obvious problems. In Peru, the expansion of the economy and a great deal of assiduous courting failed to persuade local entrepreneurs to invest all the profits they made, raising government fears of further capital flight. In Brazil, political muddle, and the strain of reinstating a vanished trade surplus to support tough debt negotiations, left the economy rumbling from one crisis to the next. In December, hopes of any further progress either in debt negotiations or in the local economy vanished with the departure of Luis Bresser Pereira as Finance Minister, following his failure to persuade President Sarney that the Brazilian economy could not survive its existing crisis without increasing taxes on the Brazilian rich. Meanwhile, the rapid deterioration of the Argentine economy looked likely to force the Alfonsín government into some form of unilateral action in 1988, however unwillingly.

Smaller countries like Costa Rica were almost powerless to wrest major concessions from the banks. Their best hope lay in a more effective debtors' cartel. But divisions between the bigger debtors continued to preclude the emergence of such a cartel, particularly given the pressure of the ruling classes closely tied to the global economy. The Mexican government was happy to continue reaping the benefits from its privileged treatment compared to other debtors, despite the social cost of five years of adjustment and its ever closer integration into the US economy. Brazil, Argentina and Peru, though all suffering extreme economic distress, still failed to perceive a common interest strong enough to weld them together into a single group. The problems were compounded by the political weakness of the Sarney government in Brazil, which effectively postponed any possibility of a decisive Brazilian move until the presidential elections in November 1988.

Nevertheless, 1987 ended with Latin American governments managing another small advance in rhetorical unity. Throughout the year, other debtors had continued to ostracise Peru. Brazil failed to consult it before the February moratorium on interest payments, and continued to preserve the formal niceties of participation in bilateral negotiations. Brazil did consult Argentina, but the possibility of Argentina following in Brazil's footsteps was headed off by another US concession — a timely announcement at the September 1987 IMF/World Bank meeting in Washington, that the US was considering reintroducing something similar to the original IMF's soft conditionality loans.

In December 1987, the major Latin American debtors met in Acapulco and brought Peru's ostracism to an end. The vehicle for this new rhetorical toughness was the Latin American peace lobby set up as a counter-weight to US policy in Central America, which included the Contadora Group countries and its Support Group.This new group of nations included 80 per cent of Latin America's population: Mexico, Venezuela, Colombia, Panama, Brazil, Argentina, Peru and Uruguay. For Mexico, the Acapulco meeting was a politically useful demonstration of its government's independence from the US. The success of Costa Rica's Central America Peace Plan had boosted morale, and the major debtors were seen to be taking advantage of its diplomatic gains.

Thus, in the wake of Black Monday, the Presidents of the Eight issued a strong statement calling for interest rates to be cut to the levels of the late 1970s, or half their present level, and a debt service burden reflecting the devaluation of the principal of their old debts on secondary markets. But they continued to reject any concept of a debtors' cartel able to agree on joint unilateral action. Nevertheless, for the first time since the Baker Plan was introduced in Seoul in 1985, they gave Peru open political support, and promised similar treatment to any country which took unilateral action to reduce debt service payments in line with its capacity to pay. In early 1988, Argentina looked likely to give the Acapulco declaration its first active test.

Immediately after, Mexico signalled its willingness to adopt the new option offered by US banks, thus again undermining any possibility that Latin American solidarity might be preceived as real, and demonstrating its relative complacence with the status quo by accepting a deal clearly much more beneficial to the US banks and the US Treasury than to the Mexican government.

The Peripheralisation of Latin America

By the end of 1987, the situation facing the eight Presidents was grim. The 1980s had seen a growing peripheralisation of their countries within the world economy. Their share of world trade had fallen from roughly 6 per cent in 1980 to 4 per cent in 1986. Latin America's exports of manufactured goods had increased, but had nonetheless failed to keep pace with the dramatic growth in the proportion of world trade tied up in these goods, now over 70 per cent of world trade as a whole. Neither multinationals nor banks now saw the region as a likely growth point in the world economy: its share of private direct foreign investment was falling[24], and of course, it was now and in the foreseeable future, a net exporter of capital to international banks. The recycled capital of the 1970s had proved a poisoned gift.

Latin America's failure to match the performance of other NICs now left it over-dependent on primary commodity exports, which changes in modern technology were making less and less important to Western countries, so exposing the region to further falls in prices: a weak economic base from which to confront the structural crisis of the OECD countries, and the world recession which still looks its most probable result.

In the 1970s, Latin Americans had congratulated themselves on the achievement of much greater independence from the US economy. In the 1980s, this tendency was sharply reversed. Trade flows between Latin American countries had declined, as had those between Latin America and the EEC or Japan, while Latin American exports to the US increased from 35 per cent of the total in 1980, to around 50 per cent in 1985. This tying of Latin America to the US exposed the region to all the weaknesses inherent in the US economy. Peripheralisation has been coupled with another process, restructuring, defined by the US government, the IMF and the World Bank, as privatisation, deregulation and liberalisation. All three will tend to leave Latin American countries less well placed to cope with the problems of an imminent global recession, and more vulnerable to manipulation in the interests of the US struggle to maintain its own world economic hegemony. They will also worsen Latin America's already notorious inequalities in income distribution, storing up problems of further social unrest in the future.

Faced with these immense changes, the Latin American ruling elite have responded remarkably weakly. Most of the region's governments have yet to take the first step towards a regional response to the present and oncoming crisis: an end to the huge drain of real resources tied up in keeping payments going to Western banks.

Over the past five years, Latin America has suffered from a generation of conservative governments, left in place to ease the transition from military to civilian rule. The region's hope lies in the fact that many of these are coming to the end of their terms — Alfonsín in Argentina, Sarney in Brazil, Sanguinetti in Uruguay. The second round of democratically elected presidents may be more inclined to take more radical measures in the face of the crisis, as has been the case in Peru.

Coping with the new aggressiveness of a declining US world power will require greater obstinacy, greater regional integration and above all, a more radical imagination on the part of Latin American leaders. Repudiation of the debt will have to be followed by a policy of diversifying exports. Latin America cannot continue to allow its access to foreign exchange to be tied up with the increasingly unstable performance of primary commodity prices. Total withdrawal from global markets is not a real option, because the region still needs to import its capital from the rest of the world. Nor can it escape the electronic revolution. But integration into the world economy will have to be selective and carefully controlled, if Latin America is not to end up paying the final cost of instabilities in international markets on the industrial countries' behalf.

Contrary to the IMF prescription for resolving the crisis, Latin America needs above all a shift in resources to develop its internal markets. Regional integration of the existing Latin American economies is a necessary step in this direction. Without an economic model which focuses on the internal market, and the distribution of resources, the region's poor will only become poorer. By the year 2000, Latin America will have 500 million people, potentially one of the world's largest domestic markets for local production in the world. If the correct decisions are not made now, the living conditions for most of those 500 million will be disastrous.

The integrated global economy of the 1970s and its counterpart, local economies which are increasingly open to every shock unleashed by the power games now dominating the industrial world, has made one piece of Keynesian advice even more relevant for the future than it was at the end of the Second World War.

'Advisable domestic policies might often be easier to encompass if, for example, the phenomenon known as the "flight of capital" could be ruled out. The divorce between the ownership and the real responsibility of management is serious within a country when, as a result of joint stock enterprise, ownership is broken up between innumerable individuals who buy their interest today and sell it tomorrow, and lack altogether both knowledge and responsibility towards what they momentarily own. But when the same principle is applied internationally it is, in times of stress, intolerable...

But experience is accumulating that remoteness between ownership and operation is an evil in the relations between men, likely or certain in the long run to set up strains and enmities which will bring to nought the financial calculation. I sympathise, therefore, with those who would minimise rather than those who would maximise, the economic entanglement between nations. Ideas, knowledge, art, hospitality, travel — these are the things which should, of their nature be international. But let goods be homespun, whenever it is reasonably and conveniently possibly; and above all, let finance be primarily national...

The 19th century carried to extravagant lengths the criterion of what one can call for short the financial results, as a test of the advisability of any course of action, sponsored by private or by collective action. The whole conduct of life was made into a sort of parody of the accountant's nightmare... But once we allow ourselves to be disobedient to the test of an accountant's profit, we have begun to change our civilisation.'[25]

Keynes is becoming miraculously popular with financiers, in the wake of Black Monday. Let us hope his voice will be heard.

Notes

Chapter 2

1. R. Thorp and L. Whitehead eds., *The Debt Crisis in Latin America*, Macmillan, London, 1987.
2. See E. Brett et al, *The Poverty Brokers: The IMF and Latin America*, Latin America Bureau, London, 1983.
3. See E. Versluysen, *The Political Economy of International Finance*, Gower Press, London, 1981.
4. 'The Future of the Dollar as a Reserve Currency', *Barclays Bank Review*, February 1979.
5. S. Strange, *Casino Capitalism*, Basil Blackwell, Oxford, 1986.
6. IMF, *International Capital Markets, Development and Prospects*, 1982, Table 15.
7. BIS *Annual Report 1982/83*.
8. A. Ham, *Treasury Rules*, Quartet, London, 1981.
9. IMF, *op.cit.*.
10. R. Devlin, *The Structure and Performance of International Banking during the 1970s and its Impact on the Crisis in Latin America*, Kellog Institute for International Studies, Working Paper No.90, January 1987.
11. W. Darity Jr., 'Did the Commercial Banks Push Loans on the LDC's' in M. Claudon ed., *World Debt Crisis*, Ballinger, Cambridge, Mass., 1986, p.208-9; and Devlin, *op.cit.*, p.29.
12. Devlin, *op.cit.*, p.29.
13. Marko Milivojevic, *The Debt Rescheduling Process*, Pinter, London, 1985, p.24.
14. W. Cline, *International Debt and the Stability of the World Economy*, Institute for International Economics, Washington, London, 1983, pp.23-4.

Chapter 3

1. J. Kraft, *The Mexican Rescue*, Group of Thirty, New York, 1984.
2. *The Economist*, 9 January 1982.

3. C. Huhne and H. Lever, *Debt and Danger*, Penguin, Harmondsworth, 1985, p.110.
4. GATT-fly, *Debt Bondage or Self-Reliance*, Toronto, 1984, p.21.
5. SELA, *A Política Econômica dos Estados Unidos e Seu Impacto Na América Latina 1984*, Editora Paz e Terra, Rio, 1985, pp.65-6, and S. Haggard, 'The Politics of Adjustment', in M. Kahler ed., *The Politics of International Debt*, Cornell University Press, London 1987.
6. M. De Vries, 'The Role of the IMF in the World Debt Problem', in M.P. Claudon ed., *World Debt Crisis*, Ballinger, Cambrige Mass., 1986, p.116.
7. R. McCauley, 'IMF Managed Lending' in Claudon ed., *op.cit.*, p.135.
8. M. Milivojevic, *The Debt Rescheduling Process*, p.72.
9. See *Financial Times*, 8 August 1985, for the delay in Mexico's multiyear rescheduling package in 1985, due to the reluctance of one 'small unidentified British bank out of almost 560 banks owed money by Mexico' to sign.
10. H. O'Shaughnessy in *Financial Times*, 1 August 1985.
11. S. Griffith-Jones in *The Banker*, September 1987, p.25.
12. S. Griffith-Jones, *The International Debt Problem — Prospects and Solutions*, WIDER Working Papers, IDS, Brighton, June 1987.
13. *Financial Times*, 24 June 1987.
14. World Bank Annual Report, 1987, summarised in *Financial Times*, 18 September 1987.
15. IMF estimates, quoted by Michael Prowse in *Financial Times*, 27 July 1987.

Chapter 4

1. 'Latin American Debt: "I don't think we are in Kansas anymore" ', *Brookings Papers on Economic Activity*, 1984:2.
2. *IDB Annual Report 1975*, p.36.
3. R. Dornbusch, 'Policy and Performance between LDC debtors and Industrial Nations', *Brookings Paper No 2*, 1985, Table 3.
4. *IDB Annual Report 1982*, p.51.
5. *Idem*, Table 58, p.390.
6. Figures on total interest payments from *idem*, p.51, and on comparative deficits on current accounts from *idem*, Table 17.
7. *Idem*, pp.35-7.
8. J. Dunkerley, *Rebellion in the Veins*, Verso, London, 1984.
9. *IDB Annual Report 1982*, p.38.
10. *Idem*, p.173.
11. *Idem*, pp. 38-40.
12. Jaime Ros, 'From the Rise of Oil to the Debt Crisis' in *The Debt Crisis in Latin America*, Thorp and Whitehead eds., Macmillan, London, 1987. Figures on capital flight taken from the World Bank.
13. H. Schmitz, 'Industrialisation Strategies in Less Developed Countries', *Journal of Development Studies*, Vol.21, 1, October 1984.

14. See Chapter 1, *World Development Report*, 1987.
15. *IDB Annual Report 1986*, pp 27-8.
16. See note 8, chapter six.
17. *IDB Annual Report 1982*, p.71.
18. A. Maddison, *Two Crises: Latin America and Asia 1929-38 and 1973-83*, OECD, Paris, 1985, Table 18, p.48.
19. Figures from World Bank.
20. *IDB Annual Report 1982*, Statistical Appendix, Tables 5 and 50.
21. *IDB Annual Report 1985*, Statistical Appendix, Table 11.
22. See Latin America Bureau, *The Pinochet Decade*, London 1983, pp.98-101.
23. World Bank figures.
24. Debt Crisis Network, *From Debt to Development*, Washington DC, 1985, p.27.
25. *IDB Annual Report 1986*, Statistical Appendix, Table 5.
26. ILO-PREALC, *Empleo y Salarios*, Table 17, p.65.

Chapter 5

1. See Winston James, 'The IMF and Democratic Socialism in Jamaica' in *The Poverty Brokers*, LAB, London, 1983, and the Report of the Arusha Conference in *Development Dialogue*, Dag Hammarskjold Centre, 1980:2.
2. Rolando Morales, *Por qué no se hizo ni se hace lo obvio*, La Paz, *mimeo*, 1987.
3. ILO-PREALC, *Adjustment and social debt*, Santiago, 1987, p.12: minimum wage data from a sample of 18 countries, industrial wage data from a sample of 12, construction wage data from a sample of 14, public sector data from a sample of 9.
4. *IDB Annual Report 1987*, Table VIII-3, nine country sample.
5. Only Chile, Brazil, Ecuador and Uruguay have any kind of unemployment insurance: in no case is it very reliable, and Brazil's programme was only introduced in 1986.
6. *Adjustment and social debt*, p.9. *IDB Annual Report 1987*, Table VIII-3, p.124.
7. Hernán del Soto, *El otro sendero*, Instituto Libertad y Democracia, Lima, 1986: estimates cited in Latin American Regional Report (Andean), 11 April 1986.
8. ILO-PREALC, *Adjustment and social debt*, p.6.
9. *Idem*, p.14.
10. Rodríguez and Wurgraft, *La protección social a los desocupados en América Latina*, ILO-PREALC, Santiago, 1987, Table 27.
11. UNICEF, *Adjustment with a Human Face*, Clarendon, Oxford, 1987, p.83ff.
12. UNICEF, *ibid.*, p.108.
13. UNICEF, *The State of the World's Children*, New York, 1984.
14. World Bank, *Poverty in Latin America*, Washington, 1986.

15. *Idem*. See also Rodríguez and Wurgaft, op.cit., p.62.
16. *IDB Annual Report 1986*, p.57.
17. *Idem*, p.55.
18. 1982 and 1984 figures. Rodríguez and Wurgaft, *op.cit.*, p.61.
19. Morales, *op.cit.*
20. Rodríguez and Wurgaft, *op.cit.*, p.61. 1985 figures for Uruguay from UNICEF, *ibid.*, p.30.
21. UNICEF, *Adjustment with a Human Face*, p.77.
22. *Cuadernos de la CEPAL*, No.54, October 1986, p.50.
23. *IDB Annual Report 1987*, Table III-1, p.24.
24. *IDB Annual Report 1985*, p.23
25. *IDB Annual Reports 1986 and 1987*, Statistical Appendix, Table 5.
26. *IDB Annual Report 1985*, p.36.
27. *Ibid.*, Table II-2, author's calculations.
28. UNCTC Current Studies, Series A, No.3, Table 2, p.3.
29. *IDB Annual Report 1987*, Table IV-8, p.65.
30. Rolando Morales, *op.cit.*
31. *IDB Annual Report 1987*, Table IV-6, p.64.
32. *Ibid.*, Table IV-6, p.64 and Morales, *op.cit.*
33. A.G. Frank, *Capitalism and Underdevelopment in Latin America*, Monthly Review Press, New York, 1967.
34. K. Griffin, *Underdevelopment in Spanish America*, Allen and Unwin, London, 1969.

Chapter 6

1. P.C. Padoan, *The Political Economy of International Financial Instability*, Croom Helm, London, 1986, p.106.
2. A. Sampson, *The Money Lenders*, Hodder and Stoughton, London, 1982, p.286.
3. W. Cline, *International Debt and the Stability of the World Economy*, Institute for International Economics, Washington, 1983, p.38; A. Kaletsky, *The Costs of Default*, Twentieth Century Fund, New York, 1985; and from an interview with John Reed, Chairman of Citicorp, *The Wall Street Journal*, 5 February 1987.
4. S. Griffith-Jones, M. Marcel, and G. Palma, *Third World Debt and British Banks*, Fabian Society, London, 1987.
5. Kidron and Segal, *The Book of Business, Money and Power*, Pan, London, 1987, p.125; *Financial Times*, 10 September, 1987; *Wall Street Journal*, 14 January 1987; and *idem*, 23 January 1987.
6. M. Milivojevic, *op.cit.*, p.67.
7. *Financial Times*, 4 May 1984.
8. *Latin American Weekly Report*, 31 March 1983.
9. UNCTC Current Studies Series A No.3, *Foreign Direct Investment in Latin America: Recent Trends, Prospects and Policy Issues*, United Nations, New York, 1986, p.18.
10. Maria da Conceição Tavares and J. Carlos de Assis, *O grande salto para o*

caos, Zahar, Rio, 1985, p.58

11. Carlos Díaz-Alejandro, *op.cit.*, p.357; and Milivojevic, *op.cit.*, p.72.
12. *The Wall Street Journal*, 13,14 and 24 May 1985.
13. *Latin American Weekly Report*, 28 January and 31 March 1983.
14. For a comparable case involving UK banks, see *Financial Times*, 28 July 1987.
15. M. Milivojevic, *idem*, p.10.
16. B. Cohen, 'International Debt and linkage strategies' in *The Politics of International Debt*, Cornell University Press, Ithaca, 1986, p.144.
17. 'Plano Baker não reduz o endividamento' in *Gazeta Mercantil*, São Paulo, 5 May 1987; and BIS figures in Banco Exterior de España, *Extebank Monthly Economic Report*, October 1986.
18. *US Foreign Policy and the Third World: Agenda 1985-6*, Transaction Books, New Brunswick, US, 1985, p.182.
19. *The Wall Street Journal*, 6 February 1987; *idem*, 13 February 1987; and views of British banks, *The Wall Street Journal*, 27 March 1987.
20. *The Banker*, September 1987, p.31-2.
21. *The Wall Street Journal*, 4, 8 and 9 September 1987.
22. A. Nicholl in *Financial Times*, 24 March 1987; *idem*, 28 September 1987; and Jaclyn Fierman in *Fortune*, 22 June 1987.
23. Dornbusch, 'The Debt Problem and Solutions', paper delivered to the *Conferencia Internacional sobre a Divida Externa dos Paises em Desenvolvimento*, Rio, November 1986.
24. Martin Schubert in *The Banker*, February 1987.
25. *Idem*.

Chapter 10:

1. Editorial, *Financial Times*, 5 December 1987.
2. Philip Stevens in *Financial Times*, 24 October 1987.
3. *Financial Times*, 23 October 1987.
4. Harold Rose, 'The Future of the Dollar as a Reserve Currency', *Barclays Bank Review*, February 1979.
5. E. Bernstein, 'The US as an International Debtor Country', *The Brookings Review*, Vol.4, No.1, Fall 1985.
6. *Statistical Abstract of the United States, 1987*, Washington D.C., 1986. See also Díaz-Alejandro in Thorp and Whitbread, *The Debt Crisis in Latin America*, Macmillan, London, 1987.
7. William Keegan in *The Observer*, 6 December 1987.
8. Anthony Harris in *Financial Times*, 7 December 1987.
9. *The Guardian*, 5 March 1987.
10. *Financial Times*, 5 January 1987.
11. *Latin American Weekly Report*, 7 January 1983.
12. Editorial, *Financial Times*, 1 December 1987.
13. Quoted in R. Feinberg, 'Third World Debt: Toward a more Balanced Adjustment', *Journal of InterAmerican Studies and World Affairs*, Volume 19, no.1, Spring 1987.

14. *Financial Times*, 31 December 1987.
15. *The Guardian*, 30 December 1987, and *Financial Times*, 4 January 1987.
16. Debt Crisis Network, *From Debt to Development*, p.51-2, and Working Party on Third World Debt, *Managing Third World Debt*, ODI, 1987, p.43.
17. Junta del Acuerdo de Cartagena, *Evolución reciente de la deuda externa de los países del grupo Andino y de algunos países latinoamericanos*, February 1987, p.11.
18. Junta del Acuerdo de Cartagena, *op.cit.*, p.11 and Working Party on Third World Debt, *op.cit.*, p.43.
19. R. Feinberg, *op. cit.*.
20. *Financial Times*, 12 February 1987.
21. Peter McGill in *The Observer*, 20 September 1987.
22. *Far Eastern Economic Review*, 11 June 1987.
23. S. Griffith-Jones, 'Bargaining in the Debt Crises: Past Trends and Proposals for the Future', *mimeo*, ESRC Development Economics Study Group.
24. Sergio Bitar, *América Latina en el Nuevo Mapa de la Economía Mundial*, Raul Prebisch seminar *mimeo*, Buenos Aires, 1987.
25. J.M. Keynes, *The Collected Works*, Volume 21, Macmillan for the Royal Economic Society, London, 1971.

Bibliography and Guide to Further Reading

The debt crisis is now the subject of an enormous literature, much of it going rapidly out of date. For a broad survey, or special needs, it is worth consulting ECLAC's *Resúmenes de documentos sobre deuda eterna*, Santiago, Chile, March 1986 and subsequent editions.

Good material on the general development of the crisis in the region can always be found in the annual reports of ECLAC, and those of the IDB, located in Washington. ECLAC's *CEPAL Review* has good up-to-date information on Latin American perspectives on the debt, as do the many reports on the social costs of adjustment published by the ILO's regional office, PREALC, in Santiago, Chile. For general statistical updates on the relationship of the debt crisis to the world economy, see the reports of the World Bank and the IMF and their specialist studies. The World Bank's *World Debt Tables* provide overall figures.

British politicians looking at the debt crisis have had the benefits of a very good survey produced by the All Party Parliamentary Group on Overseas Development, *Managing Third World Debt*, Overseas Development Institute, London, 1987, and a wealth of statistical material on the British banks' involvement produced for the Fabian Society by S. Griffiths-Jones, M. Marcel and G. Palma, *Third World Debt and British Banks*, London, 1987. War on Want has published a good pamphlet, *Profits out of Poverty*, 1986, and runs a campaign with the same title.

GATT-Fly, which is a project of Canadian churches mandated to do research, education and action on Third World issues have produced an excellent series of reports on the debt including *Debt Bondage or Self-Reliance* (1985). A working group of the Debt Crisis Network in the US has published a short and readable study entitled, *From Debt to Development* (1985).

US analyses of the crisis are produced by the Institute for

International Economics in Washington and the Brookings Institute
(which publishes a journal, *Brookings Papers on Economic Activity*,
where advisers to the US administration and those advising Latin
American governments both publish material). See also the
publications of WIDER, the United Nations World Institute for
Development Economics Research, located in Helsinki.

The following is only a short list of books or articles suitable for
further reading in specific areas, listed in order of publication.

Background on the World Economy:

R. Parboni, *The Dollar and its Rivals, Recession, Inflation and
International Finance*, Verso, London, 1981.
E.A. Brett, *The World Economy since the War: The Politics of Uneven
Development*, Macmillan, London, 1985.
P.C. Padoan, *The Political Economy of International Financial
Instability*, Croom Helm, Beckenham, Kent, 1986.

The Banks and their Problems:

W. Cline, *International Debt and the Stability of the World Economy*,
Institute for International Economics, Washington DC, 1983.
A. Kaletsky, *The Costs of Default*, Priority Press, New York, 1985.
M. Claudon ed., *World Debt Crisis*, Ballinger, Cambridge, Mass.,
1986.
S. Griffiths-Jones and others, 'Learning to Live with Crisis', *The
Banker*, London, September 1987.

Background on the World Debt Crisis, Critiques of IMF 'Adjustment':

P. Korner, G. Maass, T. Siebald, R. Tetzlaff, *The IMF and the Debt
Crisis, A Guide to the Third World's Dilemmas*, Zed, London, 1986.
H. Lever and C. Huhne, *Debt and Danger*, Penguin, Harmondsworth,
1985.
Kaletsky et al., 'The Debt Burden' and 'Third World Futures', in
Third World Affairs 1986, Third World Foundation for Social and
Economic Studies, London, 1986.
G.A. Cornia, R. Jolly, and F. Stewart, *Adjustment with a Human
Face, A Study by UNICEF*, Clarendon Press, Oxford, 1987.

Background to the Latin American Debt Crisis:

K.S. Kim and D.F. Ruccio, *Debt and Development in Latin America*,
University of Notre Dame Press, Notre Dame, Indiana, 1985.
S. Griffiths-Jones and O. Sunkel, *Debt and Development Crises in*

Latin America, Clarendon Press, Oxford, 1986.
R. French Davis and R. Feinberg eds., *Beyond the Debt Crisis*, University of Notre Dame Press, Notre Dame, Indiana, 1986.

Country Experiences and Debt Management Strategies:

R. Thorp and L. Whitehead eds., *The Latin American Debt Crisis*, Macmillan, London, 1987.
S. Griffiths-Jones ed., *Managing World Debt*, Wheatsheaf Press, Brighton, 1988.

Index

248

251

83, 159-164, 169-79, 183, 188;
policy prescriptions, 41-47, 78,
87-89, 94-96, 99, 124, 228, 236;
seal of approval, 42, 44, 45, 140;
world economy, 17-20, 23-26, 32
Import substitution, 197, 209, 213
Import tariffs, 47
Income distribution, 78, 128, 135,
185, 236
India, 68
Inflation; Argentina, 75, 93; Brazil,
93, 140, 142, 147, 149-52, 154-
155, 157-158; Bolivia, 5; IMF,
42, 46, 88, 124; industrialised
countries, 16, 24; Peru, 93, 163-
166, 178-180, 182, 187; US, 22
Informal sector, 91, 93, 185, 212
Institute of International Finance,
40
Interest; charges, 2, 54, 57, 59, 67,
132, 134; payments, 5, 7, 14, 17,
36, 39, 41, 47, 49, 52, 54, 62,
64, 105-107, 113, 124, 127, 136,
198, 209, 220, 221, 230, 234;
rates, 34-37, 76, 87
Investment, 64-68, 74-76, 100-101,
103-104; Brazil, 130, 133, 150;
Costa Rica, 191, 196-97, 201;
Peru, 162, 164, 182, 186-190
Israel, 149, 203
Ivory Coast, 54

Jamaica, 71, 78, 81, 83, 84, 97, 98,
100
Japan, 17, 19, 26, 35, 42, 43, 63,
67, 69, 114, 220, 221, 223, 225,
229-231, 236
Johnson, President Lyndon Baines,
21

Keynes, John Maynard, 20, 25, 42,
88, 237-238

Land reform, 69, 103, 148, 153,
212
Latin American governments, 20,
39, 41, 42, 43, 48, 49, 50, 61-67,

69, 70, 87, 88, 98, 99, 102, 124,
170, 221, 234, 236
LDCs (see also Third World), 20,
32, 33, 81, 113
Liberalism, 79
Liberalisation, 236; exchange
control, 208; foreign trade, 46,
57, 70; prices, 46
Libor, 35, 36, 107, 108, 109, 114,
117, 139
Liberia, 175
Loans, 18, 19, 26-27, 29, 30, 32-34,
126, 156, 176, 186, 196, 199,
203, 217, 221, 225, 231, 232;
bridging, 40, 114; conditions,
44; commercial, 34, 35, 64, 116;
IMF, 127; involuntary, 44, 112,
113; loss provision, 118, 154,
224, 229, 233; loss reserves, 32,
120, 227; multilateral, 57, 116;
new, 33, 41, 44, 106, 107, 112,
115, 160, 161, 188, 228; non-
performing, 39, 118, 140;
portfolios, 33; private, 53, 57;
public sector, 132; sales, 121,
123; soft, 157, 217, 227, 234;
stand-by, 209; syndicated, 33,
41, 107; trade, 121; value-
impaired, 39, 174
London, 19, 49; City of, 23;
market, 19, 32

Malnutrition, 3, 18, 96, 143, 167,
191, 198, 211
Marcos, President Ferdinand, 65
Market; domestic, 47, 76, 78, 79,
88, 89, 145, 151; export, 37, 44,
87; forces, 23; levels, 46;
principles, 13; world, 5, 6, 34,
61, 81, 103, 138, 160, 233, 236
Marshall Plan, 225, 227, 231, 232
Martínez de Hoz, José, 75
Medici, General, 131
Menu of options, 120, 121, 227
Mexico; advisory committee, 40;
Baker Plan, 54, 125; band-aid,
105-108; capital flight, 60;

New LAB Books

The Great Tin Crash: Bolivia and the World Tin Market

Tells the story of tin; from the rise of the tin can to the collapse of the world tin market in October 1985, and its impact on the mineworkers and their families in Bolivia.
Price £3.70

Green Gold: Bananas and Dependency in the Eastern Caribbean

Looks at the history, recent developments and future prospects for the banana industry in Dominica, Grenada, St Lucia and St Vincent, focusing on conditions for the region's small farmers.
Price £4.70

Guatemala:False Hope, False Freedom

Draws upon recent research in Guatemala to examine the enduring chasm between the rich and the poor, the continued counter-insurgency campaign, and the policies of President Cerezo's Christian Democrat party.
Published jointly with the Catholic Institute for International Relations.
Price £5.50

The Thatcher Years: Britain and Latin America

Analyses the politics of aid, trade and debt; assesses British policy towards dictatorships and democracies in Chile and Argentina; and reveals Britain's support for US action in Central America and the Caribbean.
Price £3.50

The Poor and the Powerless: Economic Policy and Change in the Caribbean

Examines the historical legacy of colonialism in a major new survey of economic development in the Caribbean, with case studies of Jamaica, Grenada, Guyana, Barbados and Trinidad.
Price £10

Ecuador:Fragile Democracy

Traces the volatile political past of this little-known Latin American republic. Analyses the impact of President Febres Cordero's 'Andean Thatcherism' in the context of IMF-imposed austerity measures in the wake of the 1970s oil boom.
Price £4.70

Prices include post and packing
For a complete list of LAB books, write to LAB, 1 Amwell Street, London EC1R 1UL

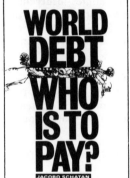

258